**Economic
Analysis for
Transport
Choice**

Charles River Associates Incorporated
is a professional service organization
in Cambridge, Massachusetts, that
specializes in economic and econometric research. CRA has conducted
research in the fields of transportation,
pollution control and abatement, and
natural resource industries, among
others. CRA's work is generally performed for long-range planning and
policy formulating groups in industry
and government.

Economic Analysis for Transport Choice

A Charles River Associates Research Study

Paul O. Roberts, Jr.
Donald N. Dewees
Harvard University

with contributions by
Gerald Kraft
Mahlon Straszheim

Heath Lexington Books
D.C. Heath and Company
Lexington, Massachusetts
Toronto   London

The contents of this report reflect the views of Charles River Associates Incorporated, which is responsible for the facts and the accuracy of the data presented herein. The contents do not necessarily reflect the official views or policy of the Department of Transportation. This report does not constitute a standard, specification, or regulation.

We wish to acknowledge the assistance of the Federal Aviation Administration in preparing portions of this report.

Published simultaneously in Canada.

Printed in the United States of America.

International Standard Book Number: 0-669-73593-0

Library of Congress Catalog Card Number: 77-151785

Table of Contents

List of Tables

List of Figures

Preface

This study of transport analysis was financed by the Office of the Assistant Secretary for policy and International Affairs of the United States Department of Transportation, and was performed at Charles River Associates, in Cambridge, Massachusetts, under contract DOT-0S-A9-003. The authors would like to thank the Department of Transportation for its support of this research, and to acknowledge the many suggestions, particularly from Dr. Howard Lapin, which influenced the final form of this work. A study such as this evolves slowly, and the interactions between DOT and CRA personnel were an important force in this evolution.

Two of the simulation models used in this study, the highway and rail models, had their genesis at the Harvard Transport Research Program, with funding by the Brookings Institution, the International Bank for Reconstruction and Development through a loan to the Ministry of Public Works of the Republic of Colombia, and the United States Agency for International Development. For use in the present study, the models were modified and several new routines added. The new routines made it possible to perform the analysis described in Chapters 6, 7, and 8 of this report. The air model, described in Chapter 9, was developed specifically for this study by Gerald Kraft, president of Charles River Associates, and Professor Mahlon Straszheim of Harvard. The programs themselves are written in *FORTRAN* IV and were run on an IBM 360/65 computer.

Gratitude is also extended to others who were vital to performance of this study particularly Dr. Jeoffrey R. Rohlfs and Ropert Trippi. Moshe Ben-Akiva did a remarkable job of writing computer programs, preparing data, and running programs without error. Robert Snyder cast a critical eye upon the early manuscripts and rendered the text more intelligible. A small army of assistants and typists, too numerous to name but nonetheless essential, worked on the many drafts of the report.

It is difficult to be very informative about who did what, as so much of the work and writing was jointly done. Chapters 1, 2, 5 and 6 were originally drafted by Roberts, while Chapters 3, 4, 7 and 8 were originally written by Dewees. However, additions and revisions to all were extensive. Chapter 9 was written by Kraft and Straszheim. Chapter 10 is, as nearly as anything can be, a joint work of both Roberts and Dewees.

Needless to say, the contents of this book do not necessarily reflect the official views or policy of the Department of Transportation. The authors take full responsibility for any shortcomings or errors that may be found in the text.

Paul O. Roberts, Jr.
Donald N. Dewees

Economic
Analysis for
Transport
Choice

1 Introduction to the Problem

The existence of an efficient and reliable transportation system appears to be crucial to development of the trade and interchange of a modern economy. Although it is clear that merely providing transportation facilities does not, by itself, initiate development, inadequate transport can serve to limit or restrict growth. Existing transport also tends to channel development in a spatial sense. Development that would have occurred along the old road can locate along a new road only if it is built. The role of transport in development is more easily understood if it is recognized that the demand for transportation is a derived demand. That is, there is no need for freight transport apart from the demand for a particular good or service and then only if there is an increase in utility as the result of the movement. There is little demand for passenger transport aside from a desire to be in another place.

An understanding of transportation system improvements is complicated by this relationship between the transport system and the production, distribution, and sale of individual commodities and services. When it is realized that the construction of a single transport project can produce shifts in the pattern of markets for many goods and changes in competition between them, it becomes obvious that the entire economy is involved. Thus the development of the region is closely related to the transport system, and changes in transportation can have a direct impact on the economy.

Efficient improvement in this transport system depends, at least in part, upon good analysis. Analysis which clarifies the consequences that result from making changes to the system and illustrates possible trade-offs contributes to an understanding of the issues raised by the various choices. However, the complex interrelationships between the transport system and the economy pose real problems for analysis, especially if a number of changes are being made simultaneously. It is difficult to examine the entire economy every time a change is proposed. As analytical and computational techniques have not existed for quantitative treatment of the problem as a whole, projects have generally been viewed independently. Methods for analyzing projects under this independence assumption have evolved and although they are not universally employed they are widely accepted.

The development of computers has placed new analytic tools at our disposal and made possible more sophisticated and comprehensive studies of systems relationships. As a result of this increasing capability and the desire to study projects within the broader systems context, a quantum jump in analytic technique has recently emerged. The combined package of philosophy, procedures,

1

and technique is generally referred to as "system analysis." Though there is no one procedure which can claim this title exclusively, there is general agreement that the technique involves selecting an objective, defining the system and its components, modeling the system, and manipulating the controllable variables so that the objective is maximized. A similar approach entitled "system simulation" has also been found to be useful.[1] To study the transport system of a country or region using this approach, computer models are built to simulate the operation of both the economy and the transport system. Alternative transport plans are conceived and their economic and transport consequences determined using the simulation models. The impact of budget constraints, time-staging of projects, pricing, user charges, and taxes on both system operation and the economy-at-large can be studied in detail. The results of such a study show year-by-year the net effect of implementing a particular set of transport projects.

The Role of Project Analysis

System simulation, however, does not eliminate the need for less complex kinds of analysis. In practice, system improvements are both conceived and implemented at the level of the individual project. During project location and preliminary design it is essential for the analysis process to furnish guidance for selecting out of the literally millions of possible projects those few designs that have promise for further consideration.

Since system analysis is comprehensive in its scope and at a high level of aggregation, it cannot efficiently consider the detailed design of the subcomponents of the system, namely the individual links where construction projects are being proposed. Yet, the design of these projects can be crucial to the operation of the larger system. A separate subtask would appear to be explicit consideration of the design of these system components. The scale of the analysis can be adjusted to match an individual project; and the data collection, analysis, and design can be tailored to the task at hand. Project analysis can thus serve as a useful input to the systems analysis process if it is properly structured.

The size and scope of a system simulation ordinarily make it an expensive undertaking, and even when the expense is worth the result there may be no agency willing to underwrite the effort. If this is the case, project analysis must be used regardless of how appropriate it is. In other cases where system effects are minor, a comprehensive system study may be entirely unnecessary. To perform the larger study would be wasteful and might even tend to obscure the major issue. Whenever a full study is impossible or impractical the gap must be filled by project analysis.

---

1. See, for example, *An Analysis of Investment Alternatives in the Colombian Transport System,* Harvard Transport Research Program, Harvard University (Cambridge, Mass., September 1968).

Project analysis is therefore a legitimate area of concern to those interested in the management and design of the transport system or some part of it. This interest in projects is founded upon the premise that in those cases where systems studies are going forward the supporting project analyses need to be specially designed to interface with them. Where systems studies are not contemplated, project analyses need to be structured so that they will allow the decision maker to perform qualitatively the analysis that would be explicitly addressed in a system analysis.

Purposes of the Study

The principal concern of this study will be with project-level analysis, addressing the traditional public finance problem of choosing among alternative investments. One specific objective is the development of both a framework for analysis of alternative transport projects and the mechanics of its realization: a framework that recognizes explicitly the varying factor endowments that exist in different developing regions. The different factor prices occurring in various countries can be reflected by changing those prices in the analysis, and by changing vehicle characteristics as they adapt to differing relative prices. Taxes and foreign exchange are explicitly included, so that the need to import fuel, vehicles, or equipment in some countries can be adequately evaluated.

Secondly, there will be a determined effort to structure the analysis so that it coordinates with the systems analysis approach. The framework used will permit separate evaluation of projects from a number of viewpoints, and will accommodate a variety of objectives. The impact of constructing a new facility is measured not only by the resulting reduction in operating cost but also by improvements in service. Methods designed to illustrate the extent to which different elements can be traded off against one another have been emphasized. Approaches for dealing with the conflicts of different interest groups have also been handled.

In addition to describing a conceptual methodology for project analysis, this study has incorporated the most important ideas into a set of computer programs that function as a coordinated software package. This package simplifies the analysis process by providing both efficient computation and useful summary results for evaluation. The programs, reported on separately, are designed for use by analysts working with developing countries, and can be adapted as necessary to any particular set of factor prices.[2]

Finally, the methodology and resulting computer programs have been applied to a series of example conditions, which although they are quite simplified,

---

2. Charles River Associates, *A Manual of Computer Programs for Project Analysis* (Washington, D.C.: Commerce Clearinghouse, 1970). Also available from the Department of Transportation and Charles River Associates.

are typical of those encountered in developing countries and serve to place the analysis into context as a decision problem in a real-world setting. The object of this application has been to test the approach, to illustrate its use, and to generate results that might provide a basis for generalizations about different kinds of transportation investments. The results, including a set of facility design optimizations, a set of project analyses, and a sensitivity analysis, are all reported on in separate chapters.

Improvements Over Traditional Project Analysis

The basic assumption underlying all project analysis is that the principal impact of introducing the project into the larger system is local and that the net effect can be determined by looking at the changed links and those immediately adjacent. This assumption will remain unchanged in this study. The basic premise is that traffic volumes are the same on all alternatives. The implications of making this assumption will be examined and the relation to systems analysis explained.

Project analysis, unlike systems analysis, is not new. Transport planners have been using various forms of project analysis for a long time. As with any well-established body of knowledge there has evolved a set of more-or-less accepted practices. Some of the features of current practice have to do with the scope of the analysis and cannot be improved until the scope is increased. This is, in part, the function performed by system analysis. Other features of current practice are merely evolutionary and can be improved and expanded to handle the analysis more efficiently and effectively in a role complementary to that of system analysis. These features have been emphasized in the analysis framework developed in this study. The more important of these features are listed below:

1. Determination of behavioral response
2. Identification of actors and actions
3. Selection of government objective functions
4. Government evaluation of taxes and foreign exchange
5. Separation of physical and economic consequences
6. Evaluation of nonmonetary consequences
7. Pricing as a control variable
8. Suboptimization of link design
9. Trade-offs in design evaluation

This list indentifies those features that can be isolated and treated separately. More generally, however, the list is a consequence of the recognition that project analysis is addressing the subcomponents of a system, namely a single link in the larger transport system.

Determination of Response to Policies

The first feature of an improved framework for project analyses has to do with the behavioral, as opposed to the normative, aspect of the transport system. Transport situations typically involve several action groups, each with its own viewpoint and goals. At a minimum there are shippers carriers, and government. Each perceives the situation in a slightly different way and reacts accordingly. There is a difference, for example, between the cost to provide a particular service and the tariff charged the shipper. The carrier incurs the cost while the shipper is only aware of the tariff. Typically, project analyses pay no attention to the incidence of cost and the resulting system behavior. Thus, though the results of the project may indicate that a particular project has the lowest benefit–cost ratio, the fact that one of the carriers has gone bankrupt has been completely ignored. This seems seriously unrealistic.

The implication for project analysis is that the real-world system and its behavioral components should be identified and attention explicitly directed to them in the analysis. Their behavior or choice of action will in many cases be determined by the economic consequences of the particular alternatives under consideration. Thus, it will be necessary to determine the incidence of revenues and costs that will allow the decision maker to predict the behavior of the system as a whole.

Identification of Actors and Actions

To be able to predict the behavior of the system it is essential to identify the action groups within the scope of the project and the range of their possible actions. In most cases it will be possible to identify their viewpoint and the incidence of costs as the actors perceive them. If this can be adequately done, their potential behavior can be predicted. Although it is difficult to predict individual behavior with certainty, a great deal more can usually be done in this regard than is generally attempted. If this incidence of cost is properly accounted for, the actions of the various entities can, in many instances, be determined fairly reliably. It will be important to the success of the project to determine which shippers will use what mode and what the net effect will be to each of the transport carriers. Although the techniques involved in this determination are fairly simple, they go far beyond project analyses as it is presently practiced.

Selection of Government Objective Functions

Project evaluation necessitates a carefully formulated objective function that views the decision from the standpoint of a government decision maker taking an unbiased look at the project as a whole. Such an objective function is frequently referred to as a public welfare function. In performing the analysis it is useful to adjust the public welfare function by taking into account foreign exchange requirements, tax revenues, construction costs, etc. It is also possible to view these adjustments from a variety of viewpoints; this has been done in this study.

Separation of Physical and Monetary Consequences

A frequently employed procedure in current project analyses is the indiscriminate mixing of physical and monetary consequences. Since everything will ultimately be reduced to dollars and cents, the reasoning goes, why not to do it at the outset? The reasons why this should not be done are subtle but important. First, if the analysis is done in a cost environment different from that for which the basic costs were obtained, the cost figures are probably meaningless. Thus vehicle operating cost figures for the United States are worthless in another country where the prices of gasoline, labor, tires, etc. are all different. It is true that before the analysis is complete, total costs must be obtained, but conversion of final cost to a different currency produces misleading results. The basis analysis should therefore, be carried out in physical dimensions; miles, gallons, or hours, and local factor prices applied subsequently.

A second reason why physical units should be used has to do with the incidence of cost. Since each of the actors in the system may evaluate physical consequences in a different way, it is important to retain physical dimensions as long as possible. The government, for example, will be interested in the physical deterioration of transport equipment because of its foreign exchange implications. The user views physical deterioration as a contributor to cost. It will, of course, be necessary to determine total costs in the final summary but preserving the breakdowns as long as possible and reporting them in detail by their incidence is useful.

Evaluation of Nonmonetary Consequences

The evaluation of proposed highway or railroad investments is most frequently performed in a feasibility study or cost-benefit analysis that computes the change in operating cost resulting from using the proposed facility instead of the existing one. Less frequently, the value of time saving for passengers is added to this cost saving to arrive at a total cost saving for the project. The present study assumes that shippers of freight may be concerned with speed of service just as passengers are, and that both passengers and freight will measure the desirability of a transport mode using several different factors. Commodity groups can weigh these different performance measures, which will be included with cost savings in the final evaluation of the project.

The formal inclusion of noncost service improvements in the models themselves permits more rigorous evaluation of this important aspect of a transportation improvement. It can be used in the evaluation of project benefits, and also to determine which of the several alternative modes or routes the particular commodities will choose. These models significantly improve the analyst's ability to predict the changes in commodity movement and to quantify the effects of transportation network changes.

Pricing as a Control Variable

Another important feature of a behavioral response system is the manner in which the pricing decision is exercised. It is possible to view this variable as controllable from the point of view of government. Frequently, regulatory bodies will control pricing although the initiative is most often in the hands of the private sector. The government's policy with respect to recovery of construction costs is also a factor in the pricing of a transport facility. Since a number of pricing policies can be instituted, the task of the analyst is to determine the consequences of each. To the extent that this variable is controllable by the government, the behavioral response of the system to a change in pricing policy can be noted and the most favorable overall pricing policy adopted.

Where the pricing policy is not under the control of government, it is still possible to explore the consequences of alternative pricing and its effect upon the behavioral response of the system. In most cases some approximation to the type of pricing policy that will normally be put into practice can be hypothesized, and the success or failure of the system can be noted. If one assumes that the private sector will price in such a manner as to maximize profits, then it may be necessary to test a number of pricing alternatives.

Suboptimization of Link Design

If a constant volume of traffic is assumed for all alternatives, it is possible to suboptimize the link design process. The total cost consequences of constructing a link of a particular design can be determined using simulation models to obtain operating costs and adding the cost of construction. As the parameters of the design are changed, both construction and operating costs on the facility will change. It is possible to manipulate the design parameters of the facility so that the total cost is minimized.

Implementation of this suboptimization process requires that models be developed for computing the construction cost as a function of the major design parameters. Models for accomplishing this have been designed and utilized in this study. Although they are simplified when compared to real-world design processes their results are still illuminating.

Trade-offs in Design Evaluation

A principal problem faced in the suboptimization of link design is what traffic volume to use, since the appropriate design features that emerge from the suboptimization process are a function of the volume initially assumed to use the facility. The traffic volume using the facility is, in turn, a function of the standards used in the design. Clearly, this is a chicken and egg problem. It is this relationship that links project analysis and systems analysis. Systems analysis can deal easily with the variation of traffic volumes over various links whereas project analysis can never do this in a sophisticated way. To perform project analyses that are useful in a systems analysis it is helpful to structure the output of the project analysis process as a study in trade-offs for various traffic volume levels.

Analyses that explicitly treat the trade-off between construction costs on the one hand and user operating cost on the other for various traffic volumes have been found useful in the systems analysis process. They are also useful in their own right as devices for showing the potential trade-offs that can be exercised by the decision maker.

Theoretical Framework

The project analysis framework used in this study incorporates the features just described. It can be summarized as follows. First, the problem must be defined by selecting the cities to be served by such a project. The existing transport facilities that would be replaced or supplemented by the addition must also be carefully identified.

Second, the traffic that will use the new facility in the future must be projected, as to both volume and commodity mix. Such a projection must, of course, be based on an assumption about the quality and cost of transportation services to be offered. Although at this point the facts have not yet been determined, some sort of first approximation must be made.

Third, the parties affected by the facility must be identified and their behavior and preferences accounted for. This is related to the second step in which shipper behavior determines which commodities will use the new facility, and to the fifth step where carrier pricing policy is considered. Studying the preferences of affected parties should reveal the interest groups that can be expected to support or oppose each project.

Fourth, the facility designs should be suboptimized by computing the costs and benefits of a range of reasonable design alternatives. Since the selection of a design will ultimately depend on traffic level and composition, as well as some weighting of the groups upon which the costs and benefits fall, it is important to determine the incidence of costs for each of the design alternatives.

Fifth, the behavior of shippers and carriers should be accurately determined based upon the specific projects resulting from the design suboptimization. This involves an understanding of both pricing policies and shipper preferences regarding costs and service aspects of transport. From this behavioral response, the projection of future traffic can be revised to reflect more accurately the expected conditions.

Sixth, a reestimate of traffic levels may necessitate redesign of the facilities, unless there are no significant changes in traffic. Thus, steps four and five can be repeated until the traffic projection and facility design converge upon a stable set of values.

Finally, the set of alternative projects must be evaluated and a "best" project selected. This will involve consideration of both the tax and foreign exchange consequences of each project, as well as the incidence of costs and benefits upon the various groups. One approach to making this decision requires definition and application of a general welfare function to the projects for evaluation of all consequences. A second involves explicit consideration of the trade-offs, with appropriate weighting of all factors and all interest groups. Both benefit by the features of analysis described above.

Study Procedure

This theoretical framework is best illustrated by a sample analysis situation in which the evaluation of alternative transport investments has been carried out. The analysis situation employed is that of choosing between investing in a new highway or railroad between two points. The problem is a general one, since the same methods can be used to analyze a highway versus an air link, river versus railroad, or conventional mode versus new mode. The explanation and discussion of the example problem is presented in Chapter 2. It is purposefully kept brief so that all points can be raised. The details of the analysis and the problems arising out of it are then analyzed more thoroughly in subsequent chapters.

The comparison of alternative projects requires complete definition of the environment in which they are to be set. The sample problem is set in a "base scenario," consisting of a pair of cities connected by an old road, along with factor prices taken from recent conditions in a particular developing country. The base scenario also employs the prevailing operating costs and methods in that country. Within this base scenario a set of environmental conditions are defined, including the terrain to be crossed, the traffic volume level, and the commodity mix to be carried. The values chosen are intended to represent reasonable quantities for the country serving as the base scenario.

The example problem is explored by designing new facilities for each alternative and simulating their operation. The problems encountered in the analysis include: how to predict travel by each mode; how to design and select appropriate facilities; how to handle the problem of different traffic volumes; how to price transport services and their effect on the viability of the mode; the incidence of costs and benefits and their measurement; and, finally, the question of appropriate objective functions for government.

After a preliminary analysis of the example problem in the initial chapter, subsequent chapters deal with the experimental conditions; the method of describing the transport links and their performance; the cost perceived by various commodities and their determination; and, using optimization techniques, the selection of appropriate facilities. In an effort to produce results for a variety of conditions, the computations of the sample problem are repeated for a variety of terrain types, traffic levels, and commodity mixes, still using the base scenario. These results are discussed in Chapter 7. In order to determine the sensitivity of these results to changes in factor prices, a second scenario is examined involving a totally different set of factor prices, but with the same terrain and traffic volumes. The complete analysis performed for the base scenario is then repeated for this second set of conditions and the results compared. Some general conclusions are reached based upon these two studies.

Finally, there is a return to the conditions of the base scenario to undertake a sensitivity analysis. Its purpose is to provide more detailed information on the elements that are important in making a highway or rail investment decision. One by one the factor prices are varied from their original value and the impact on the results observed and interpreted.

The base scenario has also been used to examine the performance of the air model. Given one set of factor prices, a number of different combinations of aircraft and airfield technology are explored to determine the impact of these choices on the performance and operating costs of the mode. Airline performance is then compared with the performance of rail and highway operations to determine their relative merits.

Summary of Conclusions

The most significant result of this study is the development and presentation of the methods of analysis that were used and the computer programs which embody them. The formal inclusion of a variety of nonmarket measures of performance in the evaluation of a project design is offered as a distinct change from existing practices. The design selection procedure and program for implementing it have been found to be quite helpful in designing and selecting the appropriate characteristics for new facilities in general. These methodological matters are summarized in Chapter 2 and are discussed in greater detail in the body of the report. It appears that it is eminently worthwhile to automate the computational process used here, and the programs are sufficiently general that they can be used in almost any situation merely with data changes.

The data used in these analyses are based upon studies of actual countries, and a wide variety of different conditions have been included to provide a broad set of final results. The results, however, imply a number of assumptions and judgments that will be interpreted differently by different persons. They do not represent final decisions on which project is best, but are instead data for decision makers to use in evaluation along with other information not formally included in the analysis. Despite the variety of conditions tested, it is unlikely that any specific real-world situation will duplicate the test conditions in all important respects, and thereby be resolved by merely observing the answers produced here.

Still, these results can be useful if properly applied. The set of conditions examined represent a series of points in the universe of possible settings for proposed transport investments. Comparison of results from the two scenarios and examination of the sensitivity analysis answers can give a good indication of how the results change with variations in test conditions. Thus, it is possible to extrapolate from the current results to an even wider range of cases, with some confidence in the relative position of the results. Real problems should be approached by finding the test conditions that seem most similar and making the appropriate interpolations; it should then be possible to see which alternatives are relatively desirable and which are out of the question. This limited set of feasible solutions can then be analyzed in detail, perhaps with these same computer programs, to find a single best solution.

With these limitations in mind, the substantive results of this study can be briefly summarized. In the example problem, the most important variables affecting the decision of whether to continue using an old facility or to build a new one was traffic volume, with greater volumes increasing the justification for the construction of a new link. Furthermore, as volume of traffic increases, the optimum amount spent on new construction increases, since operating cost savings which higher-quality facilities bring will accrue over a larger amount of traffic. Thus in one case the optimal highway for high-volume traffic costs over three times as much to construct as the optimal low-volume highway. These trends would be less pronounced if only operating cost were considered and other aspects of performance were ignored. They would also be less pronounced if the traffic consisted of lower-value goods than if it were mostly high-value goods. A corollary to this conclusion is that a single set of design standards should not be set for an entire country, but rather the standards for each facility should depend upon the expected traffic volume and the terrain conditions encountered.

At relatively low volumes, the introduction of air service can change the optimal strategy from constructing a new highway to continued use of the old road.

Air service will, in general, tend to attract high-income passengers and high-time-preference freight which forms an important part of the justification for the construction of a new road.

As between constructing a new highway or a new railroad, most conditions in developing countries favor the construction of the highway. At volumes as low as 100 tons per day in each direction, a railroad is never worth constructing; a highway will be cheaper to build in almost any terrain, will be far cheaper to operate, and will provide better service.

At 1000 tons per day in each direction, a new highway is still frequently the best alternative for most terrains and commodity mixes even where cost alone is the test. Where performance is also important, the results tend even more to favor the construction of highways, as rail performance is inferior for high-value goods and passenger movement. For bulk commodities, on the other hand, and particularly in flat terrain, railroads can be the economical choice.

At 5,000 tons per day, a railroad may be best for flat or hilly terrain if cost alone is considered, while a highway is the best choice in the mountains. If performance is considered, however, a highway is the best single choice in all cases; although with large volumes of bulk goods moving, the advantage is not large. It is sometimes better to build both a highway and a railroad than either alone, since each is best suited to carriage of different commodities.

Railroads are always more expensive in mountainous terrain at all volume levels because of the high construction costs needed to achieve low gradients or the high operating costs resulting from short trains and high gradients. Thus, it is not likely that it will be desirable to build a new railroad through mountainous terrain and in hilly terrain unless the traffic volumes are very large and the commodity mix is favorable to rail.

The choice of facility is always greatly influenced by the type of traffic as well as its volume. The predominance of low-value bulk goods, which do not care particularly about speed of service, will tend to favor railroad construction. The preponderance of higher-value commodities and high-income passengers, such as motorists, will favor a highway solution. Where the traffic volumes are low and the average value of the commodities moved is high, an air solution may be indicated.

The situation most favorable to a rail solution is, therefore, one in which relatively flat terrain is encountered and where large volumes of ore, coal, or other bulk goods are shipped a long distance between two points. Clearly, this is a rather special case, such as a line between a large mine and a port or smelter, where the mine itself is not a large center of other economic activity. Where the mine is located near a large city, it is likely that a road will also be needed.

The distance between service points is a very important determinant of costs for airline operation, since the time and cost of taking off, reaching cruising altitude, and landing are a large portion of total operating costs. Ground facility costs, on the other hand, vary hardly at all with distance. Greater distance between terminals will tend to favor airline operation over highways.

Distance is also an important factor to railroads. Railroad costs tend to decrease per unit with longer hauls. Highway costs are, by contrast, less affected by distance.

Testing the sensitivity of total costs to varying factor prices in the studies showed that the greatest impact was from changes in the prevailing interest rates. Lower interest rates tend to favor new construction rather than continued use of the old facility and affect both railroad and highway equally. They also favor more sophisticated airplanes like larger jets over the cheaper piston craft previously used.

The cost of imports is also influential, with higher import prices favoring highways at low volume and railroads at high volume. Transport wages have less impact, with higher wages favoring the continued use of the existing facilities at low volumes. Similarly, the existence of high wages tends to favor the use of railroad over highway but only slightly. Fuel costs are not a large factor in most situations, but are more important to highway operation than to railroads. Although the cost of crushed aggregate is an almost insignificant factor, high costs tend to favor railroads over road and the maintenance of existing facilities over the construction of new ones.

The results described above are applicable to conditions in the base scenario. These results are influenced, of course, by the fact that the base scenario had no particular shortages of any factor except capital and imports, which were relatively expensive. Fuel is produced domestically and is cheap; wages are rather low; crushed aggregate can be obtained in many areas; asphalt is cheap; vehicle import costs apply almost equally to both trucks and rail cars. It is not surprising, therefore, that no one factor price had a large influence on project selection. Furthermore, analysis revealed that these results did not change drastically even under some sets of quite different factor prices. Where wages, construction costs, and gasoline are much more expensive, the results will change; but the relative cost of highway and rail solutions remain similar. This is because wages affect highway operations and low-volume railroads about equally. So do construction costs in flat or hilly terrain. High gasoline costs are typically compensated for by the use of diesel trucks and buses, which tend to bring operating costs back down to those of gasoline vehicles.

One would expect significant differences from the results of this study only where factors used in one mode and not the other were in quite short supply, and, therefore, quite expensive. Where both gasoline and diesel fuel are quite expensive, this tends to favor the railroads somewhat. If asphalt, cement, and other paving materials are all scarce and have to be imported, this would tend to favor railroads, while a shortage of wood ties tends to make railroads more expensive and favor highways. Cheap domestic iron could favor railroad but it seems unlikely that real costs would be much below the world price used here. Difficult land or water access to world markets would tend to increase the costs of imports, favoring highways, unless fuel were imported, in which case its resulting high price would tend to favor railroads. Expensive tire rubber is also detrimental to highway operation.

Overall, the range of technology available for operating either a highway system or a railroad permits significant adaptations to varying factor price environments. Trucks can be big or small, depending upon the relative cost of capital and labor; they can be gasoline or diesel powered, depending upon the relative costs of capital and fuel. Railroads can use more- or less-sophisticated control equipment and can use capital- or labor-intensive maintenance procedures as costs warrant. Thus, except in specific cases of acute shortage or abundance of a factor used only in one mode, varying factor prices among countries will make only marginal changes in the results presented here. The decisive conditions will, in most cases, be terrain type, traffic volume, and commodity mix.

2

Highway-Rail Analysis: A Simple Experiment

Role of the Example Problem

The highway-rail portion of this study presents an evaluation of a number of different transportation projects in a wide variety of situations, using several measures of performance. Although the theoretical framework used is basically simple, its explanation is complicated by the number of combinations that must be explained. It would be confusing to present a full analysis for the entire range of results obtained. At the same time, a discussion of the details of the analysis, without reference to the problems solved, would be uninteresting and difficult to follow, as many of the details result from treating real-world complexities. The result, therefore, must be a compromise between reality and simplicity of exposition.

To introduce the method of analysis a single set of simple, but representative, conditions has been studied; the logic of the analysis has been traced by using this set as an example problem. In this example, average values were used for most of the parameters found in the larger study so that the numerical results discussed in this chapter are intermediate in the range of all results obtained. Later chapters will expand both data and results to describe the full range of conditions that were explored.

An attempt has been made in discussing the example to raise the major conceptual and practical problems usually encountered in project analysis. However, in most cases, the resolution of difficulties has been deferred to later chapters to avoid losing the thread of the argument. The example, therefore provides a thought-provoking overview of the material that will follow and shows the relationships of the various parts of the analysis to one another.

When studying the example, one should bear in mind that it represents only one set of conditions out of the many that could have been used. The results, therefore, are neither general nor typical, but merely the specific result for one particular set of conditions.

The Question

The highway–rail study is set in a situation where two existing cities, one-hundred airline miles apart, are connected by an old road. The road, originally built along a river valley to serve several small communities, has since declined in

15

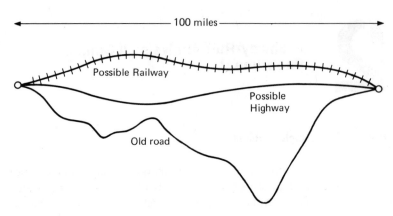

Figure 2-1. The Example Situation.

importance, but remains in use serving the traffic between the two larger cities. (See Figure 2-1). The volume of traffic moving over this old road and its distribution among commodity types are known. The condition and design of the old road are poor, but it is assumed that no further improvement to the facility should be made to the existing alignment.

Four possible courses of action may be pursued. The government could construct a new highway connecting the two cities, it could construct a railroad between them, or both facilities could be constructed simultaneously if this appears to be most appropriate. Where reconstruction of the old road is a possibility, it can be studied by treating the reconstructed road as a "new highway" of appropriate characteristics, and replacing the old with the new at the desired time. Finally, if nothing is done, traffic will continue to move over the existing highway. The purpose of the study is to develop the rationale by which the government can decide which of these four courses of actions to follow.

Analysis and Solution

Environment

Before this transportation investment question can be addressed using any type of analysis, it is necessary to obtain some fundamental information about the particular environment. To describe it several classes of variables are needed. Three such classes are: (1) the factor prices prevailing in the country or area under consideration, (2) a description of the terrain to be crossed, and (3) a statement of the volume of traffic and its commodity makeup. Note that none are under the control of the facility designer and that, with the possible exception of a few factor prices, none can be controlled by the government either.

Factor Prices. Economic analysis of any kind requires knowledge of the prices of inputs used in the construction and subsequent operation of the system. For conventional ground transport systems, these include the cost of gasoline, pavement, earth movement, railroad rails, locomotives and cars, wages, and other goods used in producing transportation. It is through these prices that the factor endowment of the country is reflected. For meaningful analysis, the prices should represent the opportunity cost to the economy of using the resources in question. The price is important because it is assumed to measure the value to the economy of the factor in its highest alternative use.

Collection of the necessary factor price data raises several difficult problems. The decision on what costs should be included in the analysis is of central importance. The incidence of these costs is also important. Construction and maintenance costs usually accrue to government bodies, while shippers typically bear the indirect cost of poor services. Chapters 5 and 10 deal with different aspects of these questions.

Another problem is that of obtaining representative prices and costs. Commodity prices, such as gasoline, may vary from one part of a country to another. Costs such as vehicle maintenance per hour or per mile vary with the equipment used, the skill of the operators, efficiency of the management, conditions of terrain crossed, and many other complex factors. The best way to avoid these difficulties is to include as many of the important determinants of cost as possible in the model itself, and to use averages for the others. The final results can be adjusted if a bias has thereby been introduced.

A further problem is the adjustment (where necessary) of the market prices found in the economy to reflect the opportunity cost of the goods, where the market does not do this adequately. This might occur where monopolies are present, where there are large government subsidies or taxes, or if there is unemployment. Gasoline, for example, may be subject to a tax that constitutes a significant portion of its final sales price, while automobiles and small trucks in many countries are subject to import duties that may be three to four times the retail price. If the country in question has a serious balance of payments problem, the foreign exchange needed to buy imported goods is scarce and imports must be artificially restricted. Should the price used include or exclude the tax? Should imported goods then be valued at the official exchange rate or should some premium or shadow price be attached to money expended in foreign exchange? These and other questions related to factor prices are considered further in Chapter 3. The factor prices actually used in this study are presented in Appendix A.

Terrain. A crucial element in determining the cost of constructing a new highway or railroad is the type of terrain over which it must pass. Clearly the cost of constructing a transport facility is less on firm, dry, flat land than in difficult mountainous terrain with unstable soil conditions. Unfortunately, the range of combinations of surface topography, soil type, underlying rock formations, and existing land use are so great as to almost defy a comprehensive description. For this study, we have considered three different terrain types covering a wide range of conditions. These three terrain types are indentified as flat, hilly, and mountainous. Although the example problem of this chapter will consider only the hilly case, the others have been studied equally thoroughly. The characteristics of each are described in Chapter 3 and the complete results of the project analysis are given in Chapter 7.

One purpose of this study is to determine, for a specific set of conditions, the relative merits of building a railroad versus constructing a highway. One might hope that modal choice and facility design questions could be answered simply by using the results for those example terrain conditions that most closely replicated the actual situation. It is probable however, that upon close examination the actual situation will be found to differ from the study condition in so many details, terrain included, that one will prefer to perform additional studies using the new data to define the actual situation more closely. Where the actual terrain is different from all three example types used here, a new type could be defined. This study has included a variety of conditions consistent with an orderly and thorough analysis and presentation of results, but it has made no attempt to be comprehensive. Still, the methods of study can be applied far beyond the data incorporated here. Any particular problem may therefore merit a separate study with data specific to that problem.

Traffic Volume and Commodity Mix.   Evaluation of the worth of a proposed transportation investment clearly depends upon knowledge of the volume of traffic that is expected to flow over the proposed new facility. In fact, volume information is essential to a determination of the costs and benefits associated with the facility. A simple figure for total tonnage, however, is not sufficient for an analysis. Some knowledge of the amounts and types of commodities moving is also important. Various commodities will typically place much different values on time savings, reliability, and probability of loss. It would, for example, be important to know whether a given total tonnage per day consisted primarily of coal, to which time is relatively unimportant, or industrial machinery, to which time is very important. Thus, the volume of goods expected to flow over the facility must be segregated by commodity type and the relative proportion of each estimated.

The volume and type of commodity affects not only the total benefits derived for each facility, but also the design and choice of the facility itself. The greater the total volume of goods flowing, the larger the initial investment that can be justified since larger investments can presumably be offset by greater savings in operating costs. Similarly, the greater the proportion of perishable or high-value commodities in the projected traffic, the greater is the investment that can be justified on the facility because of the savings in time and the reduction in loss and damage.

The investment decision is also influenced by the proportion of the total traffic in each commodity group moving in each direction. The case where similar tonnage flows in each direction over a link differs from the more fequent situation in which one type of commodity, say bulk exports, predominates in one direction, while high value goods such as imports dominate the other direction. This is particularly true where different transport equipment and different handling methods are employed in the two directions.

Changing the price and performance of moving over a segment of the network can substantially alter the volume of traffic offered for shipment over that route. Determination of the elasticity of demand for transportation as a function of price and service, however, is dependent upon knowledge of many factors having to do with the economy of the entire country. In a study of limited scope such as this one, no such knowledge is available.

This study uses three fixed traffic volume levels, which do not change when the old road is replaced by a proposed new facility. Designated as "low," "medium," and "high," they consist of 100 tons per day, 1000 tons per day, and 5000 tons per day in each direction. All are considered in the example. The complete results discussed in Chapter 7 include cases where the total flow on the link is the same as in the example, but is unbalanced, with three-fourths flowing in one direction and one-fourth in the other. Because making substantial improvements to a transportation link might actually generate large volumes of new traffic, caution must be used in applying the results of this study to real-world situations. In a case where there is evidence on which to base estimates of traffic both before and after an improvement, it would be better to use the estimated traffic volume level than the fixed level employed here. Inclusion of traffic growth in the data is explained in the *Manual of Computer Programs.* [1]

Five different commodity groupings have been identified: bulk goods, such as coal or grain; general goods, which are of higher value, such as manufactured products; special goods, which are liquid or bulk commodities; common-carrier passengers — bus, airline, or railroad; and private passengers, typically passengers in automobiles. For simplicity of presentation only one commodity mix is discussed in this chapter although the study as a whole evaluates three different mixes; balanced flow, bulk-dominated flow, and general-dominated flow. In the balanced flow of the example, the bulk and general goods flow primarily in opposite ditections, but the total daily tonnage consists of 40 percent bulk goods, 40 percent general goods, 10 percent special goods, with the remaining tonnage being 9 percent common-carrier passengers and 1 percent private passengers. The division of this traffic flow into the commodity groupings by direction is illustrated in Table 2–1.

---

1. Charles River Associates, *A Manual of Computer Programs for Project Analysis* (Washington, D.C.: Commerce Clearinghouse, 1970), Ch. 5.

Table 2-1
Specification of Commodity Mix (Balanced Traffic)

| | Total Tonnage by Direction (Percent) | | | | | |
	Bulk Goods	General Goods	Special Goods	Common-Carrier Passengers	Private-Carrier Passengers	Total
Flow A to B	60	20	10	9	1	100
Flow B to A	20	60	10	9	1	100
	Resulting Actual Tonnage by Direction					
Low Volume						
Flow A to B	60	20	10	9	1	100
Flow B to A	20	60	10	9	1	100
Medium Volume						
Flow A to B	600	200	100	90	10	1000
Flow B to A	200	600	100	90	10	1000
High Volume						
Flow A to B	3000	1000	500	450	50	5000
Flow B to A	1000	3000	500	450	50	5000

Connecting Transportation Links. A final element in the environment that will affect the volumes using the new transportation facility is the existence of connecting transportation links. If a large amount of the traffic flowing between the two cities is made up of goods moving as parts of a longer trip from cities further distant, it will be important to know by what mode they arrive at either of the terminal cities. When no other railroad exists in the country, then goods that arrive by truck at either A or B are not likely to use rail between those two cities and complete the trip by truck. If important highways or rail lines intersect the proposed link, connecting with other cities on the transportation network, this could have an important influence on the choice of mode. There is no way to generalize the infinite variety of possible flows that can exist as the result of changes in the larger transportation network. For the purposes of this study it is assumed that all traffic originates and terminates in cities A and B.

The Old Road

Evaluation of proposed investments in new transportation facilities requires that their performance be compared with performance on the existing road. To make such a comparison, it is necessary to have detailed information about the old road, including a physical description of that facility and a determination of the cost and performance of operating over it. The design parameters for the old road have been chosen to represent typical conditions for existing low-standard roads in developing countries.

While the airline distance between cities A and B is 100 miles, the hilly terrain combined with the necessity to serve the small towns between the terminal cities has resulted in substantial circuity so that the distance between them along the old road is 200 miles. The surface of the road is gravel and its design speed is 20 miles an hour with sharp turns and relatively short sight distances. The average gradient of the road is 6 percent and each of the two lanes is only 8 feet wide. The design parameters for the old road are summarized in Table 2–2.

Table 2–2
Link Physical Characteristics for the Old Road

Distance	200 miles
Surface Type	Gravel
Design Speed	20 miles per hour
Gradient	6 percent
Width of Lane	8 feet
Number of Lanes	2

To provide a standard against which to evaluate the performance of the proposed new transportation facilities, the highway model was used to simulate the operation of trucks, buses, and automobiles over the old road. Not surprisingly, the poor characteristics of this transportation link resulted in correspondingly poor performance by the vehicles using it. Under medium traffic volume conditions the average travel time for the 200-mile trip was over 12 hours, indicating an average speed somewhat under 20 miles per hour. The hills, the poor surface, and the slow speed combined to produce relatively high operating costs. Table 2–3 presents the performance and costs for a typical truck, operating on the old road. The average cost per vehicle mile for this vehicle operating over the old road was approximately $0.19 while the cost per ton mile was almost $0.08.

The costs referred to are derived from computations of the physical quantities of inputs consumed by vehicles in each of the five commodity classes. Typical figures for the vehicle carrying general goods are shown in Table 2–3. The physical inputs required to produce the vehicle movement along the highway are shown in the first column of the table. Multiplying the physical units of column 1 by the factor prices per unit in column 2 produces the costs for operating a vehicle over the entire link, shown in column 3. The results shown are those for trucks in a single commodity class at a volume level of 1000 tons per day on the old road, in hilly terrain. When the costs of roadway maintenance are added to the items in Table 2–3, one has the full list of direct costs incurred in the operation of those vehicles.

Table 2–3
Typical Vehicle Costs and Performance on the Old Road

	1 *Physical* *Units Consumed*	*2* *Cost* *Per Unit* *(dollars)*	*3* *Cost* *Per Vehicle* *(dollars)*	*4* *Percent* *of* *Total*
Crew	29.2 man-hours	0.330	9.633	25.7
Fuel	62.1 gallons	0.154	9.558	25.5
Oil	1.5 quarts	0.233	0.349	0.9
Tires	0.029 tires	101.000	2.889	7.7
Maintenance (parts)	0.000366 vehicle	13300.000	4.868	1.3
Maintenance (labor)	2.4 man-hours	0.400	0.960	2.6
Depreciation	0.000691 vehicle	13300.000	9.199	24.6
Total			37.457	100.0

Cost per vehicle mile = $0.187
Cost per ton mile   = $0.078

Note: Traffic = general truck, medium volume, flowing from A to B (200 tons/day)

Significance of Nonmarket Costs

So far we have only alluded to the fact that commodity shippers who use the old road incur costs above and beyond those for vehicle operation. Although these nonmarket consequences of travel are frequently not taken into account in the location and design of new facilities, it is clear that costs are incurred due to loss and damage in shipment, deterioration of products during long travel times, and the retention of high levels of inventory to protect against variations in shipping time. It is also clear that up to a point the shippers involved are willing to trade higher costs of vehicle operation for reductions in nonmarket cost. The choice of high-speed, high-cost truck services over low-cost but low-speed rail services is a case in point.

It seems reasonable, therefore, in evaluating the costs of providing transport services on the old road to include these nonmarket costs in the accounting. The question now arises of how this can appropriately be done. A fairly simple yet useful way in which to do this is to determine the consequences of traveling over the old road in physical terms and to allow each commodity to weight the performance individually to determine its perceived costs. When these perceived costs are added to the cost for vehicle operation, they furnish a measure of the total cost incurred by a commodity in traveling over that link. (See Table 2–4.)

It is obvious that different commodities weight the physical consequences of traveling over a link differently. This can be accounted for by specifying a different commodity weighting of performance for each class of goods. For example, speed is important to perishable items to avoid spoilage. For high-value commo-

Table 2–4
Determination of Commodity Perceived Costs on the Old Road

	1 Link Performance	2 Commodity Weightings of Performance	3 Commodity Perceived Costs = (Col. 1) × (Col. 2)
Waiting time	1.10 hours	0.514 $/ton/hr.	$ 0.565[a]
Travel time	12.16 hours	0.362 $/ton/hr.	4.402[b]
Time variability	5.12 hours	0.035 $/ton/hr.	0.179[a]
Probability of loss or damage	0.0011%	2040 $/ton	2.430[a]
Vehicle operation	15.69 $/ton	1.0 $/$	15.690[b]
Total			$23.266

Note: Traffic = general truck, medium volume, flowing from A to B (200 tons/day).
[a]Nonmarket costs.
[b]Vehicle operation.

dities, reducing travel time is important so that inventory and overhead costs can be kept low. Loss and damage is relatively less significant for low-value commodities than for high-value commodities. For lower-value commodities, the largest portion of total cost is accounted for by vehicle operation.

The commodity weightings shown in Table 2–4 are for general goods with a value of about $2000 per ton. The measures of performance chosen (travel time, waiting time, variability of time, and probability of loss) are important cost producing factors perceived by goods of this type. The cost of vehicle operation incurred by the carrier is also shown in the table, as it is typically passed along from the truck operator to the shipper and therefore is a factor in the total costs of making the shipment. For general goods, waiting time and travel time are valued fairly highly, yet the cost of vehicle operation is still quite significant. The manner in which these commodity weightings are derived will be discussed in greater detail in Chapter 5.

Once these nonmarket costs have been determined for every class of goods and added to vehicle operating costs for each class of vehicles their sum can be added to the cost of maintenance of way in each year to give a measure of the annual cost of transportation of goods on the facility. Summing these costs over the life of the facility produces the total cost of oepration. An interest rate of 15 percent is typical of a developing country, and that value has been used to discount future costs to the present. A life of 20 years is used in all analyses in the study. Items occurring after 20 years, including scrap value, have very little influence on the present when interest rates are over 10 percent. Ignoring these items, therefore, introduces only negligible error. Table 2–5 shows these figures in the form of a cost summary for the old road. As there are no construction

Table 2-5
Cost Summary For the Old Road (Balanced Traffic Flow)

	Present Discounted Value in Dollars[a]		
	Low Volume (100 tons/day)	Medium Volume (1000 tons/day)	High Volume (5000 tons/day)
Construction costs	$ 0	$ 0	$ 0
Maintenance of way	299,840	508,960	1,474,590
Nonmarket costs	2,663,150	26,028,750	379,092,030
Vehicle operating costs	4,595,880	39,237,630	451,210,940
Total costs	$7,558,870	$65,775,340	$831,777,130

[a] 15 percent discount rate, 20-year time horizon.

costs for the existing road, total costs are almost linearly proportional to the traffic volume. This total cost measure will be important in comparing proposed alternatives to the existing road.

The New Highway

The first alternative to be considered in this example is the construction of a new highway between A and B. As the old road follows the river between the two cities, its length is twice the 100-mile direct distance between them. By taking a more direct route, it should be possible to design a new roadway that would be shorter than the old road. As the terrain between the two cities is assumed to be hilly, there are a number of possible routes and modes of construction that could be used. A fairly inexpensive route could be selected to avoid the major hills at the expense of a somewhat longer alignment, or a somewhat more direct route could be followed with potentially higher costs of construction. A more direct path between the cities must also achieve a balance between higher gradient facilities and increased earthwork costs. One might consider replacing only a portion of the old road, or reconstructing it to higher standards; in either case the resulting facility would become the "new highway." It is obvious that quite a range of facilities can be designed, as the number of lanes and their width, the design speed, and the surface type, can also be varied.

In the face of such a large number of possible alternative designs, the question immediately arises of how to choose the most appropriate. In practice this is a very challenging question and deserves the careful attention of an expert design engineer. The challenge is met here by generating a large number of alternative designs using an electronic computer and selecting from among them the one with the lowest total cost as defined above. This was done as a complete substudy using the procedure shown in Figure 2-2. The substudy methodology is described in Chapter 6.

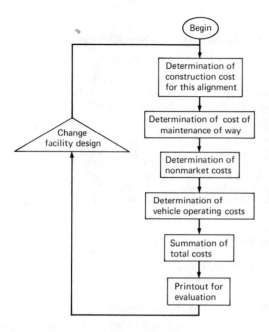

Figure 2–2. The Optimization Procedure.

The substudy concluded that there is no one design that is best for all conditions. The choice is dependent on the terrain; the traffic volume; the commodity type and mix; and the cost of earthwork, paving, and other factor inputs. For each set of conditions the trade-offs between length, gradient, and design speed will be different. This conclusion was borne out by the characteristics possessed by the minimum-total-cost new highway for each of the volume levels considered, as selected by this cost-minimization procedure. These designs are shown in Table 2–6.

Table 2–6
Link Physical Characteristics of the Highway Selected by the
Optimization Procedure for Each Traffic Volume Level

	Low Volume (100 tons/day)	Medium Volume (1000 tons/day)	High Volume (5000 tons/day)
Length	105 miles	100 miles	100 miles
Surface type	Paved	Paved	Paved
Design speed	30 mph	50 mph	50 mph
Gradient	7%	4%	2%
Width of lane	12 feet	12 feet	12 feet
Number of lanes	2	2	2

Table 2–7
Typical Vehicle Costs and Performance on the New Highway

	1 Physical Units Consumed	2 Cost Per Unit (dollars)	3 Cost Per Vehicle (dollars)	4 Percent of Total
Crew	6.076 man hours	0.330	2.005	18.1
Fuel	18.968 gallons	0.150	2.921	26.3
Oil	0.600 quarts	0.233	0.140	1.3
Tires	0.022 tires	101.000	2.178	19.6
Maintenance (parts)	0.000122 vehicle	13,300.000	1.623	14.6
Maintenance (labor)	0.800 man hours	0.400	0.320	2.9
Depreciation	0.000143 vehicle	13,300.000	1.915	17.2
Total			11.101	100.0

Cost per vehicle mile = $0.111
Cost per ton mile   = $0.047

Traffic = general truck, medium volume, flowing from A to B (200 tons/day).

The results of this analysis indicate that the low volume highway has minimum costs with a length of 105 miles, a design speed of 30 miles per hour and a gradient of 7 percent. Construction costs are $3.7 million. For the two higher-volume situations the road was essentially straight with a 50 mph design speed. There was, however, a difference in the gradient selected for traffic volume levels of 1000 tons per day and 5000 tons per day. Costs to build the facilities were $7.8 million for the medium-volume situation and $11.8 million for the high-volume case, with the increase going to reduce the gradient of the road. For flat or mountainous terrain, the best designs are entirely different from those chosen here in the hilly case.

As with the old road, vehicle operating costs for the new road were obtained by simulation. These results are shown in Table 2–7. It is interesting to compare typical truck operating costs and performance experienced on the new medium-volume highway with the figures obtained previously for the old road. Crew, fuel, and maintenance are the most important costs in both cases and all are down significantly over the same figures for the old road. (See Table 2–3.) Also significant was the saving in depreciation. An important factor here is the increased utilization of the vehicle arising from higher speeds. This is reflected in part by the fact that some 50 percent of costs were due to crew and depreciation on the old road, but on the new highway, only 35 percent of vehicle operating costs were recorded in these two categories.

The nonmarket costs to commodites for shipping over the new road were also reduced, as is evidenced by Table 2–8. Both travel time and time variability have been considerably lowered while the cost of vehicle operation is less than one-third the cost on the old road. For general commodities at least, the new

Table 2-8
Determination of Commodity Perceived Costs on the New Highway

	Link Performance	Commodity Weightings of Performance	Commodity Perceived Costs = (Col. 1) × (Col. 2)
Waiting time	1.10 hours	0.514 $/ton/hour	$0.565[a]
Travel time	2.53 hours	0.362 $/ton/hour	0.916[a]
Time variability	3.20 hours	0.035 $/ton/hour	0.112[a]
Probability of loss or damage	0.00029%	2040 $/ton	0.608[a]
Vehicle operation	4.65 $/ton	1.0 $/$	4.650[b]
Total			$6.851

Note: Traffic = general truck, medium volume, flowing from A to B (200 tons/day).
[a] Nonmarket costs.
[b] Vehicle operation.

road is a great improvement over the existing road, in all respects.

Over the 20-year time horizon used here, the present discounted value of maintenance of way, nonmarket costs to commodities, and vehicle operating costs amount to a predominant proportion of total cost. For the medium-volume road, they account for almost $20 million of the $27 million of total costs. (See Table 2-9.) In comparing the new highway using the figures obtained under any of the three traffic volumes considered with the corresponding totals for the old road (Table 2-5), the improvement provided by the new road is obvious. Before jumping to the conslusion that the new highway should be built, however, we should also examine the possibility of building a railroad.

Table 2-9
Cost Summary for the New Highway (Balanced traffic flow)[a]

	Present Discounted Values in Millions of Dollars[b]		
	Low Volume (100 tons/day)	Medium Volume (1000 tons/day)	High Volume (5000 tons/day)
Construction costs	$3.7	$ 7.8	$ 11.8
Maintenance of way	0.3	0.3	0.4
Nonmarket costs	1.4	7.5	33.4
Vehicle operating costs	2.0	11.5	54.7
Total costs	$7.4	$27.1	$100.3

[a] See Table 6-3 for detailed design parameters.
[b] 15 percent interest rate, 20-year time horizon.

Rail Alternative

Highways and railways are different in so many obvious characteristics that they are not often thought of as substitutes for each other. One or the other is frequently selected on noneconomic grounds, and then a careful analysis is used to design the facility. Unfortunately, there are no simple rules of thumb for deciding when railroads are more appropriate than highways. The construction cost of each can vary tremendously depending upon the terrain that is traversed. In any specified terrain the two will often take much different routes because of the need to minimize grades on the railroad and the greater width of right-of-way needed for the highway. It would be improper, however, to attempt to compare railroads and highways on the basis of construction costs alone because, as we noted in the previous examples, the nonmarket and vehicle operating costs are so large a component of total costs.

Trade-offs exist in railroad design that are similar to those for highways. Increased length can be substituted for high earthwork cost to achieve the lower gradients required by a railroad. The cost minimization approach discussed in the previous section can likewise be used in the design of rail facilities. The resulting facility designs are shown in Table 2–10. Not only is the railroad alignment different from those of the new highway, but the designs vary substantially between volume levels. The average railroad gradient is considerably lower than it was for the highway alternative, and the higher volumes justify a flatter roadbed than the low volume case. It is possible to have more than one size of locomotive, and the higher-powered locomotive was selected for use in the high-volume case, while the low-powered units were used for the smaller volumes. In no case were grades so steep and traffic so heavy that two locomotives were necessary. The conges-

Table 2–10
**Link Physical Characteristics of the Railway Selected by the
Optimization Procedure for Each Traffic Volume Level**

	Low Volume (100 tons/day)	Medium Volume (1000 tons/day)	High Volume (5000 tons/day)
Length	120 miles	100	100
Speed limit	20 mph	40 mph	40 mph
Maximum gradient	3%	1.25%	1.25%
Average gradient	2%	0.25%	0.25%
Number of locomotives per train	1	1	1
Locomotive horse-power	800 hp	800 hp	1500 hp
Number of passing sidings	12	10	10

Table 2–11
Typical Train Costs and Performance on the New Railway

Average cars per train		
Bulk	8	
General	8	
Special	1	
Passenger	6	
Total	23	
Average speed	25.7 mph	
Trains per day	2.7	
Operations cost per ton-mile	$0.0142	
Total annual costs by rail	(Thousands)	
Vehicle maintenance	$17.8	3.3%
Locomotive maintenance	13.5	2.5
Fuel and oil	20.6	3.8
Crew	32.3	5.9
Depreciation	62.5	11.5
Traffic and overhead	135.1	24.8
Maintenance of way, station, yards, and other	$252.3	48.2
		100.0%

Note: Traffic = general goods, medium volume, balanced flow.

tion appearing sometimes at high volumes could be reduced, and operating speeds increased, by increasing the number of passing sidings, which raised construction costs. Constructing railroads in this terrain was more costly than roads: $9.8 million for the low-volume case; $16.0 million for the medium- and high-volume cases. These costs are typical for this scenario for a one-track, narrow-gauge, manual-signal system railway, employing diesel locomotives.

Train costs and performance for the medium-volume case are shown in Table 2–11. A typical train is made up of eight bulk cars, eight general cars, one oil tank car, and six passenger cars. The average speed of 25.7 miles per hour while the train is moving compares favorably with the speeds achieved by trucks on the new highway. The delays from yard operation and switching, however, give the train a much longer total travel time. At 1000 tons per day there are a total of 19 trains per week. Operating costs are quite low, approaching $0.015 per ton mile. Operating costs are not the principal costs, however, since traffic and overhead, maintenance of way, station yards, and other costs account for 73 percent of the total. (See the listing of Annual Costs in the lower portion of Table 2–11.) The cost per ton mile for railroad transport is still low, however, when compared to the $0.047 per ton mile for highway transport.

It is interesting to examine the commodity perceived costs incurred by general goods traveling over the railroad, as was done in the highway case. This

Table 2-12
Determination of Commodity Perceived Costs on the New Railway

	1 Link Performance	2 Commodity Weightings of Performance	3 Commodity Perceived Costs = (Col. 1) × (Col. 2)
Waiting time	4.48 hours	0.514 $/ton/hr.	$2.303[a]
Travel time	9.21 hours	0.362 $/ton/hr.	3.340[a]
Time variability	1.37 hours	0.035 $/ton/hr.	0.048[a]
Probability of			
loss or damage	0.000457%	2040 $/ton	0.933[a]
Vehicle operation	1.42 $/ton	1.0 $/$	1.420[b]
Total	—	—	$8.044

Note: Traffic = general goods, medium volume, balanced flow.
[a]Nonmarket costs.
[b]Vehicle operation.

information is presented in Table 2-12. Commodity weightings of performance are identical to those used for the highway case since they are assumed to be constant over all modes. Link performance, however, is considerably different for the railroad than it was for highway and the resulting commodity perceived costs are somewhat larger, principally in waiting and travel time.

A summary of costs for the new railway is presented in Table 2-13. For the low-volume case the cost of construction is approximately 50 percent of the total, while for the higher-volume cases it accounts for a decreasing percentage of total cost. Nonmarket costs were important in all cases. For high volumes, however, nonmarket costs were significantly larger than both construction costs or operating and maintenance costs.

Table 2-13
Cost Summary for the New Railway (Balanced traffic flow)

	Present Discounted Value in Millions of Dollars[a]		
	Low Volume (100 tons/day)	Medium Volume (1000 tons/day)	High Volume (5000 tons/day)
Construction costs	$ 9.9	$16.0	$ 16.0
Nonmarket costs	4.9	22.5	74.1
Vehicle operating costs and way maintenance	5.2	6.8	23.8
Total costs	$20.0	$45.3	$113.9

[a]15 percent interest rate, 20-year time horizon.

The construction cost of different railroad facilities varies widely, and the high-volume design costs almost twice as much as the low-volume design. It is important to note that this design solution was selected in response to the particular conditions of this case. With different topography or with variations in the cost of earthwork, ties, railroad, rails, or aggregate, the solution could be greatly altered. It is also interesting to note that the nonmarket costs are significant in the total, particularly for the high-volume cases. This suggests that the commodity mix is an important factor in determining overall cost as the commodity preference weightings for higher-valued goods are in general sensitive to long waiting or travel times.

Analysis of Alternatives

It is useful to compare all the alternative courses of action that have been studied to this point. The comparison should include the old road as its continued use represents a possible alternative. If the new road is built along a completely separate alignment it is unlikely that the old road will be completely removed in any event. The appropriate comparable figures for each alternative from Table 2–5, Table 2–9, and Table 2–13 are summarized in Table 2–14. The smallest cost in each of the three columns indicates the preferred choice for each volume level. For low-volume conditions the new highway appears to be best. However, given the possible error in the prediction of future traffic demand, the margin of difference between it and the old road is small and it seems questionable whether the new highway should be built. For medium-volume conditions the choice is clearer; the new highway appears to generate half the total cost of the new railway. Building either the new highway or the new railroad is much cheaper than continuing with the old road. At high traffic volumes the new road

Table 2–14
Cost Summary Comparisons for the Old Road, the New Highway, and the New Railroad: Total Costs (Balanced traffic flow)

	Present Discounted Value in Millions of Dollars of Total Costs[a]		
	Low Volume (100 tons/day)	*Medium Volume (1000 tons/day)*	*High Volume (5000 tons/day)*
Old road	$ 7.6	$65.8	$451.2
New highway	7.4	27.1	100.3
New railway	20.0	45.3	113.9

[a] 15 percent rate, 20-year time horizon.

is still best, but the difference in cost between the railroad and the new highway
is less than at medium volume.

Some analysts might have omitted the nonmarket costs from the comparison
entirely. Although we believe that this is inappropriate, it is interesting to consider what the answers would have been had nonmarket cost been left out of the
computations. This has been done in Table 2-15, which includes only the sum of
construction costs, vehicle operating, and way maintenance costs. A decision
based upon the minimum of these among the three alternatives produces answers
quite different from those that arise from consideration of all costs. For the low-
volume facility the old road is superior, while in the medium- and high-volume
cases the new railroad is best. Omission of nonmarket costs thus tends to bias
conclusions in favor of a railroad solution.

Table 2-15
Cost Summary Comparisons for the Three Alternatives: Nonmarket
Costs Omitted (Balanced traffic flow)

	Present Discounted Value in Millions of Dollars of Construction Plus Operating Costs[a]		
	Low Volume (100 tons/day)	Medium Volume (1000 tons/day)	High Volume (5000 tons/day)
Old road	$ 4.9	$39.7	$452.7
New highway	8.0	19.6	66.9
New railway	15.0	17.8	39.8

[a]15 percent interest rates, 20-year time horizon.

Selection of a best alternative requires more than deciding whether to consider total cost or just market costs. Various decision makers will have quite different objective functions, and thus may wish to weight the many consequences
of a project differently. A single cost or benefit may be valued one way when it
falls on one group and differently when it falls on another. The matter of
objectives will be dealt with more fully in Chapter 10. Here, we will examine the
viewpoints of the four groups most directly involved: the trucker, the railroad,
the shipper, and the government.

The Trucker. From the viewpoint of the trucker, the proper solution is obvious; he would like the new highway. Almost every aspect of his operating cost
and performance are improved by moving from the old road to the new highway.
Costs per vehicle mile are reduced from $0.1807 per vehicle mile to $0.111 per
vehicle mile. Moreover, if the railroad were built instead, the trucker would lose
traffic to the railroad. This can be verified by comparing the figure for commodity perceived costs on the new railroad from Table 2-12 with those for the old

road in Table 2–4. The trucker using the old road would not be able to compete with the new railroad.

The Railroad. Railroad preferences are also easily determined, though feeling may not run as high as that of the truckers because this railway line is not yet in existence and, therefore, could not be "hurt" by the construction of a new road. For the low-volume case, railroad management would not be interested in constructing a new facility because they would lose money; but, for the two higher-volume cases, railroad management would undoubtedly be in favor of the construction of the rail alternative instead of the highway. The figures indicate that if a new railroad is built, traffic can be attracted from the old road and the railroad would be a profitable financial venture. Moreover, the railroad can argue that this is the lowest cost solution to the problem of regional transport as construction cost plus operating costs are lowest for the rail alternative. The railroad management would be opposed to the construction of a new road in addition to the railroad because of the probable deleterious effect on railroad traffic. As railroad operations have significant economies of scale, maintaining high traffic volume levels is important.

The Shipper. From the viewpoint of a shipper the decision is not quite so clear. There could easily be a difference of opinion among shippers of different types of goods as to what facilities should be constructed. General goods, with their high preference for low travel times favor a very fast mode. Passengers also have a high time preference. Bulk goods and special goods are not as concerned about time or loss and damage. Commodity perceived costs provide a measure of the way in which each of these commodity groups is likely to view the alternatives. The results of this computation for both facilities in the hilly terrain at high volume are presented in Table 2–16. The preferences here indicate clearly that bulk goods prefer railway while general goods and passengers prefer the highway mode.

Table 2-16
Commodity Perceived Costs Used in Determination of Modal Choice (Dollars Per Ton)

Commodity Group	Costs For Traveling by:	
	New Highway	New Railway
Bulk goods	0.752	0.520
General goods	1.612	1.872
Special goods	0.819	0.326
Common carrier passengers	2.340	4.190
Private carrier passengers	12.108	18.75

Note: Market plus nonmarket costs; high volume; balanced traffic flow.

The Government. The government could be expected to adopt a "neutral" point of view by weighting the benefits associated with each of the above groups on an equal basis. It appears that using only operating plus construction cost as the criteria, the rail project is the best choice at high volume, while the figures in Table 2-14 (incorporating nonmarket perceived costs) indicate that construction of a new highway is the best alternative from a total cost point of view for all volumes. This must be qualified, however, as the problems associated with pricing, taxes, foreign exchange, and others which are discussed elsewhere have not been taken into account.

A Combined Alternative

One alternative still has not been evaluated, that of both the highway and the railroad being built simultaneously. It could be possible that the construction of both facilities — even with the resulting higher total cost would lead to savings in nonmarket costs that are larger than the additional construction cost involved. This possibility seems sufficiently intriguing to merit investigation.

Although the idea of a combined alternative is simple, some complications arise when it is more closely examined. First, if the appropriate design of a facility is a function of volume, then the proportion of total volumes selecting each facility must be known before the design can be finalized. Before the choice of mode can be determined, however, the performance level for each facility must be known. This presents a chicken and egg problem requiring either an iterative or a trial and error solution. There is also a problem in pricing, particularly with rail. If the railroads are required to cover their full cost, then the lower volumes generated on the rail portion of a combined alternative imply that the tariffs charged must be higher than those for the rail alternative alone. Although these problems are real and pose complex analytical issues in the real world we would hope that the simplicity of this sample situation may allow us to jump ahead to an appropriate final solution, rather than having to converge on it iteratively.

If, for the moment, the cost of construction is ignored, so that fares cover only operating and maintenance, the commodity perceived costs can be used as a measure of the manner in which each commodity group view the modes between which it is expected to choose. Using the commodity perceived costs presented in Table 2-16, travel by each of the commodity groups on each of the modes can be analyzed. In each case the costs are based on a split of traffic volume between the modes. It is clear from examination of this table that bulk and special goods prefer to travel by rail while general goods and passengers will select the highway mode given the performance characteristics demonstrated. Thus, for the case in which all construction costs are borne by the government, a combined alternative is preferred by rail shippers over a highway solution.

Table 2-17
**Cost Summary for the Combined Highway and Railway Projects
(Balanced traffic flow)**

	Present Discounted Value in Thousands of Dollars[a]		
	Low Volume (100 tons/day)	Medium Volume (1000 tons/day)	High Volume (5000 tons/day)
New Highway			
Construction costs	$ 3,689	$ 7,827	$ 11,817
Maintenance of way	282	282	347
Nonmarket costs	1,302	7,012	29,266
Vehicle operating costs	1,367	6,808	31,964
Total costs	$ 6,640	$21,929	$ 73,394
New Railway			
Construction cost	9,883	9,883	15,995
Nonmarket costs	318	1,492	5,101
Vehicle operating costs	4,859	8,341	9,959
Total costs	$15,059	$19,715	$ 31,056
Total both facilities	$21,699	$41,744	$104,450

[a] 15 percent interest rate, 20-year time horizon.

Let us now consider whether the construction of both the highway and rail projects makes sense from the standpoint of lowest total discounted value, using the distribution of traffic by mode decided above. The costs for the combined alternative are presented by category in Table 2-17. While the cost of the combined alternative at high volume is not less than building the new highway, it is very close. Apparently the amount saved by bulk and special goods when traveling by rail is almost sufficient to pay for the cost of building and operating the new railroad in addition to the new highway. The difference between total cost in the two cases is on the order of 5 percent. If the traffic volumes had been larger, or if a larger portion of the total flow had been bulk goods, the result would apparently have been to build both facilities. In order to verify this conclusion additional experiments were made with a commodity mix that was more bulk intensive, for a situation in which there were larger traffic volumes, and for an environment with flatter terrain. For each, the total cost of the combined alternative was less than either highway or rail for one or more of the volume levels.

With solutions this close together, it is difficult for the government to ignore the possibility of building both facilities. If the government announces its intention to build a highway, the railroads and the rail shippers will voice their own desires, perhaps applying political pressure, as would the truckers and the highway shippers if the government announced a rail solution instead. As a consequence, the combined alternative might have a better chance for political success than either project alone.

If it is not appropriate for the government to absorb the cost of construction of one or both of the facilities, we must examine the impact, if any, on the above results of some other means of financing. This might occur, for example, if the railroad were a private, profit-making company or a government authority responsible for recovering the cost of construction through tolls.

We have seen that in the high-volume case, with the traffic split based upon a rail fare that covers operating but not construction cost, the combined project is barely justified, based on total costs including construction. If the rail fare is raised to cover construction, however, some traffic will be discouraged from using the railroad and shift to the highway. If we assume that the construction cost is equally divided over all ton miles shipped on the railroad, its magnitude can be easily determined by amortizing the construction cost over the life of the facility and allocating this cost to the daily tonnage.[2] The figures for low volumes need not even be considered since the combined alternative is not attractive in that case. This inclusion of construction adds a toll for bulk and special goods of $0.0376 per ton mile for the medium volume case and $0.0146 per ton mile for the high-volume case. For the 120-mile trip on the medium-volume railroad this amounts to $4.51 per ton and for the 100-mile high-volume trip $1.46 per ton; clearly enough, when added to the figures of Table 2–16, to shift those goods from the railroad to the highway. Thus if the railroad must recover its construction cost from tariffs alone, the project is not feasible.

One could investigate other combinations such as where the highway is forced to cover its construction costs with tolls while the railroad is not required to do so. This is, however, a much less common situation and will not be examined here. Likewise the case where both facilities are required to pay their full costs could be examined. In principle, highway gasoline taxes may be designed to cover the costs of highway construction. Where one transportation mode covers many different links, however, it is common for one portion of the system to subsidize another. This could happen for rail as well as highway. Clearly, when there are systems effects such as these, it is no longer appropriate to continue to measure costs and benefits over the single project. The viewpoint must be broadened.

---

2. The amortized cost of construction (*TOLL*) is computed using the construction cost (*COST*), the capital recovery factor (*CRF*) for a life of 20 years, and 15 percent interest rate, the daily tonnage (*TONS*), the days per year (*DAYS*), and the length (*LENG*) as:

$$TOLL = \frac{COST \cdot CRF}{DAYS \cdot TONS \cdot LENG.}$$

The Example Problem in Perspective

This presentation of the example problem has necessarily been abbreviated. This was done so that we might get an overview of the method of analysis and attendant difficulties. Although an admittedly oversimplified problem was selected, it grew quickly in size and complexity. What appeared to be the mere selection of either a highway or a railroad has turned into a far more complex undertaking involving the selection of appropriate facility alignments and design features, as well as a study of the pricing of the transport modes.

In the interest of simplicity and ease of exposition a number of important matters have not been discussed that cannot be ignored in an actual analysis situation. The most important of these considerations — transport systems effects — was elaborated in Chapter 1, but it bears repeating. The diversion of traffic from one route to another, a change in the choice of mode, or a transport-induced growth in traffic level and composition may fall beyond the scope of a typical project analysis, but must be considered in the project decision.

The nature of the example problem also precluded detailed consideration of the impact of the length of haul and the size of shipments on carrier economics and the resulting modal choice decision of the carrier. Clearly larger shipment sizes encourage economies of scale in transfer operations and longer hauls allow this fixed terminal cost to be recovered at a lower "rate per mile." In general, terminal and transfer operations are extremely important in any transport system and should be given high priority in the analysis. For that very reason a model of the intermodal transfer process has been included in the set of Project Analyzer computer routines used in this study. The transfer model treats the fixed costs of terminal operation while the highway and rail models emphasize the variable or line-haul portion of the costs. Although transfer operations were not addressed explicitly in the example problem of this chapter their inclusion would not change the conceptual framework of the analysis in any way.

Another complexity that was not addressed in the example problem has to do with the identification of appropriate government objective functions. Although no objective was explicitly identified it is implied that the objective was minimum total cost. For accuracy, however, one must consider the effect of foreign exchange, the revenues generated by taxes and their implications for the pricing of the transport service, and the distortions of market prices that typically exist in a developing region. All of these considerations will be handled explicitly in later chapters.

In spite of the limitations of the example problem there are some general conclusions that can be drawn. The situation addressed was one where changes to an existing line-haul transport system were being proposed. The traffic volume levels and mix are typical of many developing countries and the narrow-gauge railroad was also typical. One conclusion seems to be that a railroad is not the most economical solution for most volume levels in hilly terrain at balanced commodity flows. For high-volume levels, and particularly for commodity mixes that involve large amounts of bulk commodities, it may be attractive. Perhaps the most interesting conclusion of this example problem is that where traffic levels are high enough, minimum total costs may in some cases be achieved by building both a highway and a railroad.

The principal problem in stating general conclusions is the vast number of possible variables that bear upon the optimum solution to a problem of this type. Given the basic environmental variables, the terrain, factor prices, costs of construction, modal technology, traffic levels, and commodity mix, a very large number of possible variations can exist. For this reason it is unwise to draw overly sweeping conslusions from any general study.

3

The Experimental Conditions

Terrain

The building of any proposed transportation project requires a thorough knowledge of the terrain through which the project is to be constructed as well as construction costs. The actual design of the facility will depend upon a number of features of the landscape. In the real world these features occur in what can only be described as a hopelessly large number of combinations. If this study attempted to replicate only those forms of terrain which were highly representative of the countries where this analysis could be applied, there would still be literally hundreds of different terrain types to be considered. Even if these laborious computations were performed and somehow tabulated it is quite likely that particular problems with unique local features would need to be separately considered anyway. With the large number of other variables to be explored this would lead to literally millions of answers.

The value of such a computation would be dubious in any event, because it tends to give an erroneous impression of accuracy, which can lead to unthinking direct application of the results to cases where they are simply not appropriate. In contrast, the purpose of this study is to show trends in cost and performance and sensitivity to changes in numerous parameters, and to provide example results. It is not to give precise answers to specific real-world situations. While the examples given here should be useful in pointing out possible solutions and in providing points of reference, it is expected that in any particular case a study should be made using actual data representing the facts peculiar to the situation under study.

These objectives call for a consistent and realistic definition of the terrain to be used in the study as well as other environmental conditions. We have summarized terrain description into three different basic topographic types identified as flat, hilly, and mountainous. All three are assumed to incorporate well-drained, stable soil, and to require no special treatment for construction of the facility. Because bridges are a discrete phenomenon not directly related to any particular terrain type, no bridges have been included in the analysis. In any specific application, the number of bridges needed will have to be decided separately and their cost added to the basic construction cost. While these assumptions concerning the terrain description are strong, they favor highways and railroads equally so they should not seriously alter the relative merits of the two modes of transportation.

Table 3-1
Characteristics of the Three Representative Terrains

	Flat	Hilly	Mountain
Average gradient (percent)	2%	8%	10%
Peak-to-peak distance (feet)	10,000	4,000	20,000

A brief description of the three terrain types used in this study is given in Table 3-1. The flat terrain consists in long, low, relatively smooth undulations with a 2 percent grade, conditions which are not particularly demanding of cut and fill operations to level the roadway or roadbed. The hilly terrain has much steeper grades but the distance between hilltops is considerably shorter so that the hills are not significantly higher than those of the flat terrain. The mountainous terrain has still steeper grades and a substantially greater distance between ridge lines so that the peaks are much higher. In mountainous terrain it will often be necessary to select circuitous routes up and down the sides of the mountains in order to achieve acceptable gradients because the expense of cutting and filling would be prohibitive along perfectly straight alignments.[1]

Traffic Volume

Just as an infinite variety of terrain conditions must be condensed for a general study such as this one, so also must the traffic volume and composition be briefly described to permit a manageable analysis. Again, it is not possible to replicate every conceivable situation that might occur in practice. Instead, we have attempted to provide traffic figures that will bracket the majority of cases that may be encountered.

Three volume levels are defined: low, medium, and high, consisting respectively of 100, 1000, and 5000 tons per day on the average traveling in each direction. The low-volume figure is representative of the traffic on an unimportant rural road or on the small branch lines of a railroad. This volume was selected as the lower limit in this study because it was felt that a smaller volume would rarely justify construction of an entirely new facility. At least, in most cases, it would not be sufficient to raise the question of constructing a railroad.

The high-volume level is meant to be representative of a road connecting

---

1. Technically, "gradient" is the slope measured at a point, while "rise and fall" is the algebraic sum of the absolute values of all rises and falls divided by the distance covered. The two terms are used interchangeably in this study as they are equivalent for the simplified terrain used here.

relatively large cities and carrying medium-to-substantial traffic. The two-way total flow of 10,000 tons per day is equivalent to perhaps 2000 or more vehicles per day which, while not constituting heavy traffic, is larger than typical local traffic. A flow of 10,000 tons per day is more than any segment of the Colombian National Railroad carries at the present time. In fact, it taxes the capacity of a narrow-gauge, single-track railroad with the simple switching and signalling systems that are employed in the designs used here. It seems likely that the high volume represents the upper range of volumes for which a decision between highway and railroad will be difficult.

In considering these volumes, it is important to remember that the model is designed to simulate traffic moving from one end of the link or facility completely to the other and does not include local traffic moving over only a portion of the facility. This simplification is essential to the study because the behavior of short-haul traffic with respect to choice of mode is quite different from the behavior of traffic moving over much longer distances. Therefore, the results of these studies are most applicable to a link of a transportation network where there are substantial cities at either end of the link and little population between. It is more difficult to apply the results to situations in which significant transportation links intersect those under study. If the proposed facility is to pass through densely populated areas that generate large amounts of local or urban traffic, the local traffic would have to be considered separately from the analysis here.

In addition to noting the spatial distribution of traffic over portions of the transportation link, it is important to consider the distribution of traffic over time. In most actual situations there are cyclical variations in traffic level which vary over hourly, daily, or seasonal flows. It is appropriate therefore to consider separately the type of facility that can best accomodate this varying traffic level.

Where information is available on seasonal traffic variations they can be represented using a time period of one season and adjusting traffic volumes seasonally.

In addition, in the evaluation of alternatives projected over a 20-year time period in most countries, traffic volumes can be expected to rise continuously if not predictably over such an extended period. In the absence of specific information about the particular economy addressed it is impossible to predict what the rate of increase in traffic volume might be; that is, what an appropriate shape for this curve would be.

For any particular growth curve it is possible to substitute a constant traffic stream that is equivalent in a discounted present value sense. Conversely, a single constant stream can be converted into a large number of equivalent growing series using different starting values, annual growth rates, and discounting factors. In order to have a common basic unit of traffic measure in this study we have used a traffic volume that remains constant over the 20-year period. In a particular real-world analysis situation information will typically be available which will allow the traffic growth over time to be estimated and, at that time it is this anticipated growth curve which should be used.[2]

To compare the results of studies made under various growth assumptions it will be necessary first to convert the stream of traffic to an equivalent uniform annual volume. This can be done in two steps using interest formulas. First, the yearly volumes are discounted to find their present value using an interest rate representing the social rate of time preference, which, without inflation, would be the rate at which all future costs are discounted. Their sum gives the total present value. Then, the yearly equivalent can be found using the appropriate discounting formula for determining the annual amount equivalent to a present sum. Thus the equivalent uniform annual volume serves as the common basic unit of traffic measure by which different growth situations can be compared.

The composition of the simulated traffic volumes by commodity type is very important to any analysis of proposed transportation facilities because of the different types of vehicles used by different commodities and the different weightings placed by these commodities on the various aspects of the performance of the trip. This commodity valuation is discussed in greater detail in Chapter 5. In this study traffic is divided into five different commodity classes based upon the value of the commodity, its perishability, the type of vehicle used to transport it, the method of loading and unloading, and other factors. A detailed description of these commodity types is contained in Chapter 6 in the derivation of commodity weighting of performance. The commodity classes are labeled Bulk, General, Special, Common (passenger), and Private (passenger). Each class may actually include many different commodities. However all the commodities in a class will travel in identical vehicles, separate from other classes, and be handled in the same manner, also separate from others. Costs and performance measures are computed and printed out individually for each class.

In some cases, it might seem desirable to have more than five commodity categories, particularly if there are several goods that travel in special vehicles or receive special handling such that the costs and other aspects of shipping the good are quite different from other goods. Developing countries, however, generally have a standard general-purpose-vehicle fleet and simple, uniform cargo handling facilities, so the need for more classes is less pronounced than it would be in more advanced nations. In the event that all five classes were not needed, one or more could simply be ignored. More classes can also be added if necessary.

---

2. See Charles River Associates, *A Manual of Computer Programs for Project Analysis* (Washington, D.C.: Commerce Clearinghouse, 1970), pp. 117–121.

Commodity Mixes

Just as three different terrain types and three different volume levels have been considered, so we will analyze three different combinations of the five basic commodities. These three combinations, as we have designated them, or "commodity mixes," are: balanced flow, bulk-dominated flow, and general-dominated flow. The total number of tons of each commodity flowing each direction for each of these given mixes under the medium volume level are shown in Table 3–2. Passenger traffic has been converted from tons to numbers of persons for this presentation. For the low-volume level, all tonnages are one-tenth as great as they are in Table 3–2, while the high-volume level has numbers five times as great. In the balanced case, the total tonnage of bulk goods traveling both directions is equal to the total tonnage of general goods traveling in both directions. In the bulk-dominated case, however, the total tonnage of bulk goods is larger than that of general goods. In the case of general-dominated flows, the reverse is true. For all cases, the total tonnage of special goods and of common and private passengers flowing in both directions remains unchanged. The balanced case has equal amounts flowing in each direction while for the bulk and general cases flows are unbalanced.

An important influence on operating costs and performance is exerted by this balance of traffic in the two directions, since unbalanced loads mean that vehicles must make empty nonrevenue backhauls. Here we have assumed that there is some empty backhaul for both bulk and general goods even in the case described as "balanced." This difference could represent raw material exports moving in one direction and manufactured import products moving in the other.

In any particular application, the vehicle load factors actually observed might be quite different from those used here. In addition, the mix of commodities could be quite different from the mix that we have chosen. The values that have been used in this study are considered to be reasonable values for the conditions of the base scenario, but they are not necessarily the correct values for any particular case. The impact that directionally balanced traffic can have on load factors and therefore on operating costs can be seen by noting that filling the backhaul in the balanced case would increase vehicle operating costs very little, but it would reduce the average cost to the shipper 33 percent. Similarly, if there were no backhaul at all costs would increase on the average by 33 percent per ton.

Factor Prices

The factor prices used for the base scenario are derived using data from Colombia, South America. These figures were used in earlier simulations of the

Table 3–2
Volume of Commodities by Class in Tons Per Day for Three Commodity Mixes
(At Medium Volume: Average 2000 Tons/Day Both Ways)

Class Commodity Mix	Direction	Bulk (tons)	General (tons)	Special (tons)	Passenger		Total Tons
					Common (persons)	Private (persons)	
Balanced mix	To A	600	200	100	900	100	1000
	To B	200	600	100	900	100	1000
Bulk dominated	To A	900	300	150	1350	150	1500
	To B	100	300	50	450	50	500
General dominated	To A	300	100	50	450	50	500
	To B	300	900	150	1350	150	1500

Note: The total two-way flow of 2000 tons per day averages to 1000 tons each way. The text often refers to medium volume as "1000 tons per day," though in some cases it consists of the unequal flows of 1500 and 500 tons.

Colombian transportation system and have been calibrated for accuracy against aggregate statistics for that country. The Colombian costs were converted from pesos to U.S. dollars at the official exchange rate in 1967, when the various statistics were gathered, and adjustments have been made for inflation to the present time. Prices for the second scenario represent Israel. They were similarly derived.[3]

Even though the data used here are the most accurate available, it is necessary to recognize the assumptions implicit in their use. Most operating costs such as vehicle maintenance cost per vehicle mile and yearly maintenance cost per vehicle depend not only upon individual goods prices but also upon methods used and technology employed. For a single country these may vary from one area to another and may change over time. They can even be changed as the result of investing in a new transportation facility. If, for example, a new railroad link is built and stocked with new locomotives and cars, the new link may experience quite different operating and maintenance costs from those over the remainder of the systems, particularly if old equipment or poorly maintained road beds are employed there. Managerial efficiency or the productivity of a different labor force may cause a new facility to operate substantially more or less efficiently than an existing facility even though the same technology and equipment are used. Thus when applying the results presented here to a proposed transportation investment it is important to consider how the operation of the proposed facility might differ from the operations on which the existing cost data are based.

It is frequently tempting for Americans or Europeans to project the operation of their own transportation systems into situations proposed for developing countries. This projection can lead to seriously erroneous results as, even if the same equipment were used, the method of operation, the maintenance, and many other factors are likely to be quite different in a developing country. These pitfalls are avoided here by the use of price data and information about existing operations from the country to be studied. Every attempt has been made to create overall cost and service performance that is similar to that of the particular developing country under study.

In the example problem in Chapter 2 the role of taxes in determining factor prices was mentioned briefly. Because taxes can amount to a significant portion of the total cost of operating a facility it is important to consider their relationship to operating cost and the effect on prices of other factor inputs. Excise taxes are viewed as a cost to the shipper but they are also a revenue to the government. They therefore constitute a transfer payment to the government rather than an actual consumption of resources. In this study we have chosen to include taxes in all appropriate prices so that intermediate figures such as

---

3. See Charles River Associates, *A Manual of Computer Programs for Project Analysis* (Washington, D.C.: Commerce Clearinghouse, 1970), pp. 117–121.

vehicle purchase costs and operating costs would appear as perceived by operators and shippers. In preparing final results, however, one set of cost summaries
(called "adjusted total" in tables in this report) has been computed with taxes
removed so that their effect can be isolated from other aspects of the model.
This matter is discussed further in Chapter 10 which discusses evaluation and
objective functions.

Finally, it is important to consider in this study the meaning of the prices
being used, the desirability of adopting shadow prices, and the treatment of
foreign exchange. Price data are employed in a study such as this for two reasons.
First, the behavioral response of each of the factors to market forces in the
economy is being sought. Secondly, it may be important to reflect the real cost
to the economy of consuming the resources necessary to provide a particular set
of transportation services. The prices should represent the opportunity cost of
alternative uses of the resource. In some cases, however, it will become apparent
that the price does not in fact represent the true cost to the economy. This will
occur where ideal competitive conditions do not occur, frequently in the presence of monopoly, or where there is substantial unemployment.[4]

If, for example, there were a severe shortage of skilled managers in the
country, and operations of a railroad required a large proportion of these skilled
managers for its complex coordination, it is quite possible that the wages paid
to managers would not reflect the real cost to the economy of using them in this
way. Alternatively if there were severe unemployment in the country, then
wages paid to those hired to construct and operate the facility might grossly over-
state the real cost to the economy of the project, particularly if the man thus
employed would otherwise not be engaged in a productive occupation.[5] Generally speaking, the prices used in this study have not been adjusted for these
hidden values, but in any country where a new investment is planned some
thought should be given to this matter to determine whether there are obvious
cases where the use of a shadow price is warranted.

One case which generally merits correction is foreign exchange. Because
many developing countries have severe balance of payments problems the expenditure of foreign exchange often represents a much greater cost to the
economy than is indicated by the official exchange rate. Since foreign exchange
is of such importance it is useful to examine it for each case. Therefore, in addi-

---

4. A thorough treatment of the appropriate prices to use is beyond the scope of this
report. For a careful and helpful analysis of this subject, see M. Feldstein and J. Fleming,
"Shadow Prices in Industrial Project Evaluation," U.N. Industrial Development Organization,
Evaluation of Industrial Projects, 1968.

5. For an example of how project costs may be adjusted to reflect the use of underemployed labor, see R. Haveman and J. Krutilla, "Unemployment, Excess Capacity and
Benefit-Cost Investment Criteria," *Review of Economies and Statistics,* 1967. The basic
premise of this article is that when labor is used that would otherwise be unemployed, its
shadow price should be zero, not the prevailing wage.

tion to printing directly computed costs for projects, this study has separated out the foreign exchange component and applied to that component an adjustment representing a shadow price for foreign exchange. A second performance measure is then presented utilizing this reevaluation of foreign exchange to the project, and titled "Adjusted Total."

In developing countries, because of the great shortage of capital, the return to capital investment is often quite high. While the prevailing interest rate in the United States without inflation might be in the order of 4 to 6 percent, in a developing country it could run as high as 15 to 20 percent. We have used 15 percent for this study, feeling that it is not too high for many countries in which these results would be used. Because this rate is so different from that prevailing in the United States and Europe, it is worth noting since this could substantially alter the apparent cost and benefits of projects having large streams stretching into the future. The importance of this interest rate is discussed further in Chapter 8 on sensitivity analysis.

Summary

This chapter has shown how the environmental setting for this study was selected, and how it relates to conditions that might be encountered in an actual application. The prices and technology of both scenarios represent existing countries. The terrains used could occur in almost any country, but do not represent any specific geographic location. The traffic volumes and commodity mixes are intended to be representative of goods movements that could be found in many locations. The conditions studied here could of course be modified to describe an actual project to be evaluated or a widely differing set of initial conditions.

4

Description and Performance of Transport Links

Determining the cost of constructing and operating a transportation project requires a complete description of that link in some form. The descriptive parameters used in this study, already introduced briefly in the example problem in Chapter 2, will be further developed here. This list is different for each of the transport modes so each will be addressed separately. One can also distinguish between characteristics associated with the traveled way and characteristics of the vehicles using it. In the measurement of performance it is necessary to distinguish between performance from the point of view of the transporter and that experienced by the shipper.

Description of the Traveled Way

Highway Link Characteristics

The basic parameters used to define a highway link include length, surface type, design speed, average gradient, and the width and number of lanes. These parameters are listed in Table 4-1 to describe the existing road assumed for each of the three terrain cases of the sample problem. The link descriptions for all new projects evaluated in this study are presented in detail in Chapter 6, Designing the Facility.

Transportation links will not typically be uniform over their entire length, but will be flat in some sections and hilly in others, or paved near the cities at the ends and gravel in the middle. The descriptive procedure used here, however, admits to only one value for a characteristic over the entire length. If the facility is not homogenous, it may be necessary to divide the link into several separate homogenous links and select a set of characteristics to describe each adequately.

Looking at the figures for the flat-terrain case of Table 4-1 it is apparent from the highway length of 150 miles that this highway is somewhat circuitous since the two cities are located only 100 airline miles apart. Surface type, which affects the rate of fuel consumption, tire wear, and maintenance costs for both the vehicle and the road, can be unpaved, gravel or paved. In this study, the existing road in each case has a gravel surface and all new roads will be constructed with a hard pavement such as asphalt or concrete. The third parameter in the list, design speed, affects a variety of design characteristics of the road, such as sight distance, minimum radius for horizontal and vertical curves, maximum gradient,

Table 4-1
Descriptive Information for Highway Link
(Data for the Old Road)

		Terrain	
Parameter	*Flat*	*Hilly*	*Mountain*
Length	150 miles	200 miles	250 miles
Surface type	Gravel	Gravel	Gravel
Design speed	25 MPH	20 MPH	15 MPH
Gradient	2%	6%	8%
Width of lane	10 feet	8 feet	8 feet
No. of lanes	2	2	2

and so forth. It is also used by the highway simulation model to specify the maximum speed at which vehicles may operate over the road.

The average gradient on the road is a measure of the overall steepness of its grades. The gradient of the road will never be steeper than that of the terrain over which the road crosses, although it can be less if the road is circuitous or if a lot of earthwork was needed to cut through the hills. In this study, the old highway in flat terrain has an average gradient of 2 percent. This is the same as that of the terrain itself, indicating that no cutting and filling was done.

All of the roads examined in this study have two lanes, as in no case does the traffic density require three or four lanes, and a road with less than two lanes is impractical except in very special situations. Lane width, however, can be varied where this is appropriate. Lane width affects the speed at which vehicles move when traffic volumes rise. The 10-foot width used for flat terrain conditions on the old road is barely adequate for free movement and the 8-foot width used in the hilly and mountainous cases will inevitably cause some congestion at medium and high volumes.

Railway Characteristics

The detailed information required to describe a railway facility is somewhat different from that used to describe a highway, although the overall format is the same. The descriptive information for a railroad link is shown in Table 4-2. In this table the parameters describe the new railroad designed for the hilly terrain, low-volume situation.

The distance is simply the length along the facility from end to end. The fact that it is 120 miles indicates that this railroad was not constructed on a straight line between the cities. This circuity was necessitated by hills that were sufficiently steep that it was cheaper to angle up them than to cut straight through.

Table 4-2
Descriptive Information for Railroad Link
(Data for New Railroad, Low Volume, Hilly Terrain)

Parameter	Value
Length	120 miles
Speed limit	20 MPH
Max. gradient	2.5%
Avg. gradient	2.0%
No. of sidings	12
Signal type	manual block
Switch type	manual
Locomotive type and HP	Diesel, 800 HP
No. of locomotives/train	1

As in the highway case, the speed limit can be viewed as a parameter affecting the original design of the facility as well as its operation. It influences sharpness of curvature and also limits the top speed of trains operating over the facility. On a railroad, the maximum speed may often be imposed not only by curvature but also by the condition of the track and roadbed, because providing a roadbed smooth enough to permit high speeds may be substantially more expensive than constructing one for lower speed operation. Thus, even this new railroad, built on moderately hilly terrain has a maximum speed of 20 miles per hour. Only when relatively heavy traffic densities are encountered will it be efficient to design and construct a railroad for higher speed operation (see Table 6-4).

A quantitative description of the railroad requires the specification of two different gradients along the link. The maximum gradient, here 2.5 percent, specifies the ruling grade of the alignment which, in turn, sets an upper limit on the number of cars that can be carried in a single train. The unlimited power of a locomotive and the possibility of wheel slippage under heavy tractive effort effectively limit the hauling power. The second of the two gradients specified, the average gradient, is the average of all slopes on the rail link. This figure determines the average speed at which the train moves over the entire link.

The passing sidings on a railroad interact with the directional density of traffic to determine the level of congestion that will exist on a line. The more trains that travel the line, the greater the number of meets between trains, requiring more sidings. Generally, one passing siding was used for every 10 miles of mainline track although at high volumes more sidings were found to be desirable.

Both signal type and switching type affect the amount of time required for the train to perform passing maneuvers or to do any switching operations. At the relatively low traffic levels carried by the single-track railroads studied here it has been assumed that manual signal and switching operations would be used almost exclusively. If higher traffic densities were encountered and congestion appeared, a more sophisticated type of switching and/or signaling system might provide an alternative to the construction of additional passing tracks.

It has been assumed that a single type of locomotive will be used over any particular link. This is reasonable in light of the assumption that the link itself is homogenous over its entire distance. Only diesel locomotives have been considered since steam is not practical except where existing steam locomotives are already available. Three alternative specifications of locomotive horsepower are available in the present data, 800, 1200, and 1500 horsepower. Because this table is for the low-volume case, a small 800-horsepower locomotive is required to carry a relatively short train. Generally only one is used, but in mountainous terrain where the rail gradients are steeper it is often more economical to attach two large locomotives to a train to permit longer train lengths.

Vehicle Description

Highway Vehicles

Five different classes of highway vehicles have been designated to handle the five commodity classes. These are bulk and general truck, special truck, a common-passenger bus, and a private automobile. The vehicles represent actual models in use in the base scenario, and the descriptive data has been obtained from field observation and manufacturer's specifications.

The most important characteristics for highway vehicles are shown in Table 4-3. They include the payload, empty weight, horsepower, number of tires, and fuel cost. Parameters not shown here include crew size, oil consumption rates, maintenance cost rates, and a number of price items. The bulk and general trucks are similar in design, but the bulk truck is somewhat larger, carrying a payload of 10.3 tons compared to 7.16. The special truck is equipped with a tank body for liquid transports. The bus, as is frequently the case in developing countries, resembles a U.S. school bus, with a long, flat frame carrying the body on top. All

Table 4-3
Highway Vehicle Characteristics

	Bulk	General	Special	Common	Private
Payload (tons)	10.3	7.16	5.0	3.57	0.35
Tare weight (lbs.)	9000	8000	10,000	9000	3600
Horsepower	275	195	170	170	150
Tires	6	6	6	6	4
Fuel cost ($/gallon)	0.154	0.154	0.154	0.154	0.154

Table 4-4
Railroad Vehicle Characteristics

	Cars			
	Bulk	*General*	*Special*	*Common*
Payload (tons)	30	30	20	6
Tare weight (tons)	13	13	13	20
Average life (years)	35	35	35	35

	Locomotives		
	Small	*Medium*	*Large*
Horsepower	800	1200	1500
Weight (tons)	80	90	100
Average life (years)	15	15	15
Number of axles	6	6	6

five vehicles in the base scenario are powered by gasoline engines. In the second scenario all but the automobile are diesel. A complete data listing for vehicles is contained in Appendix C.

Railroad Vehicles

The railroad carries four classes of vehicles. There is no rail car corresponding to the private automobile; consequently, private rail passengers ride in common passenger cars. The vehicles used in this study are representative of the more recent ones in use in Colombia, on the narrow-gauge national railroads. Table 4-4 shows their major characteristics. The bulk and general vehicles carry 30 tons each, much less than boxcars or gondolas of a modern standard-gauge railroad. The common passenger car has a listed capacity of 6 tons. In this study the numbers of passengers are converted to tons at 200 lbs. each, so this is equivalent to 60 passengers.

Three different locomotive sizes have been included. The appropriate vehicle is chosen on the basis of steepness of grades and traffic volumes. They range from an 800-horsepower locomotive that could be used in yards or for light traffic, to a 1500-horsepower line engine suitable for mountain freight hauling. Further information about all three locomotives is presented in Appendix C.

Vehicle Performance Measures

Once the environmental conditions have been fixed, and the physical characteristics of the transportation link and vehicles have been defined, it is possible to determine the performance of this link of the transportation system. The simulation of performance for this portion of the study was done for the highway model and the rail model. Only a rough outline of those models can be presented here. These models and the computer programs that implement them are described in detail in a separate report.[1]

Highway Model

The highway model begins by determining the number of vehicles per day needed to carry the traffic volume specified for the highway link under consideration. It then uses several equations of vehicle performance to determine the time required for these vehicles to travel from one end of the link to the other, allowing for the design speed, the gradient of the link, the width of the lanes, and the congestion caused by these factors and interaction with other vehicles on the link. For each class of vehicle it also determines the physical quantity of every input factor required, such as the number of gallons of fuel, the hours of driver time, the amount of maintenance accumulated, and so forth. Using the number of vehicle loads to be carried per day and the time required to traverse the link, with other information about loading and unloading, down time for maintenance, and number of operation hours per day, it is possible to determine the total number of vehicles required to provide the necessary service in each class. The size of this vehicle fleet then determines the annual depreciation charges.

The cost results produced by this simulation are summarized in Table 4-5, which shows the physical units consumed for each of a number of categories including crew, fuel, oil, tires, maintenance, and depreciation. These physical units we have referred to as vehicle performance measures as they are concerned with the individual vehicles and the way they perform. Applying the cost per unit, which is part of the factor price environment for the particular country concerned, to the physical units consumed produces the total cost per vehicle. A variety of cost measures can be obtained for comparative purposes, including the average cost, the marginal cost, the cost per vehicle mile, and the cost per ton mile. These operating costs are summed over all five commodity classes and added together to provide total operating costs per year for the entire link.

Computations were also made for the cost of maintaining the highway. For comparing projects, the present discounted value of this stream of operating costs and maintenance-of-way cost is taken over a 20-year period at the specified interest rate. The resulting present discounted value of operating cost and maintenance-of-way costs are the figures that are used in the market cost figures of Chapter 2.

---

1. Charles River Associates, *A Manual of Computer Programs for Project Analysis* (Washington, D.C.: Commerce Clearinghouse, 1970).

Table 4-5
Highway Cost Performance: Sample Output

	Bulk				
	Number of Units	*Cost Per Unit*	*Cost Per Vehicle*	*Total Cost*	*Comparison*
Crew	7.059	0.330	2.330	135.700	0.158
Fuel	38.016	0.154	5.854	341.034	0.397
Oil	0.450	0.233	0.105	6.108	0.007
Tires	0.018	140.000	2.537	147.808	0.172
Maintenance	0.000	16400.000	1.230	71.651	0.083
Labor	0.500	0.400	0.200	11.651	0.014
Depreciation	0.000	16400.000	2.501	145.680	0.169
Total			14.757	859.632	1.000

	General				
	Number of Units	*Cost Per Unit*	*Cost Per Vehicle*	*Total Cost*	*Comparison*
Crew	6.076	0.330	2.005	168.029	0.181
Fuel	18.968	0.154	2.921	244.777	0.263
Oil	0.600	0.233	0.140	11.715	0.013
Tires	0.022	101.000	2.178	182.490	0.196
Maintenance	0.000	13300.000	1.623	135.972	0.146
Labor	0.800	0.400	0.320	26.816	0.029
Depreciation	0.000	13300.000	1.915	160.454	0.172
Total			11.101	930.253	1.000

Note: Hilly terrain, medium volume, base scenario, hew highway, one way, selected portion of computer printout.

Railroad Model

The railroad simulation model is similar in structure to that of the highway model though the details are quite different. The tonnage per day in each commodity class is divided by the payload of the vehicles needed per day to carry the existing traffic. Locomotive horsepower and number of locomotives to be used per train are specified in the link description. From this information and the number of cars to be carried each day, it is possible to determine the maximum tonnage of the train that can be moved over the ruling gradient on the rail line and the total number of trains needed per day.

A train performance equation then determines the average speed of this typical train over the average grades found on that link. It also computes the amount of fuel and other input factors necessary to operate these trains. The resulting time required to run a train from one terminal to the other is used together with switching time, yard time, loading and unloading time for the

Table 4-6
Railway Cost Performance: Sample Output

	Locomotive Cost	Bulk	General	Special	Passenger	Total Cars	Season[a] Total
Tons/season[a]	0	218999.88	72999.94	36499.98	36499.98	364999.63	364999.63
Cars used	3.000	17.00	17.00	5.00	15.00	54.00	
Cars needed in this direction	3.000	17.00	6.00	5.00	15.00	43.00	
Depreciation	19982.004	9181.65	3222.84	2612.58	27801.74	42818.80	62800.81
Operation and maintenance	13375.371	280297.44	93432.50	46716.23	46716.23	467162.19	480537.56
Load factor	0	1.00	0.33	1.00	1.00	0.78	543338.31
Use factor	0	0.70	0.24	0.58	0.61	0.52	
			(FC3)		(FC2)		(FC1)

	Season Cost	(FC3)	(FC2)	(FC1)
Car depreciation	42818.80	0.079	0.152	0.293
Car maintenance	17782.15	0.033	0.063	0.122
Locomotive depreciation	19982.00	0.037	0.071	0.137
Locomotive maintenance	13375.37	0.025	0.048	0.091
Fuel	17469.84	0.032	0.062	0.119
Oil	2942.15	0.005	0.010	0.020
Crew	31952.81	0.059	0.114	0.218
Total 1	146323.00	0.269	0.520	1.000
Overhead	134800.69	0.248	0.480	
Total 2	281123.69	0.517	1.000	
Way Maintenance	262214.63	0.483		
Total 3	543338.31	1.000		

Note: Hilly terrain, medium volume, base scenario, new railroad, one way, selected portion of computer printout.
[a] Season = 365 days of a 365-day year.

cars, and other factors in railroad operation, to compute the total number of cars needed to carry the specified traffic. This information is also used to determine equipment depreciation charges. Other equations compute the cost associated with maintaining the track given the tonnage that is carried over it. Operating and maintenance-of-way cost, along with the separately computed overhead and traffic cost are added for the entire year. As with the highway model, the present discounted value of this stream of operating and maintenance costs is entered into the table of total costs. A sample of the performance measures and the annual costs for operating the rail link are shown in Table 4–6.

Link Performance Measures

Shippers consider several measures of performance, including monetary costs, in deciding what mode of transportation or what carrier to use. The way these measures are used to value shippers' choices is discussed in Chapter 5. To permit this evaluation within the model as well as to allow for computation of benefit based on other than strictly cost savings, the model produces several indices of performance besides operating costs. These are referred to here as link performance measures since they collectively describe travel conditions on the link. (See Table 4–7.)

The first of these is waiting time. This is defined as the average amount of time that a commodity or passenger must wait from the time it is ready for shipment until the vehicle or train on which it is to be carried is available. For the highway mode, waiting time is taken as one-half of the average time between truck departures, which in turn is the number of hours in a day divided by the number of vehicles in each class per day. For the railroad, waiting time is the average length of time between train departures, which is the number of hours in a day divided by the number of trains per day.

This may appear to be somewhat extreme since, if trains depart regularly, it should be possible to place the goods on the loading platform just minutes before departure. In fact, however, railroads and other transport operations in developing countries do not generally attain the precision that is found in North America or Europe. Even with scheduled departures there is a problem with the delay introduced by inability to adapt to the schedule. It seems reasonable, therefore, to assume random arrivals and departures.

The second element of nonmarket performance is travel time. This comes directly from the modal model simulation of running time over a particular link. In the rail model, travel time includes not only time in motion but also time spent in switching operations and yard time required to make up the train. Similarly, in highway operations travel time is meant to include not only the line-haul travel time but also delays en-route.

The third element of performance is variability of time, which is a measure

Table 4–7
Link Performance: Sample Output

	Link Performance Vector – Direction 1				
	Bulk	General	Special	Common	Private
WT^a	1.14	1.10	1.40	0.32	0.26
TT^b	2.94	2.53	3.01	2.80	2.20
VT^c	3.36	3.20	3.90	1.69	1.47
PL^d	0	0	0	0	0
$	1.43	4.65	2.40	3.14	18.17
	Link Performance Vector – Direction 2				
	Bulk	General	Special	Common	Private
WT^a	1.14	1.10	1.40	0.32	0.26
TT^b	2.47	3.00	3.01	2.80	2.20
VT^c	3.27	3.29	3.90	1.69	1.47
PL^d	0.00	0.00	0.00	0.00	0.00
$	3.55	1.84	2.40	3.14	18.17

Note: Hilly terrain, medium volume, base scenario, new highway, both ways, summary per ton.
[a] Waiting time.
[b] Average travel time.
[c] Variability of time.
[d] Probability of loss (magnitude too small to appear here).

of the variation in total lead time. It depends not only upon the characteristics of the link but also on waiting and travel times. Many shippers value variability of time differently than they value waiting and travel times alone. For some goods, stockpiling is possible and scheduling is not as important. In these cases the variance of time is important. For others, travel time is relatively unimportant but absolute regularity is crucial.

The fourth measure of nonmarket performance is the probability of loss, a measure of the chance that a ton of commodity shipped over the link will be either lost, destroyed, or stolen. Partial loss or damage are also included in this probability. Multiplying the probability of loss by the value of the commodity indicates the anticipated dollar damage that occurs on the average. This figure is a function of the type of roadway, the type of vehicle, the time involved, and a number of other factors that differ from mode to mode.

The final item in the set of link performance measures is the monetary cost of operating the transport system. For most modes there is a difference between the cost of providing the transportation and the tariff actually paid. The models used for this study actually generate both whether or not there is a direct relation between costs and prices. The Project Analyzer Routine is capable of implementing a variety of pricing policies as desired. For our purposes in this study, the differences between price and monetary cost is merely an income transfer from the shipper to the carrier and we have chosen to ignore it. Therefore the price charged has been set equal to average operating cost.

Summary

This chapter has described in some detail the techniques used to define transportation links, vehicles, and performance for this study. The quantities included are those which were thought to be most important for project analysis, although it is possible that some studies would wish to modify somewhat the type of input used or produced. If we wished to perform a more general systems analysis of a transportation network, or to combine such an analysis with a simulation of the entire economy, the same methodology used for describing the transportation system would be employed.

5 Commodity Perceived Costs and their Determination

Importance of Nonmarket Costs

It is generally acknowledged that transportation costs are an important expense in the conduct of many businesses. Mineral deposits may lie unexploited for years because the cost of transportation to a point of consumption would be prohibitive. Factory sites are carefully selected to provide access to satisfactory transportation systems. Many large firms have a transportation department devoted exclusively to securing the best possible mode of shipment of raw materials and finished products at the least cost.

When transportation costs are discussed, usually the cash price paid for the service is the focus of attention, with all other characteristics grouped together as the "quality of service." Yet the fact that companies often pay more, sometimes several times more, than the tariff for the lowest-price form of carriage indicates that this service quality has a quantifiable monetary value. If a shipper pays $60 for air freight, rather than $20 for truck delivery, it must be because the better service is worth at least $40 more to him. In other words, the slower mode of travel must be causing some invisible, or "nonmarket" costs at least equal to the fare differential. Thus a complete analysis of the cost of shipping some goods should really include not just the monetary costs, but also an evaluation of the nonmarket costs, as well.

An evaluation of the nonmarket costs incurred on each mode of travel requires a set of physical measures of the relevant aspects of performance, and an evaluation of these performance measures by the shipper, all reduced to a single quantity that adequately describes the total shipping. This chapter proposes a scheme for determining the value of commodity perceived costs of shipping that can be used to choose the mode of travel that various commodities will select. An important by-product will be a method of estimating the benefits that accrue from improving the "quality" of transport.

Measures of Performance

The first task in evolving a scheme for determining commodity preferences is to identify those factors that are important to shippers and to organize them in a useful way. There appear to be four general causes for concern by shippers: time, time unreliability, loss and damage, and monetary costs.

Time is important to shippers for a number of reasons. One is that commodities tend to deteriorate with time. Those that do not deteriorate physically may lose value because of changes in market conditions, or because of obsolescence. Time can also be important because consumption by an industrial process or human consumer may not wait. Failure to deliver the commodity on time may halt the process or inconvenience the consumer. Shippers may also value time because goods in transit represent capital that could be put to another use.

Time can be divided into at least two different categories associated with the different portions of a trip. First, there is travel time. This includes the time that the vehicle is moving, its yard time, or switching delays, and its delays en-route. During travel time, the good is characteristically inaccessible to the shipper or receiver and may be unlocatable as well. It is almost always difficult to determine its shipping status, that is, whether it will arrive on time or late and if so, by how much.

The second category is waiting time. Waiting time is the delay experienced at the beginning of the trip due to the slow arrival of a pick-up vehicle or delay caused by having to conform to the departure of a scheduled carrier. It can even occur with company-owned equipment because of joint use. During waiting time, goods are typically accessible to the shipper although they may be packed or otherwise committed to the use anticipated.

A very important time-related factor is the unreliability of time. Since total travel time is affected by random factors, it is best described by a probability distribution. If schedules were always rigidly followed and there were no breakdowns or interruptions, there would be no variance of time. Because of the uncertainty, however, contingency plans must be made which depend upon the variability of the arrival. It may be necessary, for example, to carry goods in inventory to defend against the variability of arrival.

Loss and damage of the commodity being shipped is associated with all transport modes. Some modes however have a higher record of loss than others. Losses may be due to leakage such as with a pipeline or spillage as with bulk wheat movements. There may also be pilferage. Finally, there may be damage due to breakage, overheating, contamination, etc. To the costs that occur as the result of loss of product must also be added inconvenience and loss of time for reordering and retransporting. The incidence of loss and damage is more significant for some goods than for others. For high-value items, pilferage is more probable than for low-value goods. Delicate or perishable items are more likely to be damaged than are bulk commodities like wheat or oil. Loss and damage is represented here by the mean of the loss distribution.

The traditional costs of transportation will be referred to here as monetary costs. These costs consist in a number of factors in addition to the tariff paid by the shipper, including the cost for packaging, pick-up and delivery, loading and unloading, and insurance. They should also include the cost of operating the traffic department, expediting shipments, and providing transit storage. Packaging requirements must be directly related to the choice of mode, since for some modes the opportunity for damage and for pilferage is different than for others. Air freight, for example, normally requires less packaging than shipment by sea. Charges for pick-up and delivery may be made in addition to the ordinary transport tariff. These services do represent a cost to the shipper even where company-owned equipment is used. Loading and unloading must also be accounted for. For many movements these handling costs are more significant than the cost of the line-haul transport itself. Including insurance as a cost may be double counting since it has already been accounted for above under probability of loss or damage. It may also be traded-off against the cost of packaging. It is included here for completeness. Finally, the transport tariff must be included. It is still the largest and most visible cost associated with most transport movements.

There are other considerations that may or not be included in the cost-producing measures of performance listed above, but that are important to the shipper in choosing transport. In-transit storage of goods, diversion in route, through-rates and joint-rates, as well as special expediting or the use of special-ized equipment may all be important. Shipment of oversized or exceptionally heavy articles may be possible only on a single mode. There are undoubtedly other factors that are operative in special cases. For most cases, however, it is one or more of the measures of performance described above that are evaluated by the shipper in making his choice of mode and routing.

Components of Total Cost

With the identification of the important cost-producing items of transport now complete, we are ready to advance a scheme for using them to determine weightings of performance for a particular shipment. This may be done in the following manner. A list or vector of the measures describing the performance on a transport link can be prepared. The link performance vector (LPV) is:

$$LPV = (P_i, P_2, \ldots, P_n) \qquad (5.1)$$

where P_i is the performance measure in physical units on a single transport link or set of links. In addition to the vector of performance we can define a second vector that contains the weights assigned to each of the performance measures by the shipper of a particular commodity. We will designate this second vector, which contains the commodity weighting of performance, as the commodity preference vector. The commodity preference vector (CPV) is:

$$CPV = (W_i, W_2, \ldots, W_n) \qquad (5.2)$$

where W_i equals the cost per unit of encountering the corresponding performance measure per ton of commodity.

The product of the two vectors is thus a measure of the perceived costs for a single ton to make a trip over the link under consideration. The computation of perceived cost is thus:

$$RFAC = LPV \cdot CPV' = \sum_{i=1}^{n} P_i W_i \qquad (5.3)$$

Perceived cost for a given link will also be referred to as its R factor since it is a measure of the relative resistance to flow of goods along this link in comparison with another.

The cost of transport perceived by a commodity moving between two points is therefore the summation of the product of the physical units of performance and the "cost" weighting of this performance. Performance measures for a given transport connection are generally known by the shippers of commodities. They are also easy to simulate using models of the transport facilities.

To use this approach, an actual set of variables must be selected for each of the elements in the link performance vector and it must be possible to determine appropriate commodity preference weightings for each. Our earlier discussion concluded that the important variables were time, time unreliability, loss and damage, and monetary cost. Expanding the time variable to include those sub-classifications which are important, a reasonable link performance vector would include the following variables.

TT = average travel time in hours to traverse the link
WT = average waiting time in hours for a vehicle in which to make the trip
VT = variability of time in hours expressed as a measure of the spread of the distribution of overall transit time (which equals travel time plus waiting time)
PL = probability of loss expressed as a mean of the distribution
CST = monetary cost in dollars per ton.

Determining Commodity Weightings of Performance

Determining an appropriate commodity preference weighting for each item in the vector is difficult because it is hard to find an empirical situation that lends itself to the computation of these variables using econometric techniques. This requires for each commodity a situation in which there are a variety of physically different alternative routes, each with distinctly different values of performance measures. Using the choices made by a commodity among a large number of end points with different spacings it should be possible to determine the weightings assigned to each factor using multiple regression. However, to be useful this would have to be repeated for every commodity. If factor prices changed, these figures would have to be recomputed.

It is possible, however, to impute a cost weighting on commodity preferences for transport performance starting from a few important commodity characteristics and some observation of standard inventory practice. Although this approach is theoretical rather than empirical, it seems to describe how people behave and appears to produce good results as well.

Commodity preference weightings are fundamentally related to the value of the commodity and to the changes in this value as the result of its being transported. They are also influenced by the need to have a supply of the commodity on hand to avoid a stockout or to suffer its consequences.

Every commodity has a potential value deriving from the market in which it is sold or in which it could be sold. The potential value at the factory or mine is therefore the value in the marketplace minus the cost of transport. The value of a ton of the good in the marketplace may be somewhat different than that for a shipping ton because of packaging or cubage, and may therefore need to be adjusted. Most commodities deteriorate with time, and thereby decrease in value, although some goods suffer more than others. Finally, there are costs to the receiver of running short of a good because of delay in the transport system. These costs can be very large in some instances and are therefore important enough to deserve our attention.

The variables implied by this discussion can now be introduced. The commodity preference weighting assigned to travel time is attributable to three separate factors including the deterioration of the good in transit, the opportunity costs of the good tied up while traveling, and the cost of inventory to account for the variability of usage during travel time. Thus:

W_{TT} = deterioration + opportunity cost of goods tied up + variability of usage during travel time.

Or, in terms of variables:

$$W_{TT} = \left(\frac{VALUE}{DT} \right) + \left(\frac{VALUE \cdot RATE}{HRSPYR} \right)$$

$$+ \left(\frac{VARUSE \cdot VALUE \cdot RATE}{HRSPYR} \right) \cdot PROTFC \qquad (5.4)$$

where

$VALUE$ = price of the commodity in the market in dollars per shipping ton
TT = travel time over the link in hours

DT = deterioration time in hours

$RATE$ = interest rate in percent per year

$HRSPYR$ = hours per year

$VARUSE$ = percentage variation in daily commodity usage which will be exceeded no more than a specified proportion of the time (see Figure 5-1)

$PROTFC$ = one-half the number of standard deviations of daily stock usage variability needed to protect against outage except for the specified proportion of the time ($PROTFC$ = 1 for 98.5 percent protection, if stock usage is normally distributed)

Deterioration of a commodity is not usually linear with time. There are, however, computational advantages to assuming that it is, since then the deterioration time in hours (DT) divided into a specified travel time (TT), is the proportion of the total value that has been lost. The value DT can be adjusted to be linear within the range of interest of the problem at hand.

The opportunity cost of the goods while traveling is merely the interest on the money tied up during travel time. The money involved could have been invested at the prevailing interest rates during this time to produce an income. The appropriate interest rate will depend upon the economic situation. Because the good is real property, it need not include inflation.

The logic behind the final term of equation 5.4 is that it is necessary to carry extra goods in inventory to provide protection against stockout as a result of fluctuations in the usage rate. The amount that has to be carried in order to provide this protection is related to the variability of the usage rate of these goods and the degree of protection desired. Since each day's usage rate is a probabilistic figure, the rate can be thought of as a distribution with a mean and a standard deviation. One measure of the variability of this distribution is its standard deviation. This variation defined by numbers of standard deviations from the mean is converted, by use of a normal curve, to the more convenient form of a percentage flow. (See Figure 5-1.)

The commodity preference weighting for the waiting time is similar to that for travel time.

W_{WT} = deterioration while waiting + value of goods tied up while waiting + variability of usage during waiting time + cost to provide shipping space

The first three terms are the same as in equation 5.4 above. Thus we can express:

$$W_{WT} = (W_{TT}) \cdot FACUSE + SPACE \qquad (5.5)$$

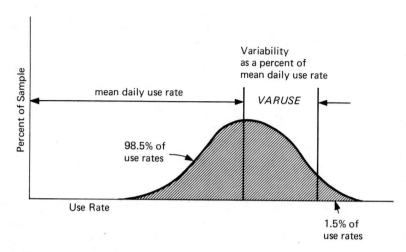

Figure 5-1. Definition of Variable *VARUSE*.

where

FACUSE = a factor which reduces the cost of goods during waiting
  SPACE = the cost to provide shipping space

Because goods may be rediverted or used during the waiting period it is perhaps reasonable to provide a reduction in the perceived cost of waiting. This can be done by adjusting *FACUSE* to an appropriate figure. Since space is always required to store goods that are ready for shipment, it also seems logical to add this cost, though it is typically small.

The value for the commodity preference weighting associated with variability of time is related exclusively to variability of lead time and the safety stock necessary to protect against a possible stockout. Thus:

$$W_{VT} = \frac{PROTFC \cdot VALUE \cdot RATE}{HRSPYR} \qquad (5.6)$$

Note that this equation is similar to the third term in the waiting and travel time computations except that here the variability involved is not that of the usage rate but of the overall transit time. If shipments always arrived exactly on schedule there would be no time variability and therefore no variability in lead time, and hence a reduced necessity to provide protection against a stockout.

The probability of loss generates a commodity preference weighting which accounts for both direct loss of property and safety stock required in case the shipment is lost. The equation is:

$$W_{PL} = VALUE + \left(\frac{VALUE \cdot RATE}{HRSPYR} \right) \cdot VARPRB \qquad (5.7)$$

where

$VARPRB$ = variation in the probability of loss from day to day defined in percentage terms.

The direct loss of property is represented by the term $VALUE$ in equation 5.7. The safety stock required to cover stockouts caused by loss or damage in a shipment is affected by the variability of the probability of loss ($VARPRB$). Since the probability of loss can be thought of as the mean of a distribution, the variability of probability of loss is a measure of the dispersion of this distribution.

Finally, the commodity preference weighting for monetary costs must be estimated. Since the link performance measure includes only the tariff for the transport link, it is appropriate to include the other costs as the percent increase over tariff required to cover the item. Thus:

$$W_{CST} = 1.0 + (PCTPAK + PCTPDL + PCTLDU + PCTINS) \qquad (5.8)$$

where

$PCTPAK$ = percent increase in tariff to cover packaging
$PCTPDL$ = percent increase in tariff to cover pickup and delivery
$PCTLDU$ = percent increase in tariff to cover loading and unloading
$PCTINS$ = percent increase in tariff to cover insurance

Representative Commodity Parameters

The theoretical foundation for commodity perceived nonmarket costs just developed can now be applied. To do this we will select a set of typical commodities and develop the commodity weightings of performance. Finally, it will be instructive to use these commodity weightings of performance to develop typical commodity perceived costs for an example highway and rail link.

This study has dealt with five general classes of commodities: bulk commodities, representing large shipments of basic commodities in unpackaged form; general commodities, which consist primarily of manufactured items packaged in an ordinary way; special commodities, principally bulk petroleum; common carrier passengers, who were assumed to be low-income travelers; and private-carrier passengers, who are high-income passengers. Although the characteristics of various commodities vary over extremely wide ranges, even within a single commodity class, it is assumed here that a single commodity value, deterioration rate, flow rate variability, and protection against stockout can be selected to adequately represent each class of item. Although it would be useful to break the classes into smaller, more homogeneous subclasses, employment of more than five basic commodity types would involve unduly complicated analysis and data collection.

In order to get a feel for average commodity prices by class, a number of commodities were selected and grouped by price as low-value goods or high-value goods, and by physical characteristics as petroleum, general goods, and bulk goods. By and large, those commodities with characteristics that would place them in the class of bulk goods had prices similar to the low-value goods. Those thought of as general goods contain a fairly large percentage of high values.

In different countries, different regions, or even different highways of a given city, the relative volumes of different commodities carried will vary widely. Thus, there is no rigorous way to translate a set of data for particular goods into characteristics for the five commodity classes used here without data on the relative volumes of the various commodities within each class for the area to be analyzed. To preserve the generality of this study, a set of values were chosen as representative of each class such that most of the goods typically carried could be placed in one class or another. The resulting parameters are shown in Table 5-1. Special goods were assigned a value of $0.01 per pound, bulk goods $0.10 per pound, and general goods $1.00 per pound. Thus, an entire order of magnitude exists between each of the three classes. The widespread differences in this table are indicative of the extreme ranges that prevail in actual practice.

Table 5-1
Characteristics Representative of Each Commodity Class

	Bulk	General	Special
Value[a]	204 $/ton	2040 $/ton	20.4 $/ton
DT	5520 hr.	6480 hr.	12,250 hr
RATE	15%	15%	15%
VARUSE	10%	35%	10%
PROTFC	1.0	1.0	1.0
FACUSE	1.0	1.0	0.75
SPACE[b]	0.008	0.152	0.00001
VARPRB	10%	10%	10%

[a] 10¢ /lb = 204 $/ton.
[b] $/hr./ton.

Also shown in Table 5-1 are the values for deterioration time, variability of flow, and the factor indicating typical protection against stockout. These were the most important variables needed as input to the equations given in the preceding section. Other variables were set to zero. In an analysis of a particular transportation problem, it would be desirable to survey the major goods moving to determine whether their characteristics would justify changing the representative class values employed here.

Passengers must be handled in an entirely different manner from freight. The performance measures used above, in the computation of perceived costs, are more appropriate for freight than they are for passengers. Nevertheless, waiting time, travel time, variability of time, and monetary cost are meaningful factors in terms of passenger preferences. Probability of loss could perhaps suggest some measure of safety but it has been omitted here because of the difficulty in evaluating this subjective factor. Values for the commodity preference weighting assigned to time by passengers was based upon the value of time. A surrogate for the value of time is the wage rate of each of the passenger classes. Though choice of this value is not ideal, it has been used by a number of other authors.[1] Also, since the major emphasis here is on freight movement and the traffic volume represented by passengers is extremely small, the latter probably does not deserve greater refinement. For urban areas, however, the situation would be completely reversed. There is of course nothing to preclude the incorporation of other performance measures that are more directly relevant to the determination of passenger perceived cost should this prove desirable.

Computations establishing the value of the preference weightings for each of the performance measures in the commodity preference vector have been carried out for the three freight classes, and the resulting commodity weightings of performance for each commodity class are shown in Table 5-2. Preference weightings for passengers were assumed directly as described above. With the exception of the passenger vectors, the elements in the commodity preference vectors are smiliar but scaled approximately an order-of-magnitude apart.

Use of Commodity Perceived Cost in Choice of Mode

The information contained in the commodity preference vector can be used to determine the path that will be preferred by a commodity which must travel from one point to another where there are a number of competing possibilities. This is accomplished by multiplying the commodity preference vector by the

---

1. See, for example, Leon N. Moses and Harold F. Williamson, Jr., "Value of Time, Choice of Mode, and the Subsidy Issue in Urban Transportation," *Journal of Political Economy* 17 (June 1963): 247.

Table 5-2
Commodity Weightings of Performance (*CPV*)
for Each Commodity Class

	Bulk	General	Special	Common	Private
Travel time (\$/ton hr.)	0.041	0.362	0.00205	1.0	5.0
Waiting time (\$/ton hr.)	0.049	0.514	0.00154	1.0	5.0
Variability of time (\$/ton/hr.)	0.003	0.035	0.0003	0.5	4.0
Probability of loss (\$/ton)	204	2040	20.4	2500	2000
Monetary cost (\$/\$)	1.0	1.0	1.0	1.0	1.0

performance of a link to produce the total cost, both monetary and nonmarket, of using that link. Summing this information link by link over alternative paths between origin and destination produces the cost of alternative routings. The smallest is, of course, the preferred alternative.

Using the link characteristics and volume levels described in Chapters 3 and 4, the link performance for each mode can be obtained by means of the simulation models. This information is then used in conjunction with the commodity preferences derived in this chapter to illustrate the choice of mode computations. This has been done for the example problem in Table 5-3. A set of sample performance data for each class of commodity for the new railroad and new highway links in hilly terrain at medium volume is given as the left-hand list in each set of Table 5-3. The right-hand list of each set of computations in Table 5-3 is the commodity preference vector determined above. For each class of goods the resulting perceived cost for traveling on each alternative is the right-hand figure of each computation series. From these computations it is easy to determine the choice of mode for each class of commodity given these specific conditions. Here special goods prefer rail, while the other four classes all prefer highway. This result is, of course, dependent upon the particular link characteristics, traffic volume levels, commodity mix, pricing policy, and commodity preference used here, and could be quite different under other conditions. It may be recalled that in Chapter 2, when the combined construction of both highway and railroad was considered, "bulk" as well as "special" preferred railroad. The difference between that case and the present is that in the former, the traffic was at high, not medium volume; and with the greater flow the cost per ton on the railroad was substantially lower. Where there is sufficient traffic to justify building both a highway and a railroad, it is probable that "bulk" and "special" will choose the railroad.

Table 5-3
Computations to Determine Modal Choice: Total Dollar Cost Per Ton by Commodity Class

		Highway				Railroad		
		Performance	× Weighting	= Total		Performance	× Weighting	= Total
Bulk	TT	2.94	0.041			9.21	0.041	
	WT	1.14	0.049			4.48	0.049	
	VT	3.36	0.003			1.37	0.003	
	PL	0.00011	204.0			0.00017	204.0	
	$	1.43	1.0			1.42	1.0	
				Σ = 1.64				Σ = 2.06
General	TT	2.53	0.362			9.21	0.362	
	WT	1.10	0.514			4.48	0.514	
	VT	3.20	0.035			1.37	0.035	
	PL	0.00011	2040.0			0.00017	2040.0	
	$	4.65	1.0			1.42	1.0	
				Σ = 6.47				Σ = 7.45
Special	TT	3.01	0.00205			9.21	0.000205	
	WT	1.40	0.00154			4.48	0.00154	
	VT	3.90	0.0003			1.37	0.0003	
	PL	0.00011	20.4			0.00017	20.4	
	$	2.40	1.0			1.45	1.0	
				Σ = 2.41				Σ = 1.48
Common	TT	2.80	1.0			8.21	1.0	
	WT	0.32	1.0			4.48	1.0	
	VT	1.69	0.5			1.27	0.5	
	PL	0.00011	2500.0			0.00017	2500.0	
	$	3.14	1.0			2.13	1.0	
				Σ = 7.38				Σ = 15.88
Private	TT	2.20	5.0			8.21	5.0	
	WT	0.26	5.0			4.48	5.0	
	VT	1.47	4.0			1.27	4.0	
	PL	0.00011	2000.0			0.00017	2000.0	
	$	18.17	1.0			2.13	1.0	
				Σ = 36.57				Σ = 71.00

Note: Hilly terrain, medium volume, balanced flow.

Use of Commodity Perceived Cost in
Benefit Measurement

While it is clear that nonmarket perceived costs are important to the choice of mode, it is not as obvious that they should be included in the measurement of benefits. The argument could be made that since they are nonmonetary in nature, they do not belong in a strictly economic analysis.

There are at least two reasons, however, why they should be included. First, the fact that shippers will often choose a carrier that charges more than the least-cost carrier for a trip between the same origin and destination can only be explained by the existence of nonmonetary costs: the higher monetary price is paid to avoid some other nonmarket costs, generally a real, tangible money cost that is paid elsewhere than to the carrier. The weighting of nonmarket costs derived above is based upon the indirect cost of travel time, waiting time, time variance, and probability of loss. Changes in the transport system that modify its performance and thereby create nonmonetary savings will in fact result in increased output per dollar of input and by this device will be transformed into monetary savings. These costs could therefore be found in an economists' input-output table, but not in the transportation row or column. Secondly, the fact that producers will change their locations in order to take advantage of the improved service characteristics following a transport improvement, often without a corresponding lowering in transport cost, is an indication that changes in transport service are inducing overall increases in efficiency. Cost savings due to transport can therefore be traded for increased sales or lowered costs of operations.

Thus, one conclusion of this study is that the costs accounted for in benefit analysis should include nonmarket perceived costs as well as monetary costs. The differential between the cost streams of alternative projects can be interpreted as the benefit that accrues as the result of building one rather than the other. While it is clear that work remains to be done in quantifying these nonmarket costs for a wider variety of commodities and under a larger range of conditions, the scheme proposed here should be useful even with present data. It should, as well, offer a framework for future empirical and theoretical development.

6 Designing the Facility

The Problem

A transportation facility connecting two points can vary enormously in both construction cost and in the performance and operating cost of vehicles using it, depending upon its design parameters. Once these parameters are selected, and the facility has been constructed, the performance is fixed, at least until major reconstruction is performed. Because the economic life of a facility may be many decades, and the cost implications of different designs so widely divergent, the selection of the facility design should be carefully considered.

The design problem is made difficult by the interdependence between any given link under consideration and the rest of the transportation system, or the economy as a whole. The appropriate design characteristics are a function of the traffic volume and composition. At the same time, the traffic volume that will find it convenient and useful to use the facility is a function of the performance, which depends in turn upon those design features. As a consequence the facility cannot be designed without knowing the traffic volume, yet the volume cannot be determined until the facility design is set. The full range of interdependencies is rarely accounted for because facilities are typically designed one link at a time. Also, the agency designing and constructing the facility may be more interested in minimizing construction cost than in choosing a design that balances construction cost against operating cost and performance.

Still, higher level goals could be set than merely minimizing facility construction costs given a set of standard specifications. The overall responsibility for design usually rests with an agency of local or national government. Depending upon the charter of the responsible body, it seems appropriate to consider at least the cost of constructing and maintaining the facility and the cost of operating transport vehicles over it. In most cases, the nonmarket cost associated with shipping over the facility should be considered as well. Even where the facility is privately owned, such as a railroad, the nonmarket costs are important considerations in design because they will affect the price shippers will pay for service.

Although it is possible to detail these cost categories further, the principal trade-offs affecting design are between the cost of constructing and the cost of using the facility. The important variables manipulated by the designer are the length, the gradient, and the average design speed. While present design practice does not make explicit the procedure for varying these parameters to optimize the cost of constructing the facility and using it, it is possible to identify such a procedure. This procedure might be costly and time consuming in practice, but it is essentially straightforward. The steps are:

1. Select the facility alignment and basic design characteristics.
2. Estimate the traffic volumes that will use the facility.
3. Compute the construction cost, maintenance cost, and operating cost; and use these costs in determining the pricing policy.
4. Determine the performance of the facility for shippers and the resultant non-market cost.
5. Examine available alternative modes and routes and revise the original estimates of demand.
6. Repeat steps 3, 4, and 5 until a stable answer is obtained.
7. Repeat the entire process starting with step 1, selecting an entirely new alignment and/or design standards; continue until a wide range of alternatives is available.

This procedure for design differs in two important respects from the process used in present practice. First, designers typically shortcut this approach by using design standards based on expected traffic volumes. Designers rarely investigate the use of widely different sets of design standards and their effect on traffic use of the facility. However, it must be conceded that it is quite difficult at the level of a particular project to take into account changes in the overall traffic volumes that will be experienced as a result of the adoption of a different set of design standards. Present practice is also discouraged from the use of more elaborate design procedures by the fact that computations are time-consuming and boring.

In the present study, it becomes necessary to adopt some explicit design procedure at that point where one would begin to evaluate a potential new facility, either railroad or highway. If the old road is inadequate, there are many different new highways that might replace it, as well as a large number of rail alternatives. Selecting a facility design for each condition treated in this study is a problem similar to that faced by the typical designer, except that the setting here is described with an example rather than an actual problem. There is no reason to suppose that there exists an actual situation that is exactly like one studied here, and therefore, the final designs adopted in this study do not purport to be ideal except for the particular situation assumed. Still, the procedure for selecting a design should be of general usefulness, and the solutions here indicate the direction and magnitude of the consequences of selecting alternative design parameters.

There are three problems posed by this exploration. First, there is the question of how to evaluate changes in traffic implied by changes in link performance. Secondly, a terrain representation must be employed that will be responsive to the trade-offs and designs that are typically employed by the designer and yet useful in an analytical determination of construction cost. Finally, we must devise a scheme for manipulating facility characteristics to obtain a range of designs that can be evaluated.

The solution to the first problem, that of changing demand, is to perform the analysis of facility design over a range of volume levels, assuming that traffic volumes are determined exogenously. The design that will be selected is the optimum for the volume level and commodity mix specified at the outset. This approach will allow us to determine the break points at which major changes in design are required by a change in traffic volume. In effect, the result is the optimum design as a function of volume.

A solution to the second problem is to devise a representation of terrain that can be dealt with analytically. This is not particularly difficult, and several terrain model representations are in common usage. However, because the terrain models used in current practice are extremely cumbersome, a new representation will be explored here.

A solution to the final problem of generating alternative designs is not difficult if depth of detail and comprehensiveness are kept within reasonable limits. The major pitfall is the combinational nature of the problem. There are many variables, each of which can vary over a fairly broad range. Discretion must be used in picking the variables to be explored and determining the number of discrete points within each range that will be tested.

The following procedure will be used to select designs for the facilities to be evaluated. First, a price scenario will be selected, utilizing the factor prices, vehicle technology, and commodity preference data of the base scenario discussed in Chapter 4 and Appendixes A and B. A set of facility design parameters will then be tried for each of the three terrain types and each of the three volume levels, holding the commodity mix constant. Costs and performance measures will then be computed for all combinations of varied parameters, and a summary of results prepared so that the most desirable design can be identified. This optimal design is used in the example problem of Chapter 2.

Construction Cost Model

Highways and railroads, while quite different in their appearance and operation, require very similar steps in initial construction. Surveying is followed by earthmoving and grading, the subbase is prepared, a base laid, and finally the running surface, either pavement or rails set down. The procedures used for computing construction costs are therefore quite similar, although the parameters for the two modes are somewhat different. Right-of-way cost will be ignored here, since it is usually low for developing countries except when passing through urban areas, and its value cannot easily be generalized. Structures and drainage can incur substantial costs, but are so entirely dependent upon specific

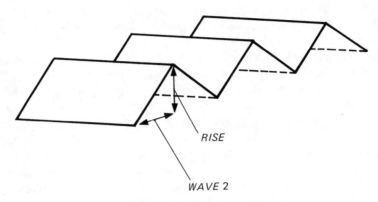

Figure 6-1. Corrugated Form of the Terrain.

features of the route location that they, too, cannot usefully be generalized. In practice, specific information about these items should be included in the cost data, but their omission here should not prejudice the highway-rail analysis, as both modes would be similarly affected.

The first task is describing the terrain that will be used as the basis for the cost models. The representation used here can be most easily visualized as a corrugated surface, like a tin roof. It extends in all directions to the horizon and appears to the observer like the illustration in Figure 6-1. The hills of this terrain can be described using the two parameters shown in Figure 6-1, *RISE* and *WAVE2*. The mnemonic *WAVE2* is a parameter representing one-half of the wave length, which is the distance from the top of one hill to the bottom of the neighboring valley. The term *RISE* represents vertical distance from the floor of a valley to the top of the next hill. The use of these two parameters allows a wide variety of terrain types to be represented. Some samples of these types are shown in Figure 6-2, where flat terrain, hilly terrain, and mountainous terrain are represented using three separate sets of the parameters.

The length, gradient, excavation and embankment quantities, and other cost elements can be computed by using this admittedly simple geometry employing a description of the alignment which follows. The two cities A and B are assumed to lie along a line perpendicular to the hills and valleys of the terrain. The shortest road or railroad between the termini would of course follow this airline projection. If the facility were built directly along this airline projection, it would encounter gradients equal to *RISE* divided by *WAVE2*. This gradient of the ground measured along the alignment of the facility will be referred to as *RFGND*. Thus, in the airline case,

$$RFGND = \frac{RISE}{WAVE2} \qquad (6.1)$$

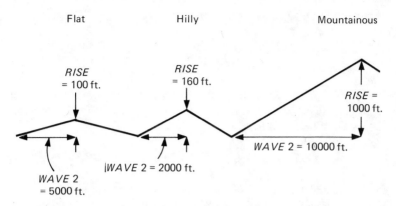

Figure 6-2. Range of Terrain Types Represented Using *WAVE2* and *RISE*.

If the gradient along the roadway is reduced relative to the gradient along the ground, the result would be lower operating costs. This can be accomplished by cutting into the ground on the hills and filling material into the valleys (see Figure 6-3). This creates a set of prisms of material that must be cut from the hills and filled into the valleys. The final gradient of the road depends, of course, upon the amount of cut material that is moved. It is possible to completely level the roadway if the size of the prism is large enough. The geometry of the prisms can be used to compute their volume and thus the cost of earth movement.

Construction cost (*CONCST*) consists of the cost of the roadway base and

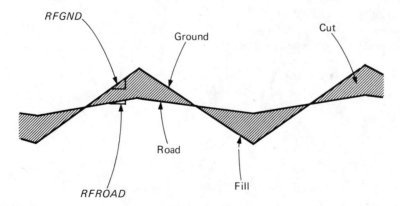

Figure 6-3. Excavation and Embankment Encountered when Gradient of Road is Less Than That of Ground.

surface paving (*SFCOST*) and the cost of earth excavation and embankment (*EMCOST*). Thus,

$$CONCST = SFCOST + EMCOST \qquad (6.2)$$

The surface cost (*SFCOST*) is the product of the length (*LENG*) in miles, the number of lanes (*TLANES*) and the unit cost per mile (*SCOST*) of a lane of this surface type (*ISURF*). That is,

$$SFCOST = TLENG \cdot TLANES \cdot SCOST \, (ISURF) \qquad (6.3)$$

Excavation and embankment cost (*EMCOST*) are the product of length, unit cost of a cubic yard of excavation (*EWCOST*) and the volume of excavation (*EWVOL*):

$$EMCOST = TLENG \cdot EWCOST \cdot EWVOL \qquad (6.4)$$

The volume of excavation can be expressed as a function of the difference (*RF*) in the rate of rise and fall along the ground (*RFGRND*) and that along the road (*RFROAD*), the number of lanes (*TLANES*) and the shape coefficients *B*, *D*, and *E* as follows:

$$RF = RFGND - RFROAD \qquad (6.5)$$
$$EWVOL = TLANES \cdot (B + D + E) \qquad (6.6)$$

The coefficient *B* represents the amount of side-to-side smoothing that must typically be done on the road. Coefficients *D* and *E* are interpreted in Figure Figure 6-4. The variable *D* is the volume in cubic yards of the parallel wedge *D* in Figure 6-4 while *E* is the volume in cubic yards of the triangular prism on the lower right side of Figure 6-4. The shapes *D* and *E* shown in Figure 6-4 are for a typical cut section in terrain that has hills with dimensions *WAVE2* and *RISE*. The equations for the geometrical figures are:

$$D = \frac{1}{2} \cdot \left(\frac{WAVE2}{100} \cdot \frac{RF}{2} \right) \cdot WDLANE \cdot \left(\frac{WAVE2}{2} \right) \cdot \left(\frac{5280}{WAVE2} \right) \cdot \frac{1}{27}$$

$$(6.7)$$

$$E = \frac{1}{2} \cdot \left(\frac{WAVE2}{100} \cdot \frac{RF}{2} \right)^2 \cdot \left(\frac{WAVE2}{2} \right) \cdot \left(\frac{5280}{WAVE2} \right) \cdot \frac{1}{27} \qquad (6.8)$$

They are obtained by multiplying one-half the area of one end of the figure by

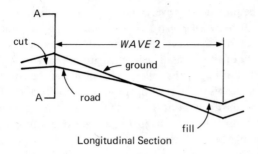

Longitudinal Section

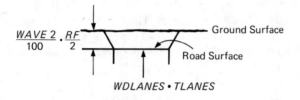

Cross Section A–A

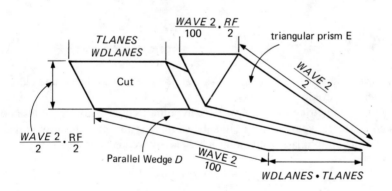

Isometric view of wedge of earth removed from the cut section.

Figure 6-4. Geometrical Relationships Used in Computing Earth Volumes.

its length, the number of waves per mile, and a factor to convert cubic feet to cubic yards. Typical unit cost for earthwork (*EWCOST*) and surface cost (*SFCOST*) must be provided for every change in the cost environment.

Since trade-offs between construction and operating cost will be of interest, we can now use the formulas developed above for determining the construction cost under a variety of situations. The original ground may be smoothed by excavating the hills and filling in the valleys. This increases the cost of construction but presumably decreases the cost of operating over the facility. The greater the difference between the gradient of the road and that of the ground, the more extensive the cut and fill and the larger the capital expenditure required to achieve it. As the hills become longer and steeper, the cost of constructing low-gradient roadways by cut and fill can quickly become very high, so design objectives may have to be relaxed.

An alternative to increasing the gradient is to allow the road to climb the hills at an angle instead of straight-on. This has the effect of reducing the gradient of the ground over which the road is passing at the expense of additional length or circuity (*CIR*). The actual length of the road can be defined precisely using the air distance and the circuity as:

$$TLENG = AIRDIS \cdot CIR \tag{6.9}$$

For the terrain defined here, with its series of perfectly uniform corrugations, the ground gradient can be computed for any circuity using:

$$RFGND = \frac{RFAIR}{CIR} \tag{6.10}$$

Thus, when the length is doubled (*CIR* = 2), the gradient of the ground along the alignment is halved.

In the geometric world that we have hypothesized until now, the hills never end no matter how far we move laterally, so there is no way to go around them. In order to approximate reality a bit more closely we may consider using:

$$RFGND = RFAIR \cdot CIR^{(-A/V)} \tag{6.11}$$

in which *V* stands for design speed and *A* is a parameter controlling the shape of the curve. The effect of changing the parameter *A* or the design speed *V* can be appreciated by referring to Figure 6–5 in which plots of rise and fall along the ground (*RFGND*) versus circuity (*CIR*) have been prepared for a variety of *A*s and *V*s.

In general, the greater the circuity one is willing to tolerate, the lower will be the rise and fall along the ground (*RFGND*) underneath the alignment. Also, with

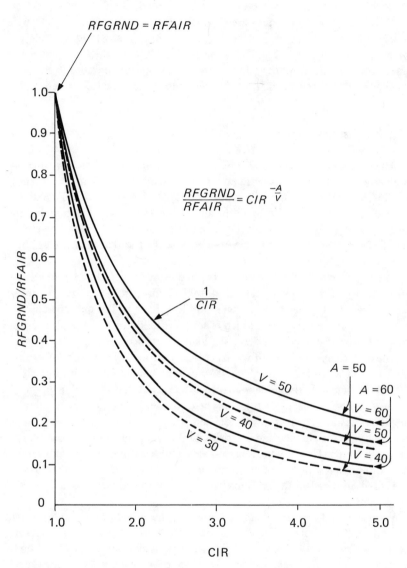

Figure 6–5. The Role of Circuity in Determining the Gradient of the Ground Under the Alignment.

lower design speeds, favorable rise and fall may be obtained with less circuity. The upper curve in Figure 6–5 is observed for perfectly regular corrugated topography. The lower curves are those representing less regular hills, i.e. hills with a more weathered character, plotted for several design speeds, and with the parameter A set equal to 60 and 50 respectively. Although the equations presented here are not calibrated, they do represent, in a behavioral way, the effect that changing the circuity will have on the ground gradient encountered.

Other Cost Components

The procedure by which the construction cost and its various sub-components were derived has been discussed in rather great detail, because the construction cost determination and the method of computation are key to understanding the example presented here. The operating and way-maintenance cost models, however, will not be described in this detail since they are fully documented elsewhere.[1] Their characteristics will merely be described so that their use can be understood.

The highway model is designed to compute three types of cost that arise during the use of the highway. These are vehicle operating cost, way-maintenance cost, and commodity perceived nonmarket costs. Each will be described in greater detail in the paragraphs which follow. Figure 6–6 shows the place occupied by the highway model in the design selection procedure.

The cost of maintenance-of-way is critically important only when there is very little traffic, where its fixed elements can dominate both the cost of construction and operation. Maintenance costs vary widely depending upon terrain, weather, drainage conditions, type of roadway, and the traffic volume using the roadway. The highway model computes road maintenance cost using a fixed cost per year per lane and a variable unit cost component that is a function of traffic volume. These two parameters vary with the surface type, and can be made to represent a variety of environmental conditions and road types. The values used must reflect fluctuations from country to country as well as over time.

Vehicle operating costs computed by the highway model depend upon many factors including the size and composition of the vehicle fleet, the local factor prices, traffic volume levels, and the detailed design characteristics of the roadway and its surface. Vehicle operating costs are developed by simulating the operation of a fleet of five vehicle types (corresponding to the five commodity

---

1. Charles River Associates, *A Manual of Computer Programs for Project Analysis* (Washington, D.C.: Commerce Clearinghouse, 1970).

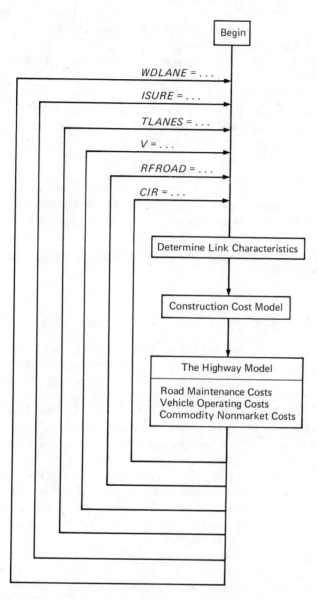

Figure 6-6. Procedure and Variables Used in the Selection of Highway Design Characteristics.

classes) over the alignment, and computing the amount of fuel, oil, and other inputs used, along with values for travel time and vehicle depreciation and maintenance, all under a range of volume conditions. Resulting physical quantities are then multiplied by unit costs to develop a total cost for the vehicle movement. Costs per vehicle mile and cost per ton mile are summed for vehicles in all classes. The final result is the total cost of vehicle operation for an entire year of traffic flow.

Information necessary for the determination of commodity perceived nonmarket costs is also obtained from the highway performance model, which generates travel time, waiting time, time variability, and probability of loss and damage for each commodity class. Multiplying each of these performance measures by the appropriate commodity weighting of performance for each class of goods produces a set of commodity perceived nonmarket costs. When summed over all classes of goods for the entire time period under consideration, they give a measure of the total cost to shippers for shipping their goods over the highway link in question. The role of this highway model and the costs and performance measures it generates in the larger process of determining facility designs will be discussed in the next section.

Rail Cost Components

The procedure followed in selecting the railway design was almost identical to that used for highways. However, one minor difference was that rail maintenance-of-way costs are combined with vehicle operating costs in the train performance calculations performed by the railway model rather than being displayed separately as in the highway model. The model, described in detail in the *Manual of Computer Programs,* consists of a series of equations which determine the size and make-up of each train and its average operating speed and fuel consumption. From the speed, block time is determined and crew, depreciation, and other costs are computed. Congestion on single-track railroads is accounted for by equations using a variable representing the number of passing sidings that are available. Fuel and oil costs are based on horsepower requirements. The determination of commodity perceived nonmarket cost is performed in the same way in the rail model as it was in the highway model.

Although the same procedure is used in the selection of the railway design as for the highway, the variables used to describe the railway are, naturally, different. The important rail characteristics include: circuity, average gradient, maximum gradient, speed limit, type of locomotive, number of locomotives, signal system time delay category, switching time delay category, and number of passing sidings. As with the highway model, trade-offs between circuity, gradient, and speed are extremely important in selecting the optimum design configuration.

Procedure for Design Selection

Now that the models have been described, it is possible to consider how they should be used to select the design parameter for a proposed new facility. This presents two basic questions: what set of designs should be considered, and how should each design be evaluated in the search for a "best" design?

One means of selecting a set of designs would be to take, for each control variable, a series of values which adequately represented the full range that variable could be expected to cover. All combinations of all values of these variables would constitute a very large set, perhaps too large to be handled even with the aid of a computer, and certainly expensive to evaluate even if possible. In addition, some of the design parameters are interrelated in such a way that a substantial number of these combinations might be impossible, inconsistent, or at least predictably inferior by any measure, to some of the others. It is therefore desirable to search for a procedure that would examine a limited set of parameter values, including only those which were feasible and not predictably inferior to others that were examined.

The definition of criteria by which designs can be evaluated to determine which is "best" is a problem about which there has been much discussion, and to which Chapter 10 of this report is devoted. Because different people and institutions may have different objective functions, it is possible for reasonable men to differ substantially in their selection of the best project for a given situation. For purposes of this study, we will take as an objective the minimization of total social cost, where this cost includes the present discounted value of construction cost, facility maintenance cost, vehicle operating cost, and commodity perceived nonmarket cost. Because cost computation will be made for many different designs, and the answers recorded, those who wish to apply some objective function other than minimizing total cost can make another selection from among the answers given.

It will be useful, however, to have a simple method of evaluating the tradeoffs that can be made between the various cost elements in highway or railroad design and to use this method to provide an intuitive feel for the type of design that will be best and to help eliminate designs that will perform poorly. To facilitate this, the four cost elements can be placed in two groups: (1) the construction costs, which are merely the costs of building the facility and (2) the use costs, which include operation, maintenance, and nonmarket costs. Using only two categories rather than the four listed above has the virtue of presenting the results in a format that is easy to visualize. Still, the results are more intuitive than a single total cost figure. Greater expenditures for construction will typically result in lowered use costs.

Using this method, designs that contribute no savings in either construction or use costs over previous designs can be discarded immediately without fear that at some higher or lower traffic volume they would be preferred. Finally, the ability to understand what is going on inside the process will allow us to develop a strategy that is considerably more efficient for searching out good solutions than total enumeration.

To understand the nature of the trade-offs that are possible between the cost of constructing the facility and the cost of using it, and to aid in the development of a strategy for manipulating the designer controlled variables in a search for good designs, let us examine the effects of making changes in the controllable variables and their effect on the cost of construction and use. In general, one would expect the following set of relationships to hold for most types of terrain. Increasing the design speed increases construction cost and decreases use cost. Increasing the maximum gradient decreases construction cost and increases use cost. Increasing lane width increases construction cost and decreases use cost. Increasing the number of lanes increases construction cost and decreases use cost. All have fairly direct and easily predicted consequences.

Increases to circuity, however, are more complex particularly if the terrain is hilly. Initial increases in circuity tend to decrease either construction cost or operating cost or both since the same gradient can be achieved with less money expended for construction or an improved gradient can be constructed with less money required for operation. This continues to be true only up to a point, however, beyond which further increases in length tend to increase the cost of both construction and operation.

Suppose a procedure was devised for systematically varying the circuity and the average road gradient for a given terrain type, while holding constant the airline distance, the traffic volume, and the volume mix. This procedure could be used to design a series of facilities that would explore the important trade-offs between circuity and gradient. The process could then be repeated for different traffic volumes, surface types, design speeds, and terrain types. Such a procedure is as follows: (1) For a given traffic volume, designate a series of increasingly more circuitous alignments, A, B, C, etc. (2) For any alignment (e.g., alignment A) designate a series of progressive reductions in road gradient to produce a series of successively smoother profiles $A_g, A_{g-1}, A_{g-2}, \ldots, A_0$. (3) Repeat the process with alignment series B, then C, etc., until the minimum cost of this series is larger than the minimum cost of the last series.

To demonstrate what such an analysis would accomplish, the procedure will be applied to a new highway in the mountainous terrain of the base scenario. Alignment A_g is assumed to sit at or near the surface of the ground and is thus costly from the standpoint of use, but not from the standpoint of construction as virtually no earthmoving is needed. The gradient of alignment A_{g-1} is less than the average gradient of the ground and involves some cut and fill to construct, thereby reducing the cost of using the facility but increasing the cost of its construction. Alignment A_{g-2} goes even further. Its surface is much smoother, approaching a horizontal surface. Finally, A_0 is a direct alignment between the

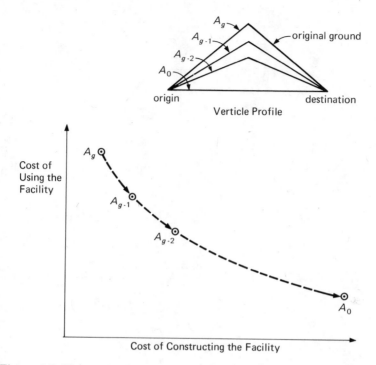

Figure 6-7. User and Construction Cost Trade-off: For a Given Circuity and Various Road Gradients

origin and destination at the minimum possible gradient (presumably zero). If the original terrain is at all hilly, this last alignment may be extremely costly to construct. This series of successively smoother vertical alignments is shown on Figure 6-7 from a position of high use cost, and low construction cost, to a situation of high construction costs but fairly low use costs.

The B series of alignments is more circuitous than A. (See Figure 6-8.) The construction cost of B_g will typically be less than that for A_g. Overall, the B series performs similarly to A, as does series C. Eventually, however, there will be some series, here series D or E, that is so circuitous that the additional length is no longer an advantage, and the cost of both construction and use begin to climb. If circuity increases are carried to an extreme, for example, series F, the excessive circuity produces alignments with very low gradients, but high construction and use costs.

The effect produced by a variety of terrain types is summarized in Figure 6-9. For mountainous terrain, the effects are much like those presented in Figures 6-7 and 6-8. For flat terrain, it is obvious that the shortest and cheapest alignment is along a straight line between the origin and the destination. The

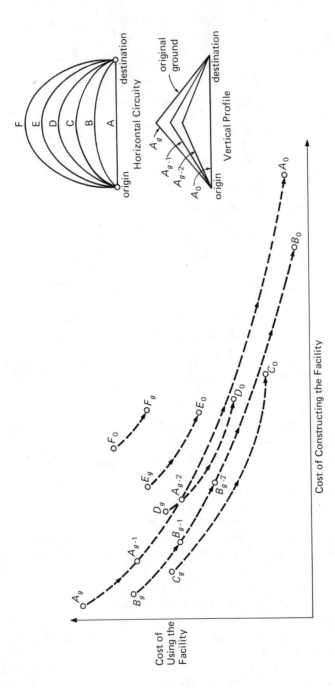

LEGEND: Capital letters denote circuity.
              Subscripts denote gradient.

Figure 6–8. User and Construction Cost Trade-off: For Various Circuity and Various Road Gradients.

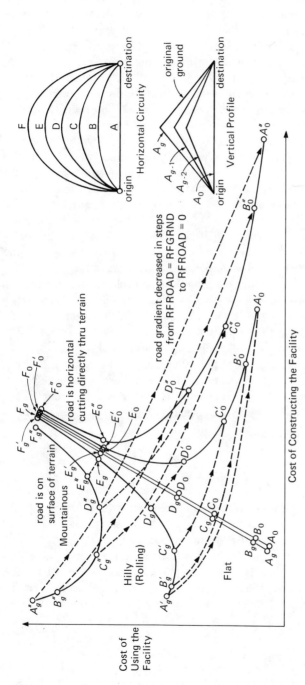

LEGEND: Capital letters denote circuity.
Subscripts denote gradient.

Figure 6–9. User and Construction Cost Trade-off: For Various Circuity, Various Road Gradients, and Three Terrain Types.

introduction of any circuity has a negative effect on both the cost of construction and operation. Furthermore, this effect is directly proportional to length. The result is a straight line inclined somewhat from the vertical axis.

Although the conclusions that can be drawn from these diagrams are by no means earth shaking, they do illustrate fairly concisely the nature of the trade-offs that are available between circuity and gradient for various terrain types. The results agree with common sense. For flat terrain, the minimum total cost alignment is along a straight line between the origin and destination. For rolling and mountainous terrain, the introduction of a moderate amount of circuity and the smoothing of the alignment vertical profile both produce economies up to a point, but not beyond. A change in the design speed has an effect similar to that of changing terrain type. One might say that an increase in design speed has a sluggish effect on the ability of the alignment to respond to changes in terrain configuration.

Both the designer and the decision maker may utilize the form of presentation employed here. By presenting the results in a two-dimensional fashion, the designer can gain insights into how changes in his design will affect costs. The decision maker will, on the other hand, find this approach useful to the problem of capital budgeting. He can see how selecting a less costly project will affect long-run use costs. Since the traffic volumes using the facility in the future are relatively harder to predict than the cost of construction, he may decide that these costs should be weighted less heavily in the selection of projects for inclusion in his capital budget. A toll authority or railroad cannot fail to notice that the cost of constructing the facility is 100 percent borne by themselves, while the use costs are partially those of shippers. In any event, the identification of the incidence of costs is a useful exercise and one that should help to improve decision making.

Base Scenario

To demonstrate application of the technique to real-world conditions and prices, an example situation was studied using the base scenario data. The problem described in detail in Chapter 1 involves selecting a highway or a railway between two cities, 100 airline miles apart. The example problem involved two modes, highway and rail; three terrain forms, mountainous, hilly, and flat; three volume levels, high, medium, and low; and three commodity mixes, bulk dominated, balanced, and general dominated. To simplify the exposition, the balanced commodity mix is the only commodity mix that will be discussed. The terrain types are identical to those that were illustrated in Figure 6-2. Descriptive parameters important to the example problem are presented in Table 6-1.

The base scenario from which this example is taken uses 1967 Republic of Colombia factor prices for the cost inputs. The choice of highway vehicles and

Table 6-1
Basic Inputs to the Example Problem

	Flat	Hilly	Mountainous
Terrain Type			
RFGND ft./100 ft.	2	8	10
WAVE2 in ft.	5,000	2,000	10,000
	Low	Medium	High
Volume Level			
Tons/day			
each direction	100	1,000	5,000

	Bulk Goods (percent)	General Goods (percent)	Special Goods (percent)	Common Carrier Passenger (percent)	Private Carrier Passenger (percent)	Total (percent)
Commodity Mix						
Flow A to B	60	20	10	9	1	100
Flow B to A	20	60	10	9	1	100

rail equipment and technology was also based upon Colombian conditions and experiences as were the facility construction costs. The factor prices used were described more thoroughly in Chapter 3, which details the experimental conditions. The derivation of commodity perceived nonmarket costs was accomplished in Chapter 5. Derivations and assumptions of basic cost elements supporting the facility cost figures are given for the highway and railway in Appendix B. Reference to the facility cost figures presented in Appendix B allows one to conclude that for the base scenario situation, the construction costs of highways are a bit less than those for railroads. However, the operating cost, which is not shown there, is typically higher for highways than for railroads.

We begin our analysis of the results by examining plots of the highway costs shown in Figure 6-10. Here the axes of the plot are the same as those used previously. However, they are quantified with scales in millions of dollars. As in the descriptive example presented earlier, the lines are plotted for increasing circuity from 1.0 to 1.7.[2] The number at the left end of each plotted line is the gradient of the roadway as represented by RFROAD. Thus, decreasing the gradient progressively decreases user costs while at the same time increasing the cost of construction, principally the cost of earthwork. Also shown on Figure 6-10 is a line of equal construction plus user costs. This line, which lies at 45° to the two axes, represents the locus of points for which the total costs are

---

2. There appeared to be no reason to explore alignments with circuities larger than 1.7. It is fairly clear from the rise of the operating cost curve that increases in length will save relatively little construction cost at the expense of a much greater operating cost.

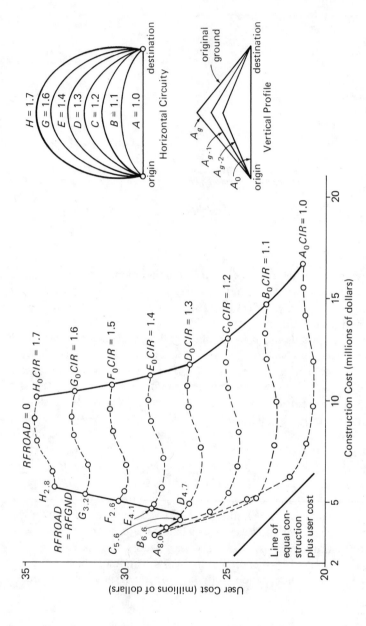

Figure 6-10. User and Construction Cost Trade-off: For Various Circuity, Various Road Gradients, Hilly Terrain, and Balanced Flows of 1000 Tons/Day Each Way.

equal. The point at which a line parallel to the 45° line intersects the plotted line represents the point of minimum total cost.

One unexpected result illustrated by the curves is the manner in which the right-hand points begin to rise rather than continuing to fall as they did in previous figures. This reflects the fact that the flatter alignments encourage higher speeds that have slightly increased operating costs. Another significant aspect of the curves is the sharp corner occurring at about 5 percent *RFROAD*. This indicates that the minimum total cost point where each curve is tangent to the 45° line occurs in a narrowly defined region.

Another interesting result is that the alignment with a circuity of 1.1 and an *RFROAD* of 5 percent has a point that is very close to the line of minimum cost. Although it is clearly not the lowest such value, the difference is small. This is illustrated in Table 6–2 where the numerical results from which the plots were made are presented. Since construction for this alignment is only $5.1 million as contrasted to $6.3 million for the minimum-total-cost alignment, it does bear careful consideration. The trade-off here involves future traffic volumes. If future traffic is uncertain and if there are other projects on which the $1.2 million difference in construction cost could be used to greater advantage, then perhaps the $5.1 million alignment should be constructed.

The results for three different terrain types for a single commodity flow level and mix are shown in Figures 6–11 through 6–14. The plot of Figure 6–14 corresponds closely to Figure 6–9 hypothesized earlier. In Figure 6–14 the mountainous terrain presents a more varied set of results than the flat or hilly terrain, since more alternative designs are possible in mountainous areas than are possible in flatter terrain. Note in particular that the mountainous plot could not be scaled to fit on any reasonable figure; achieving low-gradient designs in mountainous areas is prohibitively expensive.

To understand the overall results of the study without examining the plots of each volume level, mix, design speed, etc., it is useful to examine a table showing the design characteristics of the minimum-total-cost designs. This is presented for the highway case in Table 6–3. As expected, the higher-volume levels involve straighter alignments with higher design speeds and lower gradients.

Results for the rail alternative were obtained in a similar manner. Minimum-total-cost rail designs are summarized in Table 6–4. As can be seen, more parameters were varied in the search for a minimum, so more runs were made. Rail lines selected by the procedure were more circuitous than highways in hilly and mountainous country, and therefore somewhat longer. The results, however are more or less what one might anticipate.

In all of the cases illustrated, the total costs were lower for the highway design than for the railroad. The margin of difference is least, however, for the case of high-volume flows. The implication one might draw from this is that with higher volume levels or with a more bulk-intensive mix of commodities moving, the railroad might achieve lower total costs. The most advantageous situation

Table 6–2
Sample Results of the Iterative Design Process: For Different
Circuities and Gradients, Showing Highway User and
Construction Costs (Millions of Dollars)

CIR	RFROAD	Construction Costs	RFAC and Use Costs	Total Costs
1.0	0.00	17.0	21.0	38.0
	0.50	15.6	21.1	36.7
	1.00	14.3	21.1	35.7
	2.00	11.8	20.6	32.4
	3.00	9.7	20.7	30.4
	4.00	7.8	21.0	28.9
	5.00	6.3	21.7	28.1
	6.00	5.0	24.2	29.2
	8.00	3.4	28.6	32.0
1.1	0.00	14.6	23.0	37.6
	0.50	13.3	23.0	36.3
	1.00	12.0	23.0	35.1
	2.00	9.8	22.5	32.3
	3.00	7.9	22.6	30.5
	4.00	6.3	22.9	29.3
	5.00	5.1	23.8	28.8
	6.00	4.1	26.5	30.6
	6.61	3.7	28.2	31.9
1.2	0.00	13.0	24.9	37.9
	0.50	11.7	25.0	36.7
	1.00	10.6	24.9	35.5
	2.00	8.5	24.3	32.9
	3.00	6.8	24.4	31.2
	4.00	5.5	24.8	30.3
	5.00	4.4	25.8	30.2
	5.56	4.0	27.3	31.3
1.3	0.00	11.9	26.8	38.7
	0.50	10.7	26.9	37.6
	1.00	9.6	26.9	36.5
	2.00	7.7	26.2	33.9
	3.00	6.1	26.3	32.4
	4.00	5.0	26.8	31.7
	4.73	4.4	27.3	31.7

CIR	RFROAD	Construction Costs	RFAC and Use Costs	Total Costs
1.4	0.00	11.2	28.7	39.8
	0.50	10.0	28.8	38.8
	1.00	8.9	28.8	37.7
	2.00	7.1	28.1	35.2
	3.00	5.8	28.2	33.9
	4.00	4.8	28.7	33.4
	4.08	4.7	28.7	33.4
1.5	0.00	10.7	30.6	41.3
	0.05	9.5	30.7	40.3
	1.00	8.5	30.7	39.2
	2.00	6.8	29.9	36.8
	3.00	5.6	30.1	35.6
	3.56	5.1	30.4	35.4
1.6	0.00	10.3	32.5	42.8
	0.50	9.2	32.6	41.9
	1.00	8.2	32.6	40.9
	2.00	6.6	31.8	38.5
	3.00	5.5	31.9	37.4
	3.15	5.4	32.1	37.4
1.7	0.00	10.1	34.4	44.6
	0.50	9.0	34.6	43.6
	1.00	8.1	34.5	42.6
	2.00	6.6	33.7	40.2
	2.76	5.7	33.6	39.3

Note: Hilly terrain with balanced flows of 1000 tons/day at 30 miles per hour design speed. The results of this table for 30 mph correspond to the points plotted in Figure 6–12; note that it is different from the final design in Table 5–3, which used a design speed of 50 mph.

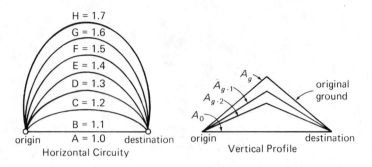

Horizontal Circuity   Vertical Profile

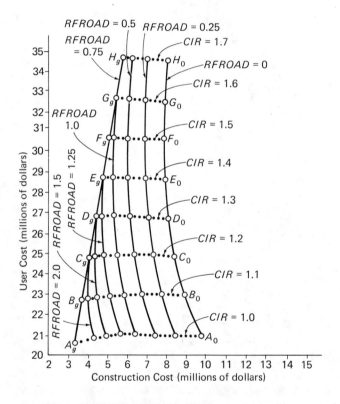

LEGEND: Capital letters denote circuity.
        Subscripts denote gradient.

NOTE: Results computed from based scenario in millions of U.S. dollars.

Figure 6-11. User and Construction Cost Trade-off: For Various Circuity, Various Road Gradients, Flat Terrain, and Balanced Flows of 1000 Tons/Day Each Way.

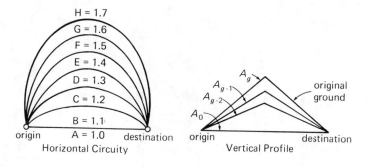

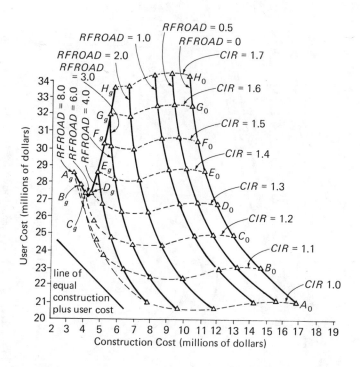

LEGEND: Capital letters denote circuity.
         Subscripts denote gradient.

NOTE: Results computed from based scenario in millions of U.S. dollars.

Figure 6–12. User and Construction Cost Trade-off: For Various Circuity, Various Road Gradients, Hilly Terrain, and Balanced Flows of 1000 Tons/Day Each Way.

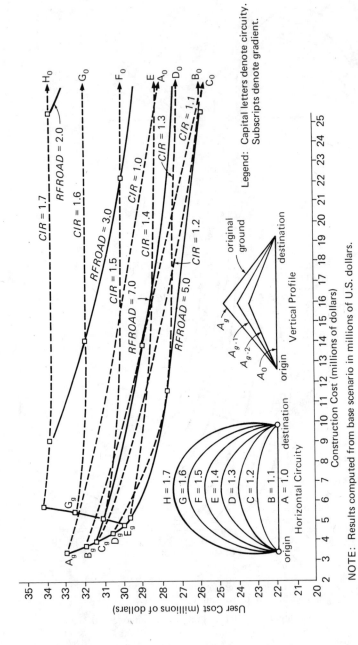

Figure 6-13. User and Construction Cost Trade-off: For Various Circuity, Various Road Gradients, Mountainous Terrain, and Balanced Flows of 1000 Tons/Day Each Way.

NOTE: Results computed from base scenario in millions of U.S. dollars.

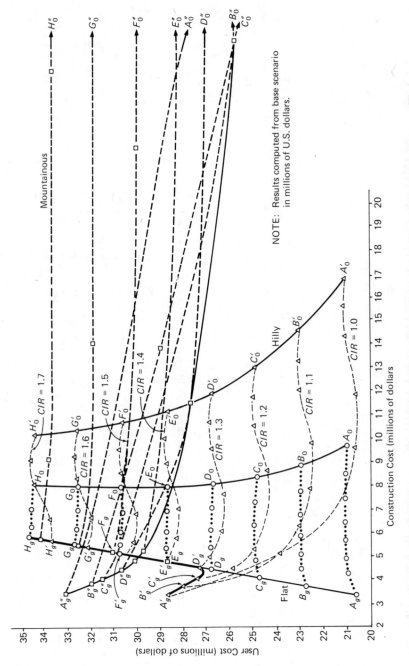

Figure 6–14. User and Construction Cost Trade-off: For Various Circuity, Various Road Gradients, Three Terrain Types, and Balanced Flows of 1000 Tons/Day Each Way.

Table 6–3
Minimum Total Cost Highway Designs for Balanced Flow Conditions Under Different Terrain Types and Volume Conditions

	Low (100 tons/day)	Medium (1000 tons/day)	High (5000 tons/day)
Flat	1.0, 50 mph, 2% $6.0 million	1.0, 50 mph, 2% $21.0 million	1.0, 50 mph, 2% $91.8 million
Hilly	1.05, 30 mph, 7% $7.4 million	1.0, 50 mph, 4% $27.1 million	1.0, 50 mph, 2% $100.3 million
Mountainous	1.30, 30 mph, 5.9% $8.5 million	1.40, 30 mph, 5.1% $34.7 million	1.30, 30 mph, 5% $169.4 million

Legend: $\dfrac{CIR,\ V,\ RFROAD}{TCOST}$

Table 6–4
Minimum Total Cost Rail Designs for Balanced Flow Conditions Under Different Terrain Types and Volume Conditions

	Low (100 tons/day)	Medium (1000 tons/day)	High (5000 tons/day)
Flat	1.0, 2.0%, 30 mph, 3, 1 $14.3 million	1.0, 0.25%, 40 mph, 1, 1 $38.9 million	1.0, 0.25%, 40 mph, 1, 1 $106.8 million
Hilly	1.2, 2.0%, 20 mph, 3, 1 $20.0 million	1.0, 0.25%, 40 mph, 3, 1 $45.3 million	1.0, 0.25%, 40 mph, 1, 1 $113.9 million
Mountainous	1.9, 3.4%, 20 mph, 3, 1 $23.1 million	2.0, 2.5%, 20 mph, 1, 2 $74.6 million	1.9, 0.5%, 20 mph, 1, 1 $276.4 million

Legend: $\dfrac{CIR,\ GAV,\ V,\ LT,\ NL}{TCOST}$.

for rail is of course the flat alignment. Here the cost of construction is significantly lower than in the mountains and the railroads were more competitive.

Although this brief analysis does not purport to present a final result, it appears that only under certain volume and mix situations is the railroad a reasonable competitor to highways. This normative statement, however, should be qualified by saying that, where existing facilities drastically alter the cost of construction or where the initial factor prices result in different costs for construction and operaton, this conclusion could easily be reversed.

The important conclusions that can be drawn from this study are that there exist significant trade-offs between the length, the gradients, and the design speed of facilities and their effects on user and construction costs. The facility must be designed with consideration of the advantages to be gained by making these trade-offs. Likewise the volume level of the facility and the basic terrain type in which the facility is situated are extremely important. The commodity mix is also a factor in some situations.

When the general economic consequences of the construction of a large-scale transport link are quite extensive this focus on careful optimization of the design may seem to be a diversion of analytic energy. However, even the potentially most advantageous project can be rendered much less beneficial if it is burdened with the excessive costs of gross overdesign; that is, to a design suited to volumes or commodities that will not materialize for decades. It is thus important to emphasize that the appropriate set of design standards is a function of the traffic volume. If the predicted level of traffic volume does not materialize, the facility is overdesigned and resources are wasted. By contrast, underdesign of facilities merely hastens the day they will need to be replaced.

In the final analysis, the designer working at the project level will undoubtedly have a less comprehensive view of the system and its performance than those who are charged with the responsibility of integrating individual projects into the total system. It is therefore appropriate for the designer to present a range of alternative designs over a variety of volume levels for use in this overall systems analysis. This chapter has attempted to illustrate both a method of approach and its possible use.

7 Results of Project Analysis

Introduction

The complete results of the base scenario study, a portion of which was outlined in Chapter 2, are discussed here, along with the results from the other scenario.[1] Evaluation of these results requires selection of a measure by which the relative merit of one solution over another may be determined. Obviously, there are a variety of such measures; Chapter 10 attempts to compare and evaluate them. For this chapter, however, we will concentrate on only three measures of overall performance: (1) the total present discounted value of the project; (2) the total present discounted value, with adjustments to include deduction of tax revenues to the government and the use of a shadow price on foreign exchange; (3) the same measures excluding the nonmarket measures of performance discussed in Chapter 5. A breakdown of the items included in these totals is given in detail in Appendix D. In all cases, a 20-year time horizon and a 15 percent interest rate are used for discounting.

This chapter will treat the adjusted total present discounted value as the preferred objective measure. This does not imply, however, that consideration of the other measures is unwarranted or erroneous. One advantage of a detailed simulation is that it can provide a great variety of output, which permits people with different objectives to make their own evaluation and conclusions — from the same base data.

Base Scenario Results

Flat Terrain, Simple Alternatives

A summary of the results obtained in simulations of the flat terrain is contained in Table 7–1. Taking as the best project one that minimizes the present discounted value of the costs incurred, it appears that for low volumes in flat terrain, continued use of the old road is better than either construction of a new highway or construction of the railroad. The total adjusted costs for the old road are approximately 20 percent lower than those for the new highway, and

---

1. A complete table of the results is contained in Appendix D, p. 199.

Table 7–1
Comparison of Project Alternatives
Base Scenario: Flat Terrain
(Present Discounted Value of Costs, Millions of Dollars)[a]

A. Market Plus Nonmarket Costs

Volume	Commodity Mix	Definition	Old Road	New Highway	New Railroad
Low	Balanced	Total	5.0	6.0	14.3
		Adjusted[b]	5.0	6.0	16.7
	Bulk	Total	4.9	5.9	13.3
		Adjusted	4.9	5.9	13.6
	General	Total	5.4	6.1	14.5
		Adjusted	5.4	6.1	14.8
Medium	Balanced	Total	39.2	21.0	38.9
		Adjusted	39.2	21.1	39.6
	Bulk	Total	39.1	20.9	35.4
		Adjusted	39.0	21.1	36.4
	General	Total	45.3	23.5	40.9
		Adjusted	45.4	23.6	41.9
High	Balanced	Total	243.1	91.8	106.8
		Adjusted	239.3	91.7	111.7
	Bulk	Total	249.0	92.5	104.4
		Adjusted	244.5	92.3	110.9
	General	Total	204.5	107.9	112.0
		Adjusted	299.6	107.7	128.6

B. Market Costs Only

Volume	Commodity Mix	Definition	Old Road	New Highway	New Railroad
Low	Balanced	Total	3.1	5.0	9.1
		Adjusted	3.1	5.0	9.5
	Bulk	Total	3.2	5.0	9.2
		Adjusted	3.2	5.0	9.6
	General	Total	3.4	5.1	9.2
		Adjusted	3.4	5.1	9.6
Medium	Balanced	Total	23.3	14.5	15.4
		Adjusted	23.3	14.6	16.0
	Bulk	Total	25.2	15.3	16.3
		Adjusted	25.1	15.4	17.3
	General	Total	27.5	16.3	16.3
		Adjusted	27.6	16.5	17.3
High	Balanced	Total	137.4	58.4	32.7
		Adjusted	133.6	58.3	37.7
	Bulk	Total	153.1	63.1	38.7
		Adjusted	148.6	62.8	45.2
	General	Total	175.3	68.7	38.8
		Adjusted	170.5	68.6	45.4

[a] 20-year time horizon; 15 percent discount rate. See Appendix D for the full set of results.

[b] Adjusted for taxes and foreign exchange. See Chapter 3.

almost one-third of those for the new railroad. As volume increases to 1000 tons per day in each direction, however, the new highway becomes the best alternative and this remains true even at the high-volume level.

Total costs for the old road at high volumes seem to be excessively high when compared to the costs for low and medium volumes because congestion has begun to develop on the old road at the high-volume condition. Congestion will become more apparent in the hilly and the mountainous terrain in subsequent results.

It is interesting to note that the selection of projects is the same whether the adjusted total or the unadjusted total is used. This turns out to be true for virtually every case reported in this chapter. In addition, the commodity mix seems to have little effect, as the balanced, bulk dominated, and general dominated mixes all result in the same project selection. This reflects the fact that the different mixes are only moderately different in their bulk and general composition, and have identical total tons of special and passengers.

Quite a different picture emerges if only market costs are considered; that is if the nonmarket measures of performance such as travel time and waiting time are ignored in the analysis. These results are presented in Table 7-1 (B). Here, for low volume the continued use of the old road is best, as it also is under the adjusted total measure; and for medium volume the construction of the new highway is best. At that medium level, however, the total cost for the new highway and for the new railroad are quite similar. In the high-volume case the railroad attains a clear superiority. Thus, at low- and medium-volume levels, the high capital investment in the railroad puts it at a disadvantage with respect to either the road or the highway when only market costs are considered. The operating efficiency of the railroad, however, gives it a substantial cost superiority at the high-volume level.

Comparison of Parts A and B of Table 7-1 shows how different the results are when nonmarket costs are included in the comparison. In Part A the railroad is *more* expensive at high volume by almost 20 percent than the new highway would be, while in Part B, with only market costs considered, the railroad is more than 30 percent *less* expensive than the hew highway at the same volume level. At the low volume, the railroad suffers not only from higher construction cost but also from operating costs that are nearly three times as great as highway operating costs. (See Appendix D for details of the components of these total costs.) Project selection will clearly depend upon whether or not it is decided to include nonmarket costs in the evaluation. We recommend that nonmarket costs be included.

Flat Terrain, Combined Alternative

Given that the nonmarket costs are an important portion of total cost in the high-volume cases for both the new highway and the new railroad, it is interest-

Table 7-2
Comparison of Project Alternatives
Base Scenario: Flat Terrain, Combined Railroad and Highway
(Present Discounted Value of Costs, Millions of Dollars)[a]

Mix	Definition	Combined Project (New Railroad/ New Highway)	Best Single Project (New Highway)
Balanced	Total	89.0^c	91.8
	Adjusted[b]	90.5^c	91.7
Bulk	Total	83.2^c	92.5
	Adjusted[b]	85.3^c	92.3

Note: Traffic = High volume only, bulk and special commodities on railroad; general, common and private on highway.
[a] 20-year time horizon; 15 percent discount rate.
[b] Adjusted for taxes and foreign exchange.
[c] Lowest total cost for this terrain type.

ing to consider whether the project would do better if both facilities were built, each tailored to the particular needs of certain commodity groups. To examine this situation, we have considered the construction of both a new highway and a new railroad, with the bulk and special traffic carried on the railroad, and general, common, and private traffic carried on the highway. The selection of this commodity split between the two modes seemed reasonable in that the higher-value commodities would prefer to use the highway, the higher-performance link, while the lower-value commodities would be better off using a mode with the lower market price. These assumptions were confirmed by running a series of tests using a variety of different modal allocations. Only the high volume was considered because neither the medium- nor low-volume cases would justify building more than one facility.

As Table 7-2 shows, the total cost and the adjusted total cost for the combined new railroad and new highway is actually lower than the total cost for the best single project: constructing the new highway. The advantage of the combined project is greater where the commodity mix is bulk dominated than in the balanced case; a preponderance of bulk goods makes it possible to take greater advantage of the low operating costs of the railroad. In fact, building both these facilities is actually cheaper than building either alone. This is even more significant when one realizes that neither facility is at all congested when constructed alone.

The explanation for this lower cost despite the large initial investment lies in the fact that the commodities can best be satisfied by facilities that respond to a particular commodity's needs. Construction of both facilities, however, enables each commodity to use the mode for which it is best suited, thereby lowering the nonmarket cost of shipment. Such economy is possible, only where there is substantial volume, so that each facility may be operated efficiently and the initial investment can be spread over a larger number of ton-miles.

When the total costs of two alternatives are quite similar, as was the case in Table 7-2, it is possible that error in the computations may exceed the difference in cost. Introducing other factors may then help in deciding which project to select. Perhaps the difference in resources required by railroad and highway will lead to a preference for one or the other that is not reflected in the factor prices. A shortage of investment funds, or an overheated economy might favor the highway over the combined project because of the lower initial investment. Fear of embarrassment in the event of a misjudgment of traffic volumes, a form of risk-aversion, might favor the project with the smaller sunk-capital investment, since the smaller investment would be better if traffic was less than expected, and even if traffic were larger than predicted there would be no serious problems. In short, a number of points might be used as "tie-breakers" if total costs are similar. If such items can be quantified, however, it would be better to include them directly in the main analysis.

Hilly Terrain, Simple Alternatives

In the hilly terrain, when both market and nonmarket costs are considered, the best strategy in all cases is to construct the new highway. (See Table 7-3.) At low-volume levels, the difference in total cost between the old road and the new highway is very small, less than 5 percent, so that the preference for the new highway is not strong. This still represents substantial shift from the flat terrain case in which, at low volume, continued use of the old road was best.

It is important to remember, however, that the relationship between the old road and the new highway is dependent upon the existing features of the old road, which were rather arbitrarily assumed in this problem. Both the new highway and the new railroad have been designed to suit the terrain, traffic, commodity mix, etc. The old road by contrast was assumed to have been constructed long ago, and is no longer optimal for existing traffic. Thus, the condition of the old road inevitably has a bearing on the comparative performance of the old and new road. Clearly, the results from this study depend upon the very specific data used as input. While the answers may be correct for this particular scenario, they will not support broader generalization such as "in hilly terrain one should always build a new highway even if the volume is low."

At the high-volume level the railroad comes within 20 percent of the total cost of the new highway, as it did in the flat terrain situation. Once again the railroad suffers not only from its somewhat higher construction costs, but also from its evaluation of nonmarket performance, which is much higher than that

Table 7-3
Comparison of Project Alternatives
Base Scenario: Hilly Terrain
(Present Discounted Value of Costs, Millions of Dollars)[a]

A. Market Plus Nonmarket Costs

Volume	Commodity Mix	Definition	Old Road	New Highway	New Railroad
Low	Balanced	Total	7.6	7.4	20.0
		Adjusted[b]	7.4	7.3	20.3
	Bulk	Total	7.4	7.3	19.0
		Adjusted	7.3	7.2	19.3
	General	Total	8.2	7.7	20.1
		Adjusted	8.1	7.5	20.4
Medium	Balanced	Total	65.8	27.1	45.3
		Adjusted	63.8	26.9	46.1
	Bulk	Total	66.6	26.9	40.9
		Adjusted	64.5	26.7	41.7
	General	Total	78.5	29.7	45.8
		Adjusted	76.4	29.6	46.6
High	Balanced	Total	831.8	100.3	113.9
		Adjusted	802.6	100.2	118.8
	Bulk	Total	920.6	101.0	111.4
		Adjusted	887.2	100.7	117.9
	General	Total	1301.5	116.3	128.0
		Adjusted	1257.6	116.2	135.6

B. Market Costs Only

Volume	Commodity Mix	Definition	Old Road	New Highway	New Railroad
Low	Balanced	Total	4.9	6.0	15.0
		Adjusted	4.8	5.9	15.4
	Bulk	Total	5.1	6.0	15.2
		Adjusted	4.9	5.9	15.5
	General	Total	5.4	6.0	15.2
		Adjusted	5.3	5.9	15.5
Medium	Balanced	Total	39.7	19.6	22.8
		Adjusted	37.8	19.4	23.6
	Bulk	Total	43.4	20.4	23.6
		Adjusted	41.2	20.2	24.4
	General	Total	48.1	21.4	23.6
		Adjusted	45.9	21.3	24.4
High	Balanced	Total	452.7	66.9	39.8
		Adjusted	423.5	66.7	44.7
	Bulk	Total	547.4	71.5	45.7
		Adjusted	514.1	71.3	52.3
	General	Total	727.9	77.1	45.8
		Adjusted	684.0	77.0	52.4

[a] 20-year time horizon; 15 percent discount rate.
[b] Adjusted for taxes and foreign exchange.

of the highway. (See Appendix D.) A comparison of the railroad operating and nonmarket costs shows that they are quite similar to those of the flat terrain, as the optimal design for this facility was similar to that used in the flat terrain.

Part B of Table 7-3 indicates that the results for the hilly terrain case, when nonmarket costs are excluded, are very much like those for the flat terrain in terms of project selection. Thus, at low volume, continued use of the old road is indicated, while at medium volume the new highway should be built, and at high volume a new railroad is appropriate. Once again it is apparent that the railroad, when given substantial volumes to carry can — even in hilly terrain — be the low-cost mode of shipment if market costs alone are considered. However, if non-market performance is properly evaluated, the railroad is found to be inferior to the new highway. As with the flat terrain, the difference due to nonmarket performance is large.

If considering and evaluating nonmarket costs in a study such as this are accepted, at least in concept, the results suggest that most feasibility studies that look only at cost savings or compare the cost between alternative designs or modes must be seriously in error. Not only do nonmarket costs make a decisive difference between choosing a new railroad or a new highway in the high-volume case, but they also exert a strong influence over the design of the facility.

It is significant to note that in both flat and hilly terrain the railroad does not come close to being the best solution in either low or medium volumes. This confirms the conventional belief that railroads are an efficient mode of trans-portation only when they can carry large quantities of traffic. This means from 1000 to 5000 tons per day each way in the present situations, although the critical volume could vary widely with terrain, commodity mix, and other factors.

Hilly Terrain, Combined Alternatives

It is possible that in hilly terrain a combination of rail and highway projects might be better than either one alone. Table 7-4 shows the results of studies conducted at all three volume levels for combined facilities compared with the single best project, which in each case was the new highway. The only case in which the combined project is superior to the new highway was for high-volume, bulk-dominated traffic. Even here, the difference is only about 2 percent. Thus, the total project cost is virtually identical, although the difference in initial in-vestment for the new highway as opposed to a combination of new highway and new railroad is very great.

Mountainous Terrain, Simple Alternatives

In the mountains, as in the hilly terrain, at low volume the choice between constructing a new highway and continuing to use the old road is very close.

Table 7–4

Comparison of Project Alternatives

Base Scenario: Hilly Terrain, Combined Railroad–Highway

(Present Discounted Value of Costs, Millions of Dollars)[a]

Volume	Mix	Definition	Combined Project (New Railroad/ New Highway)	Best Single Project (New Highway)
Low	Balanced	Total	21.0	7.4[c]
		Adjusted[b]	21.1	7.3[c]
Medium	Balanced	Total	41.6	27.1[c]
		Adjusted	42.7	26.9[c]
High	Balanced	Total	104.5	100.3[c]
		Adjusted	106.0	100.2[c]
	Bulk	Total	98.7[c]	101.0
		Adjusted	100.8	100.7[c]

Note: Traffic = Bulk, special on railroad; general, common, private on highway.
[a] 20-year time horizon; 15 percent discount rate.
[b] Adjusted for taxes and foreign exchange.
[c] Lowest total cost for this terrain type.

(See Table 7-5.) It has, however, increased to a difference of 20 percent, thus putting greater weight upon the construction of the new highway. Again, the arbitrary assumptions relative to the old road should not be forgotten in this comparison.

At medium volumes, the new highway is much better than the old road since construction cost for the medium-volume road has increased very little over the low-volume road and can therefore be spread over a much larger volume of traffic.

Finally, at high volume the old road is terribly congested, its total cost standing almost 20 times as great as the total cost incurred at medium volumes, while traffic has risen by a factor of only 5. The new railroad, which has not come close to competing in low- and medium-volume cases, still costs almost twice as much as the new highway. This reflects the great difficulties of railroad construction and operation in mountainous terrain. One must either incur enormous expenses to tunnel through mountains, bridge valleys, and cut and fill to create a relatively level roadbed, or one must be prepared to greatly increase the length of the facility to avoid the steepest hills, thus increasing the operating cost for the railroad. It seems quite clear that in terrain as mountainous as that studied here construction of a railroad is simply out of the question.

In Table 7-5 (B) it is apparent for the first time that the results are unchanged whether one considers nonmarket costs or not. The numerical answers

Table 7–5

Comparison of Project Alternatives

Base Scenario: Mountainous Terrain

(Present Discounted Value of Costs, Millions of Dollars)[a]

A. Market Plus Nonmarket Costs

Volume	Commodity Mix	Definition	Old Road	New Highway	New Railroad
Low	Balanced	Total	11.3	8.5	23.1
		Adjusted[b]	10.9	8.4	24.0
	Bulk	Total	11.1	8.4	22.2
		Adjusted	10.7	8.3	23.2
	General	Total	12.4	8.8	23.4
		Adjusted	12.0	8.7	24.3
Medium	Balanced	Total	106.9	34.7	74.6
		Adjusted	102.0	33.9	81.1
	Bulk	Total	109.0	34.7	71.7
		Adjusted	103.8	33.9	80.0
	General	Total	128.9	39.1	81.3
		Adjusted	123.5	38.3	89.7
High	Balanced	Total	1301.5	169.4	276.4
		Adjusted	1257.6	164.4	207.3
	Bulk	Total	1991.1	172.6	296.7
		Adjusted	1917.5	167.3	340.9
	General	Total	2258.3	203.6	327.5
		Adjusted	2173.4	198.1	372.0

B. Market Costs Only

Volume	Commodity Mix	Definition	Old Road	New Highway	New Railroad
Low	Balanced	Total	7.5	7.0	18.0
		Adjusted	7.1	7.0	19.0
	Bulk	Total	7.7	7.1	18.4
		Adjusted	7.3	7.0	19.3
	General	Total	8.3	7.2	18.4
		Adjusted	7.8	7.1	19.3
Medium	Balanced	Total	64.6	23.3	34.9
		Adjusted	59.7	22.5	41.5
	Bulk	Total	70.9	24.7	38.8
		Adjusted	65.7	23.9	47.1
	General	Total	79.1	26.4	38.8
		Adjusted	73.6	25.6	47.2
High	Balanced	Total	1071.9	105.5	142.3
		Adjusted	998.3	100.6	173.3
	Bulk	Total	1331.2	115.0	172.1
		Adjusted	1246.3	109.8	216.3
	General	Total	1755.3	127.3	172.3
		Adjusted	1643.0	121.9	216.8

[a] 20-year time horizon; 15 percent discount rate.

[b] Adjusted for taxes and foreign exchange.

are quite different, but the ultimate project selection is the same. The new highway is the best alternative in all traffic cases. The combined alternatives were not considered at all, since the high construction costs would have offset the gains in user costs.

General Observations

Throughout this chapter the railroad adjusted total cost has always been greater than its nonadjusted total, while just the opposite has been true for the new highway. This difference arises from the fact that railroads generally are tax free in that there is likely to be no import duty for locomotives or rails — particularly when the railroad is government owned — and railroad diesel fuel is generally not taxed. Truckers and other highway operators, however, must generally pay very substantial taxes to import their vehicles, and highway fuels quite often bear a large tax. Thus the adjustment that is made to compensate for government revenues from taxes and to reflect the shadow price on imported goods substantially increases costs for the railroad; but the two cancel out for the highway.

Despite these differences, the result in terms of project selection for adjusted or unadjusted total costs was the same in all cases except where combined projects were considered. The difference between the adjusted and unadjusted railroad cost was greatest in the situation where the railroad was least suitable, that is, in the mountainous terrain.

Results from Other Price Scenario

The second price scenario contains many prices which are quite different from those in the base scenario, as shown in Appendices A and B. Highway construction costs are three times as great per mile in the second scenario, most of this difference being in the cost of base and of paving. Railroad construction cost is increased by a factor of approximately 1.5, primarily because of the increase in the cost of ballast and ties. Since rails are assumed to be imported in both situations, their price has not changed between the two scenarios.

The second scenario, while it still describes a developing country, represents one in a more advanced stage of development. Its wage rate is 4.5 times that in the base scenario. There are smaller changes in many of the other prices which depend upon construction cost and the wage rate. Taxes and the foreign exchange component for imported materials are also different for this scenario.

Despite these changes in relative factor prices, the technology used in the second price scenario remains the same as that in the first. That is, the highway vehicles, railroad locomotives, and other railroad rolling stock all have the same physical dimensions and parameters in both cases except that highway vehicles use diesel fuel in the second scenario and gasoline in the base scenario. In addition, the project design selected for each volume and terrain case has been retained in the second scenario just as it was in the first. It would have been possible to recompute the optimal design for each facility, and these would most likely have been somewhat different than those of the base scenario because of the changes in relative prices. It was decided, however, that it would be more interesting to see a comparison between identical projects than to have a new optimum design and be unable to make precise comparisons for similar facilities. Because the volumes, commodity mixes, and terrain descriptions were originally selected to apply to any country for which these programs would be applicable, they have been retained in this second scenario.

Flat Terrain

The results of the study for the second price scenario in the flat terrain are displayed in Table 7-6. Despite the relatively large change in several factor prices between the base and the second price scenario, the selected projects have remained quite similar. In the flat terrain, the best choice according to the total or adjusted total costs is to use the old road for the low-volume level and to build a new highway for the medium- or high-volume levels. Construction costs for the new highway have tripled, as could be predicted from the input price changes, while construction costs for the new railroad have only doubled. The commodity evaluation of nonmarket performance has remained the same as it was in the base run, since the performance of each facility in physical terms is unchanged, and no changes have been made in the commodity weighting of performance. These figures are shown in Appendix D.

The total cost and adjusted total cost are, in all cases, well above those of the base scenario, and the increase is greatest for the low-volume case since the sharp rise in construction cost has its greatest effect at these volumes. For this reason, the old road is a far better choice than the new highway in the low-volume case, while in the base scenario it was only marginally better. When nonmarket evaluation of performance is not considered in the analysis, the selection of projects also remains as it was in the base scenario. That is, the old road is used at low-volume levels, a new highway is constructed for medium volumes and a new railroad is constructed for high volumes. The combined railroad–highway project was not simulated for this factor price scenario. However, since the cost of the new highway has increased more than that of the railroad, thus narrowing the gap between them, it is expected that the combined project would again be superior for the flat terrain and high-volume balance or bulk-dominated case.

Table 7–6
Comparison of Project Alternatives
Other Scenario: Flat Terrain
(Present Discounted Value of Costs, Millions of Dollars)[a]

A. Market Plus Nonmarket Costs

Volume	Commodity Mix	Definition	Old Road	New Highway	New Railroad
Low	Balanced	Total	7.7	13.2	25.2
		Adjusted[b]	7.4	13.2	25.2
	Bulk	Total	7.5	13.1	24.3
		Adjusted	7.2	13.1	24.3
	General	Total	8.3	13.4	25.5
		Adjusted	8.0	13.4	25.5
Medium	Balanced	Total	51.9	32.1	56.8
		Adjusted	51.8	31.5	56.7
	Bulk	Total	55.8	32.4	54.2
		Adjusted	52.6	31.8	54.2
	General	Total	64.8	35.9	59.7
		Adjusted	60.9	35.1	59.6
High	Balanced	Total	364.3	126.3	142.9
		Adjusted	334.8	121.5	143.6
	Bulk	Total	383.4	130.0	144.8
		Adjusted	351.0	125.0	145.6
	General	Total	471.0	152.5	162.4
		Adjusted	429.5	145.8	163.2

B. Market Costs Only

Volume	Commodity Mix	Definition	Old Road	New Highway	New Railroad
Low	Balanced	Total	5.7	12.2	20.0
		Adjusted	5.5	12.2	20.0
	Bulk	Total	5.8	12.3	20.3
		Adjusted	5.6	12.2	20.2
	General	Total	6.3	12.5	20.2
		Adjusted	6.0	12.4	20.2
Medium	Balanced	Total	39.0	25.6	33.3
		Adjusted	35.9	25.0	33.2
	Bulk	Total	41.9	26.8	35.1
		Adjusted	38.7	26.2	35.0
	General	Total	47.0	28.8	35.1
		Adjusted	43.1	27.9	35.0
High	Balanced	Total	258.6	92.9	68.8
		Adjusted	229.1	88.1	69.5
	Bulk	Total	287.5	100.5	79.1
		Adjusted	255.1	95.5	79.9
	General	Total	341.9	113.4	79.2
		Adjusted	300.4	106.6	80.0

[a] 20-year time horizon; 15 percent discount rate.
[b] Adjusted for taxes and foreign exchange.

Hilly Terrain

Table 7-7 shows the results for simulation of the hilly terrain in the second price scenario. Here, at low traffic levels, the old road is still a better choice than the new highway. In the base scenario the new highway was slightly better than the old road in this situation, but here the total cost of the old road is less than 75 percent as expensive as the new highway. This difference is primarily the result of substantially increased highway construction costs.

At medium-volume levels, the new highway is the best choice, as it was in the base case, while for high-volume levels again the new highway is superior — this time being 15 percent cheaper than the comparable railroad. When the non-market evaluation of performance is not considered, as shown in Part B of Table 7-7, the choice of project is again the same as in the base scenario, with the old road selected for the low-volume, the new highway for the medium-volume, and the new railroad for the high-volume case.

Mountainous Terrain

In this case the low volume still recommends continued use of the old highway rather than construction of the new highway. This is a major change from the base scenario in which the new highway construction was 10 percent cheaper than continued use of the old road. Now the new highway construction is 10 percent more expensive than continued use of the old road. Thus the major impact of these factor price changes seems to have been to discourage construction of new highways where traffic volumes are low.

For the medium- and high-volume cases the new highway is still the best choice, as it was in the base scenario. Even when nonmarket evaluation of performance is not considered as in Part B of Table 7-8, the old road is still the best choice for low volumes, in contrast to the base scenario where the new highway was a better choice. For medium and high volumes without the nonmarket measures of performance, the new highway is still the best choice as it was in the base run.

Summary and Comparison

The results of any finite study cannot be applied to the whole universe of real-world situations, even where, as here, a wide variety of different conditions have been examined. Generalizations can be made only if it is recognized to be valid for the specific conditions upon which the experiments were based.

With these limitations in mind, one can see that if any new facility is to be built, it is rarely advantageous to build a railroad instead of a highway if all

Table 7-7
Comparison of Project Alternatives
Other Scenario: Hilly Terrain
(Present Discounted Value of Costs, Millions of Dollars)[a]

A. Market Plus Nonmarket Costs

Volume	Commodity Mix	Definition	Old Road	New Highway	New Railroad
Low	Balanced	Total	11.7	15.9	36.4
		Adjusted[b]	11.3	15.7	36.3
	Bulk	Total	11.5	15.8	35.7
		Adjusted	11.1	15.6	35.6
	General	Total	12.8	16.3	36.8
		Adjusted	12.2	16.1	36.7
Medium	Balanced	Total	94.5	43.3	69.4
		Adjusted	88.7	42.2	69.3
	Bulk	Total	97.9	43.5	66.4
		Adjusted	91.6	42.4	66.2
	General	Total	116.2	47.4	71.3
		Adjusted	108.2	46.1	71.1
High	Balanced	Total	1364.7	141.5	155.6
		Adjusted	1215.8	136.7	156.2
	Bulk	Total	1550.5	145.1	157.5
		Adjusted	1371.9	140.1	158.3
	General	Total	2203.7	167.7	175.1
		Adjusted	1943.4	161.0	175.9

B. Market Costs Only

Volume	Commodity Mix	Definition	Old Road	New Highway	New Railroad
Low	Balanced	Total	9.0	14.4	31.5
		Adjusted	8.6	14.3	31.4
	Bulk	Total	9.2	14.5	31.9
		Adjusted	8.7	14.3	31.8
	General	Total	9.9	14.8	31.9
		Adjusted	9.4	14.6	31.8
Medium	Balanced	Total	68.4	35.8	46.9
		Adjusted	62.6	34.7	46.8
	Bulk	Total	76.6	36.9	49.1
		Adjusted	68.4	35.9	48.9
	General	Total	85.7	39.1	49.1
		Adjusted	77.7	37.8	48.9
High	Balanced	Total	985.6	108.1	81.5
		Adjusted	836.7	103.3	82.2
	Bulk	Total	1177.4	115.7	91.8
		Adjusted	998.8	110.7	92.6
	General	Total	1630.0	128.6	91.9
		Adjusted	1369.8	121.8	92.7

[a] 20-year time horizon, 15 percent discount rate.
[b] Adjusted for taxes and foreign exchange.

Table 7-8
Comparison of Project Alternatives
Other Scenario: Mountainous Terrain
(Present Discounted Value of Costs, Millions of Dollars)[a]

A. Market Plus Nonmarket Costs

Volume	Commodity Mix	Definition	Old Road	New Highway	New Railroad
Low	Balanced	Total	17.8	18.8	44.6
		Adjusted[b]	17.1	18.5	44.6
	Bulk	Total	17.6	18.7	44.6
		Adjusted	16.9	18.5	44.4
	General	Total	19.5	19.2	45.7
		Adjusted	18.6	19.0	45.5
Medium	Balanced	Total	158.2	55.1	108.3
		Adjusted	147.3	52.9	109.6
	Bulk	Total	165.1	55.9	107.6
		Adjusted	153.4	53.7	109.2
	General	Total	196.3	62.2	117.2
		Adjusted	181.4	59.5	118.8
High	Balanced	Total	3350.0	254.7	373.1
		Adjusted	2957.9	238.6	381.4
	Bulk	Total	3891.1	265.1	400.0
		Adjusted	3412.6	247.6	411.7
	General	Total	5445.7	313.4	430.7
		Adjusted	4770.0	291.1	442.5

B. Market Costs Only

Volume	Commodity Mix	Definition	Old Road	New Highway	New Railroad
Low	Balanced	Total	14.0	17.2	39.6
		Adjusted	13.3	17.0	39.6
	Bulk	Total	14.2	17.3	40.7
		Adjusted	13.5	17.1	40.5
	General	Total	15.4	17.6	40.7
		Adjusted	14.5	17.4	40.5
Medium	Balanced	Total	115.9	43.6	68.7
		Adjusted	105.0	41.5	70.0
	Bulk	Total	127.0	45.8	74.7
		Adjusted	115.2	43.6	76.3
	General	Total	146.5	49.5	74.7
		Adjusted	131.6	46.8	76.3
High	Balanced	Total	2430.7	190.7	239.1
		Adjusted	2038.7	174.7	247.3
	Bulk	Total	2964.0	207.5	275.3
		Adjusted	2485.5	190.0	287.1
	General	Total	4043.2	237.2	275.6
		Adjusted	3368.1	214.9	287.4

[a] 20-year time horizon; 15 percent discount rate.
[b] Adjusted for taxes and foreign exchange.

measures of performance are considered. The railroad is best in flat terrain, at high-volume levels with commodity mixes that consist principally of bulk commodities. Its desirability is successively reduced as the terrain becomes more hilly, the volume decreases, or if the goods shipped place higher values on shipping time. If one judges by direct market costs alone, ignoring all other aspects of performance, then the railroad appears superior to the highway at high volumes in flat and hilly terrain. Finally, in conditions where the railroad performs best considering all measures of performance, it appears desirable also to have a relatively high-performance highway.

The minimum volume of traffic needed to justify a railroad in flat or hilly terrain may be between 1000 and 5000 tons per day each way. One example would be the movement of ore or coal from a mine over several hundred miles to a smelter, refinery, or port. The long distance reduces the relative importance of terminal and yard costs, and the low value makes terminal delays less important. Another example would be the movement of agricultural products from a farming area to a port or urban consumption area. Here again, long distance is important if truck competition is to be kept to a minimum. The problem of gathering the product from many farms to a single point of departure may cause very large increases in costs. Furthermore, the flexibility of trucks, which can carry other goods between other points in off-season, may make them a strong competitor for highly seasonal flows, unless the railroad can use its rolling stock on other lines in the off-season. In any event, the terrain must be flat enough that a very level alignment can be found, or the railroad's operating costs will suffer. Costs will also rise if the railroad is compelled to carry substantial amounts of short-haul, low-volume shipments, whose terminal costs exceed line-haul savings.

The second scenario had wages 4.5 times those of the base, highway construction costs 3 times as large, rail construction costs 1.5 times as large, and a lower fuel cost, for diesel fuel rather than gasoline. This change in relative factor prices tends to favor continued use of the old road rather than undertaking new construction. This effect is strongest at low volumes. At higher volumes the increased wages offset construction cost increases more than at low volumes. The actual projects selected differ in that in all three terrains, in the low-volume balanced and bulk-dominated cases the old road is best, while in the base scenario the new highway was an improvement even at low volume in the hilly and mountainous cases. In no case is the railroad the best alternative, although in the flat terrain with balanced or bulk-dominated commodity mix the combined project is best at high volume.

Upon reflection, the similarity of results between the base and other scenario is not as surprising as it first appears, in view of the factor price differences. The labor input per ton-mile on a relatively low-volume narrow-gauge railroad is not tremendously less than needed for moving the same traffic by truck, so a rise in wages affects both similarly. Fuel costs are different, but they are low in both cases, and thus not a crucial component in total costs. The cost of capital equipment is quite large in both cases, but the prices are similar since rail rolling stock is imported and the road vehicles produced domestically in the second scenario are almost as expensive as the imported trucks in the base scenario, when import duties are included. It seems therefore that only a severe shortage of a factor that was used much more intensively in one mode than the other would cause net results to differ substantially from those of the base scenario. When such a case occurs, the result should be rather easy to predict. This will be pursued further in the sensitivity analysis of Chapter 8.

8 Sensitivity Analysis

Method of Analysis

The sensitivity analysis described in this chapter was performed to determine the impact of changes in various factor prices upon the total cost of operating the projects simulated in this study. It also permits observation of the trade-offs between railroad and highway investment resulting from changes in basic factor prices.

It is important to note at the outset that there is no single measure of performance that can record all aspects of the impact of a particular factor price change. Different persons, groups, or organizations will be affected differently by a particular set of these changes so that several measures of performance must be observed in order to record the full impact. An increase in the price of fuel, for example, may substantially raise operating costs for truckers, thereby reducing their profits. Yet, if competition from other modes prevents passing this increase on to shippers, the shippers themselves may be almost indifferent to a rise in fuel cost. This chapter will attempt to observe the impact of factor price changes from several different viewpoints in order to preserve these differences in perceived consequences.

Choice of Factors Varied

From among the many hundreds of prices confronting carriers as they purchase inputs necessary to perform their transportation functions, we have selected five fundamental factor inputs to be investigated here. Their selection was based upon their importance in overall costs and interest for this analysis. These factors are (1) interest rate, (2) price of fuel and oil, (3) cost of crushed aggregate or ballast, (4) wage rate, and (5) price of imports.

Each of these factor prices influences several data items for the models used in this study. Table 8-1 shows the relationship between changes in the five basic factor prices discussed in this chapter and the corresponding alterations in the actual input data used by the simulation models. Input data parameter names are listed in the left-hand column and the five factor prices are listed across the top. Definitions and base values for the input parameters are given in Appendix A. The numerical values in the table show how the input parameters change for a 10 percent increase in the appropriate factor price. Since only a few of the

Table 8–1

Changes in Input Parameters Due to 10 Percent Rise in Factor Prices

Affected Input Parameter	Factor Being Varied by +10%				
	Interest	Fuel and Oil	Aggregate	Wages	Imports
Construction Cost					
Highway	–	+0.25	+2.5	+ 3.5	+ 3.0
Railroad	–	+0.25	+1.0	+ 2.5	+ 5.0
Earthwork	–	+0.5	–	+ 2.5	+ 2.5
Highway Parameters					
Ck8 } maintenance	–		+1.25	+6.75	+ 1.5
Ck9 } of way	–		+1.25	+6.75	+ 1.5
OILC	–	+10.0	–	–	–
FC	–	+10.0	–	–	–
UDT	–	–	–	+10.0	–
WAGEM	–	–	–	+10.0	–
COST (of vehicle)	–	–	–	–	+10.0
RATI	+10.0	–	–	–	–
Railroad Parameters					
CARCST	–	–	–	–	+10.0
CSTLOC	–	–	–	–	+10.0
A1, B1	–	–	–	+ 6.0	+ 4.0
A2, B2	–	–	–	+ 6.0	+ 4.0
A3, B3	–	–	+0.25	+ 5.625	+ 3.75
B4	–	–	–	+10.0	–
B5	–	+10.0	–	–	–
B6	–	+10.0	–	–	–
CRF	+9.69	–	–	–	–
CRFL	+7.33	–	–	–	–

input parameters change by even 10 percent for any case, it is clear that most of these input parameters are affected by more than one of the five basic factor prices. This says nothing about the influence of other factor prices not varied at all here.

For example, the nonearthwork components of the construction cost for a highway respond to changes in all factor prices except interest rate, since construction here is assumed to occur in the first year of the analysis. It is assumed that for the nonearthwork portion of highway construction cost, 30 percent represents imported construction equipment and parts. Thus, a 10 percent increase in the cost of imports would cause a 3 percent increase in the nonearthwork cost of road construction. In the base situation, approximately 25 percent of the total construction cost is for crushed aggregate, so that a 10 percent increase in the cost of aggregate causes a 2.5 percent increase in the cost of this construction. Wages make up 35 percent of the construction cost while fuel and oil for the construction equipment are 2.5 percent. An increase of 10 percent in each of these factors brings construction cost increases of 3.5 percent and 0.25 percent respectively.

The interest rate is used for determining the present discounted value of the stream of costs simulated over the 20-year period. It is also used to determine the charges that should be made to cover capital costs invested in equipment. Fuel and oil prices, which are assumed to move together, have important effects on both motor vehicle and railroad fuel costs as well as on the cost of lubricating oil for both. They also enter into the cost of construction. Aggregate and ballast, also assumed to move together in price, are major factors in the construction costs of both railroads and highways, and have a small impact on maintenance costs for both the highway and for the railroad roadbed. The level of wages affects crew costs directly for both modes, and has a smaller impact on almost all other prices including the cost of construction and the cost of all maintenance. Since all vehicles for both modes are imported, the major impact of changes in the cost of imports is upon the depreciation charges for these vehicles, although effects are also felt in construction costs because construction equipment is typically imported. Railroad rails may also be imported.

Procedure

The procedure followed in computing this sensitivity analysis is relatively straightforward. First, a base situation must be selected for which all costs of performance have already been computed. Then one of the five factor prices is raised 10 percent from its original value, a new set of costs and performance computed, and the factor price returned to its original value. Repeating this for each factor in turn produces five simulations of the same physical situation in addition to the original base simulation run. It is then possible to compare total cost measures between the original or base run and the other five runs to see how the factor price changes have altered total cost.

If the percentage change in total costs is divided by the 10 percent change in the particular factor price, the result has the appearance of a partial derivative (or elasticity) of total cost with respect to that factor price. Thus, within reasonable limits, one could use the result shown here to predict the effect of factor price changes greater or smaller than 10 percent. Ten percent was chosen because it was large enough to make a noticeable difference but small enough to have a linear effect on cost. However, very large increases in factor price would raise that factor's share of total cost, and thus increase sensitivity of total cost to its variation. The sensitivity measured here, therefore, is valid only over a limited range. Great differences in factor prices would affect shipper behavior and other variables nonlinearly, so they should be considered as completely separate scenarios, not estimated with sensitivity results.

It must be remembered that the response of total cost to these factor price

changes is valid only for the base situation from which the changes are made. If
some other base condition is selected; for instance if traffic volumes are different
or if the facility design is different, then not only would total costs be different,
but the response of total costs to changes in a particular factor price might also
be different. For example, on a flat, straight highway the cost of the fuel and oil
is typically a very small percentage of total truck operating costs, while in steep
mountainous terrain, where it is necessary to grind up and down hills at very low
speeds, the relative importance of fuel cost is substantially greater.

For this analysis, we have taken as the base situation the base scenario factor
price data (see Appendices A and B), with hilly terrain, and a balanced commodity mix, and have examined three volume levels of 100, 1000, and 5000 tons per
day in each direction. This combination offers an average situation, and yet it
provides a variation along the most important determinant — the traffic volume
level. The relative importance of different factor prices is probably more sensitive
to changes in volume than it is to any of the other scenario descriptors. In this
base situation the old road, the new road, and the new railroad were examined,
so that differences in sensitivity to factor price changes for these conditions can
be observed and compared.

Results

Of the five factor prices tested in this analysis, the interest rate has the
greatest impact on the present discounted value of a 20-year stream of total project costs. The 10 percent increase in interest rate resulted in a change in total
costs of from 3 percent to over 6 percent in the cases tested. The price of imports
was the second most important factor. Its effect was generally more than 2 percent of overall costs except for high-volume rail cases where it was lower. The
least-significant factor price was the cost of aggregate, which, when raised 10
percent, caused an increase in total costs of no more than 1.24 percent and often
much less than that. The cost of fuel and oil was only moderately more important than that of aggregate in its total impact, while wages had an influence
ranging from 1 percent to somewhat over 2.5 percent.

The change in total cost produced by each 10 percent increase in the separate factor prices is presented in Tables 8-2, 8-3, and 8-4 as a percentage of the
base value for that cost. Thus each entry in Table 8-2 shows the percentage
change in the cost category identified at the right end of the line, when the
factor price noted at the left is raised by 10 percent, at the specified volume
condition. The bottom set of six lines gives the cost of each category before any
factor price change, in millions of dollars. The cost data from which the percentage changes were computed are presented in Appendix D, Table D-5. Sensitivity
analysis has been performed for the old road in hilly terrain, the new highway
designed for the hilly terrain, and the new railroad designed for the hilly terrain,

Table 8-2
Response of Project Costs to Changes in Factor Prices: Old Road
(Cost Change as Percent of Base Costs)[a]

Factor Price Change[b]	Volume			Cost Category
	Low	Medium	High	
Interest Rate	0	0	0	Construction
+10%	−7.7%	−7.7%	−7.8%	Maintenance/Way
	−6.2	−6.3	−5.4	Vehicle Operation
	−7.7	−7.7	−7.7	Nonmarket
	−6.8	−6.9	−6.5	Total
	−6.7	−6.8	−6.4	Adjusted Total
Fuel and Oil	0	0	0	Construction
+10%	0	0	0	Maintenance/Way
	3.1	3.3	1.4	Vehicle Operation
	0	0	0	Nonmarket
	1.9	1.9	0.8	Total
	1.4	1.5	0.6	Adjusted Total
Crushed	0	0	0	Construction
Aggregate	1.3	1.2	1.2	Maintenance/Way
+10%	0	0	0	Vehicle Operation
	0	0	0	Nonmarket
	0.1	0.01	0	Total
	0.1	0.01	0	Adjusted Total
Wages	0	0	0	Construction
+10%	6.7	6.7	6.7	Maintenance/Way
	2.1	2.4	3.7	Vehicle Operation
	0	0	0	Nonmarket
	1.5	1.5	2.0	Total
	1.3	1.2	1.7	Adjusted Total
Imports	0	0	0	Construction
+10%	1.3	1.6	1.6	Maintenance/Way
	4.0	3.6	4.8	Vehicle Operation
	0	0	0	Nonmarket
	2.5	2.2	2.6	Total
	3.0	2.7	3.0	Adjusted Total
Base Costs	0	0	0	Construction
($millions)[c]	$0.300	$ 0.509	$ 1.475	Maintenance/Way
	4.596	39.238	451.211	Vehicle Operation
	2.663	26.029	379.092	Nonmarket
	7.559	65.775	831.777	Total
	7.423	63.809	302.584	Adjusted Total

[a]Each entry shows the percentage change in the cost category at the right when the factor price at the left is raised by 10 percent.

[b]For initial values of factor prices, see appendixes A, B.

[c]The dollar cost incurred before any factor price changes. Data are for base scenario, hilly terrain, balanced traffic, present discount value for 20 years at 15 percent interest rate.

Table 8–3

Response of Project Costs to Changes in Factor Prices: New Highway (Cost Change as Percent of Base Cost)[a]

Factor Price Change[b]	Volume			Cost Category
	Low	Medium	High	
Interest Rate	0	0	0	Construction
+10%	−7.4%	−7.9%	−7.9%	Maintenance/Way
	−6.3	−6.7	−6.7	Vehicle Operation
	−7.7	−7.7	−7.7	Nonmarket
	−3.5	−5.0	−6.3	Total
	−3.4	−5.0	−6.2	Adjusted Total
Fuel and Oil	0.3	0.4	0.4	Construction
+10%	0	0	0	Maintenance/Way
	3.6	3.3	3.1	Vehicle Operation
	0	0	0	Nonmarket
	1.1	1.5	1.8	Total
	0.9	1.2	1.3	Adjusted Total
Crushed	2.4	1.1	0.7	Construction
Aggregate	1.4	1.4	1.3	Maintenance/Way
+10%	0	0	0	Vehicle Operation
	0	0	0	Nonmarket
	1.2	0.3	0.1	Total
	1.2	0.3	0.1	Adjusted Total
Wages	3.5	2.9	2.8	Construction
+10%	6.7	6.9	6.6	Maintenance/Way
	2.1	1.9	1.8	Vehicle Operation
	0	0	0	Nonmarket
	2.6	1.7	1.3	Total
	2.5	1.6	1.1	Adjusted Total
Imports	3.0	2.7	2.6	Construction
+10%	1.8	1.4	1.3	Maintenance/Way
	3.7	3.1	3.1	Vehicle Operation
	0	0	0	Nonmarket
	2.5	2.1	2.0	Total
	2.7	2.4	2.4	Adjusted Total
Base Costs	$3.689	$ 7.827	$ 11.817	Construction
($millions)[c]	0.282	0.291	0.393	Maintenance/Way
	2.012	11.454	54.669	Vehicle Operation
	1.425	7.500	33.407	Nonmarket
	7.408	27.072	100.286	Total
	7.287	26.880	100.154	Adjusted Total

[a]Each entry shows the percentage change in the cost category at the right when the factor price at the left is raised by 10 percent.

[b]For initial values of factor prices, see appendixes A, B.

[c]The dollar cost incurred before any factor price changes. Data are for base scenario, hilly terrain, balanced traffic, present discounted value over 20 years at 15 percent interest rate.

Table 8-4
Response of Project Costs to Changes in Factor Prices: New Railroad
(Cost Change as Percent of Base Costs)[a]

Factor Price Change[b]	Volume			Cost Category
	Low	Medium	High	
Interest Rate	0	0	0	Construction
+10%	0	0	0	Maintenance/Way
	−7.1%	−6.8%	−6.6%	Vehicle Operation
	−7.7	−7.7	−7.7	Nonmarket
	−3.8	−4.9	−6.4	Total
	−3.7	−4.8	−6.2	Adjusted Total
Fuel and Oil	0.4	0.4	0.4	Construction
+10%	0	0	0	Maintenance/Way
	0.1	0.5	2.9	Vehicle Operation
	0	0	0	Nonmarket
	0.2	0.4	0.7	Total
	0.2	0.2	0.8	Adjusted Total
Crushed	0.6	0.3	0.3	Construction
Aggregate	0	0	0	Maintenance/Way
+10%	0.2	0.2	0.1	Vehicle Operation
	0	0	0	Nonmarket
	0.3	0.1	0.1	Total
	0.3	0.1	0.1	Adjusted Total
Wages	2.5	2.5	2.5	Construction
+10%	0	0	0	Maintenance/Way
	5.3	5.1	3.6	Vehicle Operation
	0	0	0	Nonmarket
	2.6	1.7	1.1	Total
	2.6	1.6	1.1	Adjusted Total
Imports	4.0	3.2	3.2	Construction
+10%	0	0	0	Maintenance/Way
	4.0	4.0	3.2	Vehicle Operation
	0	0	0	Nonmarket
	3.0	1.7	1.1	Total
	3.1	1.9	1.3	Adjusted Total
Base Costs	$ 9.883	$15.995	$ 15.995	Construction
($millions)[c]	0	0	0	Maintenance/Way
	5.166	6.813	23.786	Vehicle Operation
	4.914	22.497	74.080	Nonmarket
	19.963	45.305	113.861	Total
	20.321	46.098	118.790	Adjusted Total

[a]Each entry shows the percentage change in the cost category at the right when the factor price at the left is raised by 10 percent.

[b]For initial values of factor prices, see appendixes A, B.

[c]The dollar cost incurred before any factor price changes. Data are for base scenario, hilly terrain, balanced traffic, present discounted value over 20 years at 15 percent interest rate.

all under balanced traffic flow conditions and using the base factor price scenario. All three traffic volume levels are included.

Interest Rate Sensitivity

The interest rate has the largest impact on total costs for two reasons. First,
it determines the discount rate at which the cost and benefit streams for the 20
years of simulated operation are discounted to produce a present value. Raising
the interest rate decreases the weighting of future items in the cost stream, and
thus decreases the present value of costs. Second, it determines the price that
must be paid for capital equipment. Raising the interest rate increases this cost,
but since most costs are in future years this increase is more than offset by the
increased discount rate.

It can be seen in Table 8-2 that the impact of the interest rate on total cost
of the old road is greater than a 6 percent reduction for all three volume cases. In
the case of the new highway (Table 8-3), the impact of a change in the interest
rate increases with larger traffic volumes because, as volume increases, operating
costs and performance become a larger proportion of the total cost. Therefore,
the impact of interest rate on these factors overshadows the lack of impact on
construction costs.

The same effects occur for the new railroad. Comparing the figures for Tables
8-3 and 8-4, it is clear that the sensitivity of costs due to interest rate is very
nearly the same for either a new highway or a new railroad. The sensitivity to
the change of interest rate of operating costs alone is almost constant across all
three cases at greater than 6 percent. The change in total costs, therefore, is
attributable primarily to the change in relative importance of construction and
operating costs. The major significance of a rise in interest rates is that it favors
continued use of the old facility, especially at low volumes. If a new facility is to
be built, the interest rate affects the choice between highway and railroad relatively little.

Fuel Cost Sensitivity

The impact of a 10 percent increase in the cost of fuel and oil is slightly
above 3 percent for the low- and medium-volume cases on the old road. The
high-volume case records only half as great a fuel cost increase but this is because
at high volumes the highway has become very congested. Under conditions of
congestion the other operating costs rise much more rapidly than fuel use. The
fuel cost becomes a much smaller percentage of the total cost, and therefore
sensitivity to its price is decreased. For the new road, the increase in operating
cost is again slightly over 3 percent. For both the old road and the new highway,

the total cost increase is simply a reflection of the increased operating costs from the rise in fuel and oil price.

For the new railroad, at low volume the sensitivity to fuel and oil price increases is extremely low since at this volume the fixed costs of rail operations are so much greater than the operating expenses. Even at medium volume the change in operating costs is only 0.5 percent, but in the high-volume case the impact of fuel and oil change has risen to almost 3 percent. The total cost in this case has increased by less than one percent.

Thus, it is clear that fuel costs are substantially more important for highway operations than they are for railroads. Countries with high fuel costs will find railroad solutions generally more desirable than indicated in this study, although fuel's proportion of total costs is still relatively modest. It should be remembered that the base scenario represents a country which exports oil, so the fuel costs found there may be below the average for developing countries, and well below those of oil importers.

Crushed Aggregate Sensitivity

An increase in the price of crushed aggregate has no impact on operating costs for either the old road or the new highway since maintenance of the road itself is covered under maintenance of way and not included in operating cost. Typical accounting policy for the railroad, however, places maintenance costs with other operating costs so that there is a small change in operating cost as a result of the aggregate price increase. The fact that its impact on the railroad decreases with increasing volume reflects the increased utilization of the particular roadbed by more traffic and the reality that maintenance costs are not proportional to traffic volume carried.

For the old road, the impact of increases in the cost of crushed aggregate on total cost is extremely small since only the maintenance of the road is affected. For the new highway, the cost increase on aggregate has a substantially greater impact at low volume than at high volume because it also affects construction cost. When spread over the small volume there is a much greater impact per ton. Even so, the 10 percent price increase never raises total costs by more than 1.25 percent. The effect on the new railroad is even less than that on the new highway with 0.33 percent being the maximum increase reflected at low volumes and 0.05 percent influence at high volume. In terms of overall importance, the cost of crushed aggregate appears to have effects of the same order of magnitude as the fuel cost although its relative importance varies inversely with traffic volume while the fuel and oil costs generally vary directly with volume. High aggregate costs will favor continued use of the old road, and will favor a new railroad over a new highway. Only where gravel is in short supply and much more expensive than it is here will it be an important factor.

Wage Sensitivity

When wages are increased by 10 percent, total costs for both the old road and the new highway rise somewhere between 1 percent and 2.5 percent. On the old road there is an operating cost increase between 2.5 percent and almost 4 percent, but this constitutes only about one-half of total costs so the increase in the total is correspondingly lower. The sensitivity to labor cost of the high-volume case on the old road is a reflection of the heavy congestion that occurred there. The congestion generated requirements for a large amount of labor, although fuel costs did not increase particularly. On the new highway it is interesting to note that the sensitivity to wage cost decreases with increasing volume. This reflects in part the substantial labor component of the initial construction of the new highway which is spread more thinly over the traffic as the traffic volume increases. This also explains the fact that, at low volume, the impact on total costs is greater than the impact on operating costs, while at medium and high volume the reverse is true.

For the railroad, wages are a smaller component of construction cost because of the substantial expense of importing the rails. Therefore, while rail-operating costs increase by a full 5 percent in the low- and medium-volume cases, the total cost increase only 2.5 and 1.5 percent respectively. In the high-volume case, both increases are even lower as the labor efficiency of the railroad increases.

Higher wages would favor the old road at low volumes. At high volume, the higher wage places the old road at a disadvantage, and raises costs for the new highway slightly more than for the new railroad. It should be remembered, however, that even at 5000 tons per day the railroad is not greatly less labor intensive than the highway. Only when the railroad can run long, heavy trains great distances over level terrain does it save significantly over the labor cost of trucking operations.

Import Cost Sensitivity

A 10 percent increase in import costs causes a rise in operating cost of approximately 4 percent on the old road. This reflects primarily the cost of importing the vehicles used to operate over that road. On the new highway the increase is never more than 3.6 percent and in the high-volume case is down almost to 3 percent. This is the direct result of more efficient use of expensive imported vehicles because of the much improved design of the highway.

The impact of imports on total costs for the new highway is only slightly lower than that for the old road, although the operating cost impact is substantially less. This is because the construction of the new highway requires only a moderate amount of imported construction machinery.

The new railroad has a 4 percent increase in operating costs for low and medium volumes and 3.2 percent for high volumes. This consists primarily of the

cost of imported vehicles to be used in the operation, and these are used somewhat more efficiently as volume increases. The impact on total cost is slightly
less than the impact on operating costs and decreases substantially with volume.
This is because the construction of the new railroad requires large amounts of imported rails that are quite expensive. As the traffic volume increases, this expense
can be shared by larger and larger amounts of traffic so that the relative importance of the construction cost decreases and thereby the impact of the increase in
the costs of imports also decreases.

When total costs, including operation and construction, are considered, it
appears that in the low-colume case the import price is less important for the old
or the new highway than it is for the railroad, while in the high-volume case just
the opposite is true. Thus, relatively high import prices will favor the highways at
low volume, and the railroad at high volume.

Nonmarket Costs

Nonmarket costs are a reflection of the importance to shippers of the various
nonprice aspects of the performance of the transportation link. It should be
noted that Tables 8-2, 8-3, and 8-4 include nonmarket costs in the totals. Since
they are nonmarket costs, they do not change with a change in factor prices.
They do change, however, as the interest rate changes, because of discounting in
future years. Thus the inclusion of these nonmarket costs dilutes the effect of all
factor price changes. This is, of course, a perfectly accurate and valid result since
total cost is considered to include both market and nonmarket costs. It should
not, however, be confused with the impact of factor price changes on market
costs alone, which is reflected both in operating and maintenance-of-way costs,
as well as in the construction cost figures shown in Tables 8-2 through 8-4.

Table D-5 in Appendix D shows that the nonmarket costs often constitute
one-half or more of the total costs of a project. It is interesting to note the
change in total cost associated with a variation in the perception of these nonmarket costs. If, in some way, all of them could be changed simultaneously by
10 percent, then, since they reflect half or more of the total cost, it is predict-
able that total cost would vary by 5 percent or more. This would make the
evaluation of nonmarket performance one of the most important factor prices,
and demonstrate the importance of providing accurate estimates of nonmarket
performance and its evaluation.

Conclusions

Of the five factor prices tested in this analysis, the interest rate had the
greatest impact on total project cost, with a higher interest rate favoring continued use of the old road and a lower rate improving the desirability of a new

highway or railroad equally. The cost of imports was the next most important factor price because of imported vehicles and railroad rails; increased tended to favor highways at low volume and railroads at high volume. Wages had only a moderate influence on total costs, since only transport wages were varied for this analysis. At low volume, high wages would favor the old road, while at high volume they favor the new railroad slightly more than the new highway. Fuel cost was less important, and had a larger impact on the highway than on the railroad. The cost of crushed aggregate was almost insignificant, but higher prices did tend to favor the old road or the new railroad. The evaluation of nonmarket performance, while not a factor price, is an important element in the total costs, and would rank just behind interest rates in sensitivity.

This analysis, performed for the base scenario, has several characteristics that influence the interpretation of these results. Imports, which are subject to heavy duties because of balance of payments problems, are automatically relatively expensive — a situation that is typical in many developing countries. In a case where there was a balance of payments surplus, no import duties, and cheap ocean shipping, the cost of imports could be half what it is in the base scenario, and the sensitivity, as well as ultimate results, would be quite different. In the base scenario, oil is produced domestically and exported, therefore all fuel prices are relatively low. In a country where oil was imported with heavy duties or great shipping costs, fuel could be several times its base scenario price, with a correspondingly greater impact on total costs. Note, however, that in the second scenario gasoline is much more expensive than in the base scenario; and vehicle operators responded by using diesel trucks, which more than cancelled out the difference in price.

Aggregate is widely available in many parts of the base scenario country so its price was reasonable. In many countries, however, crushed aggregate can be obtained only after shipping long distances, and may thus be very expensive. This would raise highway costs and increase sensitivity to the aggregate price. Generally speaking, however, in any case where there is a severe shortage of one factor, its price will be high, and it may become more decisive in making the investment decision.

The sensitivity analysis has shown how total cost and its components in the base scenario are affected by changes in the prices of a number of input factors. There has also been an attempt to show how the sensitivity might change in substantially different circumstances. It is important to remember that other conditions besides factor price affect investment decisions, and things such as length of the average shipment, total tonnage per day, and the mix of commodities to be shipped will often dominate the analysis, as it did here.

9

Air Model and Results

Introduction

Air cargo, because of its high cost, accounts for only a small fraction of all freight ton-miles carried, both in the United States and in less developed countries. Air passenger service is also expensive and is thus only a small part of total passenger travel, although its percentage is larger than the cargo percentage. Still, when performance characteristics such as speed are considered, the great advantage of air often places it in a favorable overall position, relative to surface modes of transportation. Speed is an important determinant of passenger demand, and also may be important to certain types of cargo such as fresh produce or spare parts for equipment used in important production processes.

In some cases, air transport may entail less capital expenditure than surface systems, thus making it an attractive solution for some transport needs. Difficult terrain, which can dictate circuitous surface routes with high construction costs, has little effect on air facilities or operation, except at airports. Where terrain conditions are especially severe and passenger and cargo volumes are low, the savings in capital costs may be sufficient to offset air's higher unit operating costs and make them competitive with surface modes. The speed of air cargo, however, depends heavily upon freight loading and distribution systems available at the terminals.

Trade-offs between air and surface modes can be examined by using the air model in conjunction with surface modal models. The air model calculates the cost, performance, and foreign exchange requirements of using air to meet a specific level of passenger and cargo demand on a specified link. Investment requirements for aircraft and fixed supporting facilities at the terminals and in route are also derived. The cost model is designed to describe short-haul air service typical of domestic operations in the lesser developed countries with routes of 100 to 500 miles in length.[1]

The air model is constructed to permit the explicit testing and evaluation of

---

1. Long-haul air service, particularly that of international operations, has been modeled elsewhere in detail. A simulation model of international jet operations for stage lengths in excess of 700 miles is in Charles River Associates, *SST Study*. This study develops cost estimates on a link basis for each component of direct and indirect operating costs for a variety of aircraft types. A statistical cost study of international airline operations using cross-section analysis of data aggregated to the firm level is in Mahlon Straszheim, *The International Airline Industry* (Washington, D.C.: The Brookings Institution, 1969), chapt. 4 and app. A, B.

a large variety of aircraft technologies. In the case of air, the range of factor proportions and possible technologies is extremely great; in addition, the technology is changing rapidly, producing rather dramatic changes in the price of used aircraft in the world market and hence in the capital intensity of alternative technologies. This ability to compare several alternative technologies in detail would appear more important in the case of air than in the other modal models. In this study, four basic types of aircraft are considered. The particular aircraft used in the illustrative simulations are shown in parenthesis: small piston (DC-3), large piston (DC-6A,B), turboprop (L-188 Electra and L-100B) and short- to medium-haul jets (DC-9). These are all aircraft types that have either proven economical for short-haul service in the past or are likely to be so in the near future.

Input data for an air link describe the physical attributes of the airport location and the aircraft being used. Volumes are defined in terms of daily averages in each direction as:

1. average daily tonnage
2. average daily volume (ft^3)
3. average daily passengers

Measures of both cargo tonnage and volume (or density) are needed, as the volume restriction will in many cases become binding before the weight capacity of the aircraft is reached.

In addition to these data that describe the characteristics and performance of the individual link, two other variables reflecting the nature of the air transportation system are required as input: (1) the average daily utilization of the aircraft, and (2) the load factor. In general, aircraft are not used only on a single link; therefore, scheduling and operating conditions of the entire system environment in which the aircraft operates must be considered in evaluating the performance of a particular link.

A single air link between two points is represented in the model by means of two air terminals and intermediate facilities such as navigation and communication aids. Portions of fixed costs for the two terminals and the en-route facilities are assigned to the link. Performance on each link is determined by three sets of characteristics: (1) the physical characteristics of the airport locations, (2) the volume of passengers and goods being carried, and (3) the performance characteristics of the aircraft themselves.

For any given air link, a variety of cost and performance measures are determined by the model. Summary measures include total costs, total investment costs, total annual charges for that investment, and operation performance. In addition, a breakdown of cost components such as fuel, crew, maintenance, depreciation, labor and nonlabor inputs associated with indirect expenses (those not involved in the direct aircraft flying operation), and costs of electronic and navigation aids are presented. The model determines total foreign exchange requirements in each of the several cost categories, based on input variables that delineate the percentage of foreign exchange for each category — fuel, aircraft, spare parts, etc. In addition to these cost measures, travel time is also derived, and is a useful measure of performance in evaluating the air link from the shippers' point of view.

The equations used in the air model are discussed in detail in Appendix E, which also contains a listing of the equations themselves. The operating cost equations are modifications of those developed by the American Air Transport Association. Equipment costs have been obtained from the FAA Logistics Service, while airport costs are developed from a separate construction cost model.

Use of the Model

The air model is useful for examining a range of possible trade-offs in the choice of technology for the less developed countries, based on differences in demand characteristics, factor prices, and input productivity levels. As with the other modal models, the number of variables of interest is large, necessitating the use of the computer program outlined in Appendix E. Because of the number of possible trade-offs incorporated in the model is quite large, they will not be described in detail here. Rather, the remarks below are intended to outline the principal technological and economic trade-offs addressed by the model, and to place these in some perspective *vis a vis* air transport planning problems in the developing countries.

Details of surface topography are much less important to air than to truck or rail. The air model, therefore, requires only a description of the airport sites rather than a complete definition of the intervening terrain. The air model, however, does include considerable detail in its description of the technological possibilities — the choice of aircraft, for example. Differing relative labor and capital costs are evaluated in the choice of an optimal technology, and can be directly incorporated in the model.

The more ambitious task of detailing costs of alternative aircraft and ground facilities will only prove as successful as the data inputs. Although published data on airline operations that are available to outside observers are as scanty as those on trucking operations, it is likely that air carriers operating in these countries have the necessary data to operate the air model with considerable precision. It is also likely that these data can be obtained for public planning purposes, since public ownership of the larger airlines is commonplace. (This is in contrast to trucking operations, for example, which tend to be a very competitive industry with many small firms.)

The model includes a large number of input variables that are useful for representing different factor prices and productivity levels. Many diverse forces will affect reported productivity. Airline management practices and institutional considerations, such as the extent of political patronage or featherbedding may be important. Public ownership of airlines almost always introduces the question of the effects of political patronage on staffing levels. Also, many of the productivity relationships employed in the model, such as aircraft utilization, flight crew productivity, the probability of maintenance, and indirect operating personnel will depend on many links in the system rather than the single link in question. The density of the route system and the number of flights from a given airport, will also affect productivity. Hence, whereas the model computes the cost for only a single link in the system, users of the model in a real application must incorporate information about the composition of a system of air links and how air operations are conducted over that system.

The model could be used directly to analyze more than one link, by simply making repeated trials. Two sorts of "systems" applications suggest themselves. One would be to compute the cost for all links in and out of a given airport. This might serve as the basis for a cost–benefit calculation on a proposed airport expansion; for example, a bigger runway to accommodate jets. The second case would be to compute the cost of a set of links that might constitute a potential network for a new aircraft, for example, a system of links to receive jet service. This would be useful in deciding whether a new aircraft should be introduced. In each case, aircraft utilization appropriate to each link constituting part of the "system" in question is a necessary input.

The model is useful in solving four broad classes of planning problems: (1) choice of aircraft; (2) airport and airways investments; (3) user pricing, subsidy, and regulation of fares or tariffs; (4) choice of mode and demand analysis. When considering these problems, it is helpful to keep in mind which variables are policy variables, controllable by the airline or by the government, and which are exogenous and must be taken as given by uncontrollable factors. Choice of aircraft is clearly controllable by the airline, while airport and airway facilities can be specified by the government or airport authority. Service frequency and fare levels are the joint responsibility of the airline and the regulatory body, while demand for air service (route density) is exogenous except as it is related to these two factors. Stage length is also exogenous, as are the interest rate and factor prices. The choice of alternative modes, at least in the short run, is also given.

Choice of Aircraft

Air technology is a production process characterized by variable proportions, permitting choice among a wide range of input combinations in response to its relative factor prices. Aircraft choice is the fundamental consideration, since the input requirements of alternative aircraft — fuel, crew, maintenance, capital, etc. — vary widely. While jets save on crew and maintenance costs, they are the more capital intensive choice. Capital costs can be an important consideration in view of the capital and foreign exchange scarcity in less developed countries. The necessary airport investments for jets are also substantial. At the other end of the spectrum, a range of smaller, used, piston and turboprop aircraft are available, often at very low prices.

Less developed countries always face the choice of acquiring new equipment, which is very capital intensive, or buying an older technology at typically low used prices. As new aircraft are introduced into North American and European markets, older equipment becomes available on the used market. The sharply discounted prices at which used piston aircraft became available soon after jets were in commercial operation in the United States and the North Atlantic is the classic example of this phenomenon. That occurrence has repeated itself all through the 1960s, as a steady stream of used aircraft became available to developing countries at very low prices. Moreover, the opportunity for developing nations to choose among technologies at widely varying relative factor prices is likely to persist.

Whether or not to buy jets is the choice that typically receives the most attention. The answer will depend on the cost of capital, including foreign exchange, and route density, which affects aircraft utilization levels (and hence realized capital costs). The availability of favorable financing from foreign sources is often important in the choice. The wisdom of investing in jets also depends on the characteristics of the market, especially whether or not there is jet competition.

The economics of this choice for medium- and longer-haul international operations have been discussed elsewhere.[2] In many cases in the early 1960s the less developed countries appeared to have been too hasty in acquiring jets and entering the very competitive long-haul routes. If anything resembling the real opportunity cost of capital and foreign exchange was used, the cost of jet operations in less developed countries had to be well above the cost of used piston aircraft (at the very low market prices prevailing at the time for most of the carriers in those countries). However, political pressure to participate with jets often pushed any consideration of the real costs of capital far in to the background. There are a number of cases where carriers appear to have overextended their entry. In many instances these nations sought to protect themselves from jet competitors by imposing restrictions on their competitors, as regards their schedule frequency or plane type.

By the late 1960s, the structure of comparative costs had changed considerably. A learning experience with jets has reduced their costs while at the same time piston aircraft maintenance has grown increasingly expensive. Where route densities will sustain high utilization rates, the jets are becoming increasingly

---

2. Straszheim, *op. cit.*, chapt. 3.

competitive with used piston aircraft, even at shorter stage lengths and high interest rates.

The model developed here is well suited to examining this sort of technological trade-off. All of the relevant classes of aircraft for short-haul operations are included in the model. Input data for any particular aircraft can be inserted into the model along with the necessary airstrip facilities. Airstrip requirements may differ significantly among aircraft and are an important component of costs, as will be seen below. The real costs of airstrips are usually greater than the nominal charges levied for their use. Different costs of construction for the two airports defining the link can be employed in the model, and differing shares of the costs of these two airports can be allocated to the link in question, perhaps, for example, because of different levels of traffic density at the two terminals. Input data include the rate of interest and the terms for writing off aircraft and airstrip investment. The load factor on each plane, a variable likely to differ if aircraft size differs, can also be specified. The simulation results described in the next section illustrate how several different aircraft can be compared over a single link.

The question of appropriate capital intensity in aircraft choice often takes the form of when and how to replace DC-3s currently used in short-haul operations. The DC-3 is becoming increasingly expensive to maintain over time, but new jets or turboprops are generally too expensive on short-haul, low-density routes. Used turboprops, available from U.S. local service carriers, may be a possibility; however, the operating costs of these aircraft in the United States have generally been high. Lower labor costs in the developing countries might help to mitigate these costs.

Another of the most obvious options is that of using larger piston aircraft as they are replaced by jets in carrier operations in the denser, longer-haul markets. These piston aircraft are worth little on the used market. Though originally designed for long-haul service, larger piston aircraft such as the DC-4, DC-6, L-1049 which have little or no depreciation cost, tend to have lower seat-mile operating costs than the DC-3 at any but the very shortest stage lengths. However, their greater size implies that lower load factors may result. How much of the potential cost savings will accrue in the form of lower passenger-mile costs will depend on load factors. In addition, these larger aircraft require additional runway investments, whose costs may be quite significant at low traffic densities. Additional airstrip investment can thus be traded for lower operating costs by the airlines and perhaps even a savings in capital and foreign exchange if new aircraft must be bought to replace the DC-3.

Again, the trade-offs are numerous, but they are well suited to examination by the model, which delineates the costs of different alternatives. The model also differentiates between aircraft investment and operating costs (which typically accrue to airline operators) versus airstrip and facilities costs. The trade-off between airport investments and airline operating costs can therefore be examined.

Public Airport and Airways Investments

Because different aircraft have different runway requirements, airport investment proposals often go hand in hand with proposals to introduce new equipment on a link or set of links. A simple cost–benefit analysis of an airport project can be made with the model by computing the cost for operating alternative equipment types on all links to and from the airports.

This modeling capability can be quite useful in airport planning in less developed countries. Such planning is always under substantial political pressure; new jet airports are important public works projects and are often used for patronage purposes or as a means of distributing funds regionally (perhaps as part of regional unification programs). It is often difficult to evaluate the benefits of such projects aimed at social, "external," or development goals. To be able to estimate the cost implications at least puts this portion of project evaluation in familiar and understandable terms.

There remains the question of how the demands for air service will change as a result of introducing new equipment. It is often claimed that jet service is a big stimulus in these markets because it is felt to be safer — though this has not been substantiated. Also, economic development stimulated by the airport construction or existence of improved service may affect demand. The air cost model does not address these macroeconomic or system effects influencing demand.

The inclusion of navigation aids and air traffic control inputs in the model permits limited examination of the trade-offs implicit in the choice of this technology. Here the technology is complex and the trade-offs are subtle. The results depend to a very considerable extent on local weather conditions. The wisdom of investing in instrument landing capability or equipment for night airport operations will depend on traffic density, with a higher number of flights raising the payoff of instrument-controlled approaches and takeoffs; and on prevailing fog and ceiling conditions, which define the limits of visual flight operations. These can be important in mountainous terrain. For example, because of low ceilings an important airport in Colombia at Bucaramanga in the Andes Mountains is inoperative one to two months a year.

The available air traffic control system together with local weather conditions and terrain will determine the number of days an airport can be utilized during one year, and also will affect the average utilization of aircraft operating to and from that airport. Being unable to operate an airport affects operating to and from that airport. Being unable to operate an airport affects both demand for air service and the costs of providing that service. Two factors increase costs: lower aircraft utilization rates and reduced productivity of inputs associated with indirect operating expenses. The latter are largely due to personnel stationed at the airport and associated fixed costs of operating the facility regardless of its use. Both of these cost effects can be reflected by the model. Aircraft utilization as an input variable for direct operating costs reflects in part the scheduling effects of relying on visual flight rules (or instrument flight rules) at any site in question. With respect to indirect operating costs, the model delineates labor and nonlabor requirements on any link, and these can be adjusted upward to reflect the added costs of being unable to operate an airport a certain percent of the time. These procedures, which estimate the cost effects of visual versus instrument flight procedures, or day versus day/night operations, together with estimates of the costs of air traffic control investment can be used in evaluating such proposed investments. Two factors that the model does not consider are safety implications and the effects of service reliability on demand.

Investments in navigational aids are generally associated with an entire system of links rather than a single link or airport site. Determining the effects on aircraft and airport utilization of such investments will likely require a fairly extensive examination of a system of city-pair markets in which the estimated scheduling of likely aircraft movements is compared before and after the investment. This is a task for both airline and air traffic control management. The air model can be used to estimate the implications on airline operating costs over the system (both direct and indirect costs, as outlined above) by running the model for each link. The resultant operating cost savings over the system of links can then be compared to the necessary investment in navigational aids.

User Pricing, Subsidy, and Fare Regulation

The procedures for pricing public facilities and the ownership and regulation of airline operations vary widely among countries. The air cost model can provide useful inputs in addressing a variety of public policy questions pertaining to pricing and subsidy. First, airport facility costs, as determined by the model, might serve as the basis for airport user charges. Prices might be set in any relation to costs, of course, and any sort of price discrimination among users or on a geographic basis might be employed. For example, geographic discrimination may be an important means of pursuing regional development ovjectives. The model indicates nothing as to the advisability of these alternatives, but can be useful in delineating airport and navigational costs in such a way that the extent of price discrimination implicit in any airport pricing scheme is made explicit.

Similarly, the costs of airline operations given by the model can be useful in fare or tariff regulation. The model delineates costs as a function of the stage length and density of operations, but does not suggest any particular pricing strategy. Of course, any pricing strategy will affect demand, and transport planning must attend to this interrelationship lest the pricing policies adopted prove inconsistent with initial demand forecasts.

Modal Choice and Demand Analysis

Passengers and freight shippers decide which of the available modes of travel to use by evaluating the cost of service characteristics of each alternative and minimizing the weighted total of these factors. Other chapters, particularly Chapter 5, have described in detail how this process is thought to work and how it is represented in the surface models. The air model computes operating cost, travel times, and other data necessary to construct a description of the cost and performance of the air mode. Whether a particular commodity traveling between specific points will use an air or surface carrier can be determined by comparing the commodity's evaluation of the air performance with its evaluation of the available surface modes.

In practice, there is no fixed relationship between costs incurred by an airline for moving a specific commodity over a single link and the tariff charged for that movement, although some average or marginal cost calculation certainly must enter into the fare-setting process. Therefore, the modal choice question is related to fare regulation and pricing issues, and can be evaluated only after fares are set. This can be done in an iterative process in which traffic is assumed, costs and performance computed, fares set, modal choice determined, and thus a new set of costs and performance computed for the traffic flow that results from the model choice operation. All steps are repeated until the traffic flow converges. The air model does not perform this iterative process, but it can provide the necessary cost and performance data for the operation.

Simulation Data and Results

The primary object of the simulation runs is to reveal how the model works and to provide some feel for the sensitivity of the cost results to the several most important variables. Therefore, an extensive parametric analysis of the many variables of interest in the air model will not be done here. As in the other model analyses, the input data describe hypothetical situations; however, these examples have been chosen with some care, based on data from actual countries and hence the results are suggestive of results that could be obtained from a study of a similarly situated country.

Two examples were run; they can be briefly described as follows:

Base Scenario: less developed country with wages one-fourth to one-third U.S. levels, with productivity levels much lower as well, and with high capital costs.

Other Scenario: fast developing nation with wages one-half to two-thirds U.S. levels, and labor productivity almost comparable to U.S. levels.

Input data pertaining to factor prices and productivity for these two cases are shown in Table 9-1. Two rates of interest were used, 8 percent and 15 percent.

The assumption for the less developed country, denoted here as the base scenario, is that the productivity of both maintenance and flight crew personnel

Table 9-1
Input Data for Air Model Simulation Runs: Selected Labor Wage and Productivity Variables

Variable	Base Scenario					Other Scenario				
	DC-3	DC-6	L-100	L-188	DC-9	DC-3	DC-6	L-100	L-188	DC-9
*Crew costs/hour	$9.	$20.	$20.	$20.	$24.	$9.	$15.	$15.	$15.	$24.
Maintenance labor ($/hour)	0.96	0.96	0.96	0.96	0.96	1.44	1.44	1.44	1.44	1.44
Maintenance labor productivity (relative to U.S.)	0.5	0.5	0.5	0.5	0.5	1.0	1.0	1.0	1.0	1.0
*Aircraft engine parts (current/original prices)	4.0	3.0	1.0	1.0	1.0	4.0	3.0	1.0	1.0	1.0
*Airframe parts (current/original prices)	4.0	3.0	1.0	1.0	1.0	4.0	3.0	1.0	1.0	1.0
Nonlabor cost relative price factor (foreign to U.S.)			0.25					0.67		
Indirect operation labor personnel ($/year)										
Passenger servicing employees			$1,500					$3,500		
Aircraft and traffic servicing employees			1,500					3,500		
Promotion and sales employees			1,500					3,500		
General and administrative employees			1,500					3,500		
Nonassigned employees			1,500					3,500		
Air traffic control personnel ($/year)										
Radio operation			$1,400					$2,800		
Flight service specialist			2,600					5,200		
Air traffic controller			2,600					5,200		
Electronic technician			3,400					6,800		
Electro-mechanical technician			2,000					4,000		
Weather forecaster			3,400					6,800		
Airport management personnel			2,600					5,200		
Crash-rescue personnel			1,400					2,800		
Unskilled			1,400					2,800		

*A variable that takes on different values for each aircraft.

is quite low. Maintenance labor wages are assumed to be $0.96 per hour. Jet crew costs in the other scenario are $24 per hour; a typical figure for a U.S. two-man crew would be more than twice that level.

This difference reflects two factors that have opposite effects on cost: (1) a substantial difference in pilot salaries between the base scenario and the United States — (a 3 to 1 ratio is not uncommon);[3] (2) crew utilization levels in the base scenario are perhaps one-half the levels achieved in the United States, where 70 to 80 flying hours a month is typical. This difference in crew scheduling is typical of the experience of carriers in developing countries, a factor that lessens the cost advantage arising from lower pilot wages of these carriers relative to their counterparts in the developed countries.

The simulation of costs was done for link stage lengths of 100, 300, and 500 miles and a range of route densities, beginning with a mixed passenger-cargo operation of 1000 passengers/year and 73 tons of cargo, extending to a mix of 25,000 passengers and 913 tons annually. All-cargo operations analyzed range from a low of 73 tons/year to 5478 tons/year. The link is assumed to connect a larger city having a major manufacturing component to a smaller, outlying city. Airstrip costs in the latter were assumed to be much lower, reflecting the lower opportunity cost of land. Also, airport facility costs for the link are prorated differently in the two cases; in the case of the large city with presumably many air routes to other points, 5 percent of the airport costs are assigned to the link. For the smaller, outlying city, 20 percent of airport costs are assigned to the link.

The format for describing the model results is largely self-explanatory. A portion of the output of one run, for direct operating cost only, is shown in Table 9-2. The full output for a run, more of which is contained in Appendix E, covers almost a dozen pages with detailed cost and performance information. For each cost category, total costs, labor requirements, nonlabor costs, and foreign exchange are presented. All foreign exchange costs are delineated. Costs are divided into three categories: total annual costs; total annual debt service charges (including the debt service charge or the capital recovery factor applied to all investments, commonly referred to as "debt amortization" — a constant charge representing the sum of "interest" and "principle repayment"); and total investment requirements.

The simplest means of presenting the results of the analysis of these projects and to reveal the sensitivity of costs to different variables is by a graphic display of several key parameters.

A brief comment is in order regarding the graphs for mixed passenger and cargo operations. The model assigns cargo to passenger holds until excess cargo capacity is utilized at a level indicated by the assumed load factor for cargo traffic. It then adds all cargo flights to the link to serve the remaining cargo volumes. There is no satisfactory means of assigning all costs to either cargo or passenger

---

3. Straszheim, *op. cit.,* p. 70.

Table 9-2
Portion of Air Printout: DC-9, Other Scenario

DC-9 IN COUNTRY A   00261700   PAGE 10

		PASSENGER/YEAR	1000.
		CARGO TONS/YEAR	73.
		CARGO CU.FT./YEAR	11231.
		COST OF CAPITAL	0.08

SHARE OF ANNUALIZED CAPITAL COSTS FOR
NAVIGATION, EQUIPMENT, AND PERSONNEL REQUIREMENTS ALLOCATED TO LINK

	DAY ONLY		DAY/NIGHT	
	VFR	IFR	VFR	IFR
NAVAIDS	410.07	4626.45	2102.93	4626.45
AIRPORT LIGHTS	0.0	314.05	646.69	646.69
METEOROLOGY	0.0	43.81	0.0	43.81
COMMUNICATIONS	1349.38	1484.90	1349.38	1484.90
ATC	3587.84	3587.84	3587.84	3587.84
AIRPORT VEHICLES	295.83	69.61	295.83	69.61
PERSONNEL	14199.99	24919.99	15919.99	26639.99
TOTAL	19843.11	35046.64	23902.65	37099.28

SUMMARY OF TOTAL AND FOREIGN EXCHANGE COSTS

	DAY ONLY				DAY/NIGHT			
	VFR		IFR		VFR		IFR	
	TOTAL	FOR.EXCH.	TOTAL	FOR.EXCH.	TOTAL	FOR.EXCH.	TOTAL	FOR.EXCH.
ANNUAL CAPITAL RECOVERY COSTS	47793.	29895.	49913.	31615.	47369.	29471.	47597.	29698.
OPERATING AND MAINTENANCE COSTS	133913.	42443.	140806.	38674.	131806.	38674.	139412.	35607.
TOTAL ANNUAL COSTS	181706.	72338.	190320.	70289.	179176.	68145.	187009.	65305.
TOTAL INVESTMENT	449203.	262960.	465604.	279361.	446616.	260373.	450046.	263803.

DC-9 IN COUNTRY A

00261T00   PAGE 11

PASSENGER/YEAR   1000.
CARGO TONS/YEAR   73.
CARGO CU.FT./YEAR 11231.
COST OF CAPITAL   0.08

ANNUAL FOREIGN EXCHANGE COST

| | DAY ONLY | | DAY/NIGHT | |
	VFR	IFR	VFR	VFR
FUEL & OIL	13003.79	13003.79	13003.79	13003.79
AIRFRAME MATERIAL	3624.66	3624.66	3624.66	3624.66
ENGINE MATERIAL	2839.64	2839.64	2839.64	2839.64
AIRPORT CAPITAL	7670.79	7670.79	7670.79	7670.79
FLEET CAPITAL	15406.89	12839.07	12839.07	10748.99
GROUND EQUIPMENT & NAVIGATION AIDS	6521.39	11035.47	8665.26	11208.83
GROUND VEHICLES	295.83	69.61	295.83	69.61
AIRCREW WAGES	0.0	0.0	0.0	0.0
MAINTENANCE WAGES	0.0	0.0	0.0	0.0
INDIRECT LABOR COST	0.0	0.0	0.0	0.0
TOTAL COST	49362.98	51083.02	48939.03	49166.29

traffic; moreover, without a common "output" measure, an "average cost" (e.g., ¢/ton-mile) cannot be derived for mixed cargo-passenger operations.[4] Because average cost curves are most familiar to analysts, the cost curves for mixed operations presented in relate average costs per passenger mile (defined as total costs/passenger miles) to either distance or route density. This use of "average costs" is merely for illustrative purposes. It does *not* endorse the all too common procedure utilized for investment, pricing, or other public policy planning purposes of assigning all costs to passenger operations.

Results for the Base Scenario

While the results are based to some extent on hypothetical data, it is interesting to compare the direct operating costs in the simulation for the base scenario with available data on aircraft direct operating costs in Colombia. Since wages and productivity in Colombia are probably a reasonably representative case of the base scenario, this provides a limited check on the relevance of the simulation results. Table 9–3 presents average direct operating costs for several planes used by Avianca, the national airline of Colombia, for February 1967, and the simulated costs for the base scenario over a 300-mile network and medium traffic density (5000 passengers and 183 tons/year). Since the reported costs for Avianca are for a single month and are averages for a route system that is unspecified, this comparison cannot serve as the basis for any detailed "calibration" of the model. What it does indicate is that the model can approximate the structure of costs by component for the three aircraft classes — small piston, large piston, and jets — when appropriately calibrated by use of variables denoting the wage, flight crew and maintenance, labor productivity, utilization, and maintenance parts prices.

Figures 9–1 and 9–2 show costs related to stage length and route density for the DC-6 and DC-9, at two rates of interest for VFR day operations. The familiar downward slope of these cost curves has two explanations. Certain portions of both direct and indirect costs are associated with ground operations and hence decline on a per-mile basis as stage length increases. Some direct operating costs, such as those for depreciation and crew, depend on flight time, which is a nonlinear function of stage length. Fuel costs are also related to stage length in a nonlinear fashion since a disproportionate share of total fuel consumption is consumed in take-off and climb to cruising altitude.

Here, assuming fairly low aircraft utilization levels, the DC-6 is cheaper. At

---

4. If the DC-3 is used, an aircraft which has limited capacity for belly cargo, the mix of passenger and cargo operations analyzed here requires a significant number of all-cargo flights. Approximately one-third as many all-cargo flights are needed in addition to the passenger flights to serve the cargo demand. For the bigger aircraft which have more belly storage space and a greater weight allowance for residual cargo, the number of all-cargo flights is much less.

Table 9-3
Comparison of Simulated Direct Operating Costs in Base Scenario to Colombia Experience ($/Block Hour)

	Simulation[a]			Avianca[b]			
	DC-3	DC-6	DC-9	DC-3	DC-4	L-1049	Boeing 720 B
Flight crew	18.00	40.00	48.00	18.99	27.26	53.17	58.17
Fuel and Oil	13.61	60.95	113.50	17.62	42.39	104.64	176.66
Maintenance	48.60	101.00	107.65	44.56	97.47	257.83	262.03
Depreciation	4.73	37.98	206.44	2.10	35.44	7.59	166.80
Insurance	6.73	27.62	190.15	1.15	5.79	13.84	48.45
Total[c]	91.67	267.54	665.74	84.42	208.33	437.06	712.10

[a]Simulated costs for 300 miles, VFR day, 5000 passengers and 183 tons/year, 8% rate of interest.
[b]Avianca costs for February 1967. Source: Mahlon R. Straszheim, "Air Passenger Technology and Public Policy in the Developing Countries," Proceedings, *Transport Research Forum*, Ninth Edition, 1968.
[c]Totals may not add due to rounding.

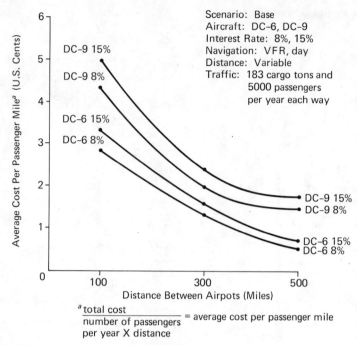

Figure 9-1. Cost as a Function of Distance

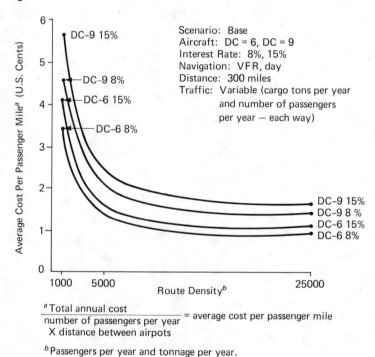

Figure 9-2. Cost as a Function of Density.

150

higher utilizaiton levels or lower interest rates, this conclusion is reversed. At longer stage lengths, the DC-9s comparative cost position improves as well. Higher rates of interest raise the costs of operating each aircraft, and raise the costs of the DC-9 relatively more than the DC-6 since the former is more capital intensive.

Figure 9–3 illustrates costs of a range of aircraft for mixed passenger-cargo operations over a 300-mile stage length and a range of traffic densities. At a 15 percent interest rate the DC-3 and DC-6 are almost equal in costs. However, at an 8 percent rate of interest shown in Figure 9–3b, the cost advantage of the DC-6 is rather pronounced at higher volume levels. Also, lower interest rates yield a relatively greater cost saving for the capital intensive choices like the DC-9 and L-188 for the older piston aircraft. This can be seen by comparing the cost differences in Figure 9–3b with those of Figure 9–3a. Again, under higher utilization assumptions, the cost position of the DC-9 would be improved. This illustrates the advantages to developing countries with high capital costs of using noncapital intensive planes like the DC-3.

Figure 9–4 illustrates costs for all-cargo operations over a 300-mile stage length, as a function of traffic density and the rate of interest. As would be expected, larger, more capital intensive aircraft are cheaper for higher route densities. At low densities, the DC-3 is preferred; as density rises, the DC-6 becomes cheaper, and at even higher densities, the L-100 is preferred. The L-100 is a very capital intensive choice relative to the DC-6. High utilization rates must be achieved for the L-100 to be economical. This in turn requires high traffic density recalling the complex trade-offs between these two parameters. The interest rate also affects the density levels at which it becomes cheaper to shift to a large aircraft. In Figure 9–4a, for a 15 percent rate of interest, the L-100 is preferred over the DC-6 at cargo volumes of about 3000 tons/year, whereas at an 8 percent rate of interest shown in Figures 9–4b, the point at which the costs curves intersect is at a cargo volume of only one-third that level. Larger all-cargo aircraft like the L-100 have the promise of reducing costs and hence stimulating growth in demand. The results of Figure 9–4 suggest that a subsidy of the capital costs is an obvious way to encourage the less developed countries to choose more capital intensive means.

Foreign exchange costs are determined in the model. These are summarized in Table 9–4 for the case of VFR day operations; a 300-mile stage length; medium traffic density; rates of interest of 8 percent and 15 percent; and two aircraft, the DC-6 and DC-9. This illustrates the magnitude of foreign exchange differences involved in the most fundamental choice confronting the less developed countries, the switch from piston to jet aircraft.

Foreign exchange costs are typically incurred where the investment is made in aircraft and the associated support facilities. The extent to which these costs can be deferred or met throughout the useful life of the aircraft or facilities will depend on financing arrangements. At the one extreme, all of the investment out-

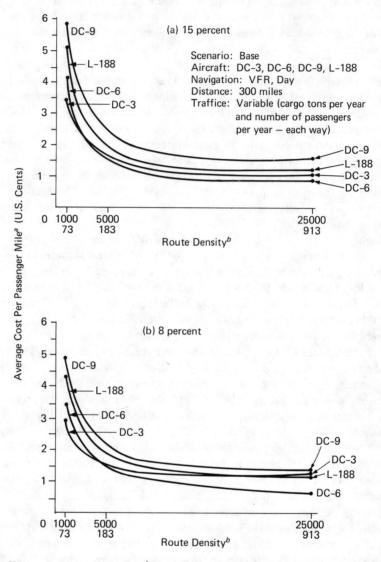

Figure 9-3. Cost as a Function of Density: Four-Aircraft Comparison.

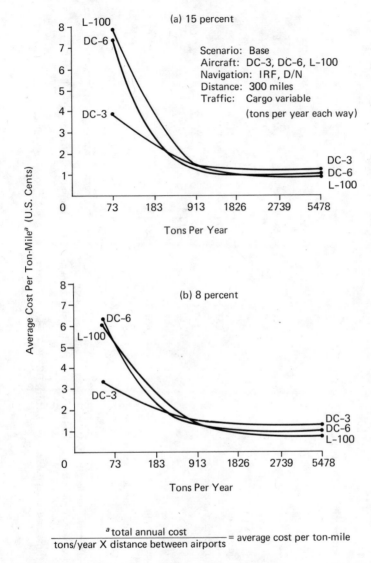

$$\frac{^a\text{total annual cost}}{\text{tons/year X distance between airports}} = \text{average cost per ton-mile}$$

Figure 9-4. Freight Cost as a Function of Density: Three Aircraft.

Table 9–4
Foreign Exchange Requirements (Thousands of Dollars)

Aircraft: Rate of Interest	Other Scenario[a]		Base Scenario[a]	
	Total Costs	Foreign Exchange Costs[b]	Total Costs	Foreign Exchange Costs[b]
DC-6B				
Total investment requirements	368.1	185.6	411.8	226.0
Annual operating costs	251.2	79.3	164.3	34.9
Total annual costs (operating plus debt service)[c]				
8 percent	292.4	102.9	212.2	64.9
15 percent	313.9	113.4	236.1	77.5
DC-9				
Total investment requirements	661.9	475.6	860.4	663.4
Annual operating costs	296.0	122.6	207.2	76.9
Total annual costs (operating plus debt service)[c]				
8 percent	369.8	178.4	304.9	155.6
15 percent	407.4	204.7	353.3	192.0

[a]VFR day operations, 300 mile stage length, 5000 passengers/year and 183 tons/year.
[b]The different foreign exchange components in the two scenarios result in part from differences in aircraft utilization rates and different fuel import conditions.
[c]Expected aircraft life (time used in capital-recovery factor): DC-6B, 7 years; DC-9, 13 years. Assume no salvage value.

lays must be paid for with foreign exchange. Subsequent operations may produce foreign exchange receipts if the aircraft is used in international operations. On the other hand, it may be possible to finance equipment purchases in such a way as to permit repayment in foreign exchange over a period of years. Thus, the nature of financing requirements will determine in part the importance of foreign exchange charges.

Both total investment costs and annual operating costs, to include operating plus debt service charges, are shown in Table 9-4. The foreign exchange portion of these costs is also shown. For the base scenario, the less developed country, foreign exchange costs for the DC-9 are 51.1 percent of total annual costs at an 8 percent rate of interest versus 30.6 percent for the DC-6 at the same rate of interest. At either rate of interest, the foreign exchange components of the total investment requirement is 54.8 percent for the DC-6 and 77.1 percent for the DC-9. If foreign exchange constraints are serious, the real costs of jet technology are significantly increased relative to piston aircraft. Moreover, this burden is greater if financing terms cannot be arranged which permit the foreign exchange component of the investment to be repaid over a period of years.

Results for Other Scenario

The results for the other scenario, denoting a rapidly developed nation with high potentiality, will be more briefly summarized. Again, the cost curves have the familiar shapes. In this case, the higher labor wage and productivity levels leads to a shift in the comparative cost structure in favor of a more capital intensive technology. As shown in Figure 9-7, the DC-3 is not competitive except for low route densities and at an 8 percent rate of interest. Countries whose factor prices and productivity are similar to those of this scenario have been rapidly replacing the DC-3 and other smaller, older piston aircraft for some time. In this example the DC-9 is not competitive with the DC-6, but the cost difference is less than in the case of the less developed countries exemplified by the base scenario. This reduction in the relative advantage of the DC-6 occurs because labor wages in the other scenario are higher and hence the high labor component required to maintain older piston aircraft has a greater effect on costs. Finally, Figure 9-8 for all-cargo operations shows that the L-100 is the preferred choice at lower cargo volumes than for the base scenario. Again, the explanation lies in the fact that the L-100 is labor saving relative to the DC-3 and DC-6.

In short, more advanced countries such as illustrated by the second scenario, will find it economical to switch to the most advanced technology at lower volume levels than carriers in the less developed countries. The more rapidly advancing countries will also most likely find the foreign exchange burden less difficult to finance.

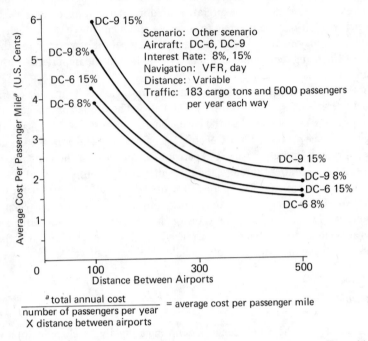

Figure 9–5. Cost as a Function of Distance: Other Scenario, Two Aircraft, Two Interest Rates.

Surface–Air Comparison

It should be clear that even where traffic volume can be accurately predicted, the choice of equipment for airline operation depends upon a sufficiently large number of variables to make analysis of the choice quite complex. In this respect the choice of aircraft and airport design is of the same order of difficulty as the decision between rail and highway, and their specific designs on the ground. Comparing performance of the ground modes with airborne movement combines all these complex threads into a single Gordian knot.

It is impractical to attempt to compare every optimal ground colution for the many different conditions studied with every corresponding optimal air solution, particularly in view of the qualifications presented in Chapter 10 regarding the existence of single optimal solutions. Instead, we have compared two ground situations with a single air situation and examined modal choice, studying the desirability of each project. These results are then extrapolated to ascertain the values of critical parameters that would cause a shift in project selection

It should be noted that the traffic volumes studied with the air model are

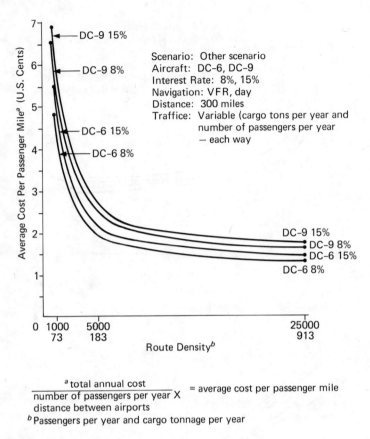

Figure notes:

Scenario: Other scenario
Aircraft: DC-6, DC-9
Interest Rate: 8%, 15%
Navigation: VFR, day
Distance: 300 miles
Traffice: Variable (cargo tons per year and
         number of passengers per year
         — each way

$$\frac{^a\text{total annual cost}}{\text{number of passengers per year} \times \text{distance between airports}} = \text{average cost per passenger mile}$$

[b] Passengers per year and cargo tonnage per year

Figure 9–6. Cost as a Function of Density: Other Scenario, Two Aircraft, Two Interest Rates.

generally below those used in the highway–rail analysis. This reflects the empirical observation that cities that generate a moderate amount of ground traffic demand much less air traffic, and the few towns that have no ground access at all do not develop economic activities that require large amounts of air shipment.

First, consider two cities in hilly terrain separated by 300 airline miles, and generating a low volume of balanced flow on an old road. Here, the new railroad was not a desirable alternative, so we will examine construcion of the new highway, which was the best alternative in Chapter 2, continued use of the old road, and introduction of air service. Highway performance is the same as in the 100-mile case, except that cost and travel time are tripled to reflect the longer distance. The distance along both the old and new roads is greater than 300 miles,

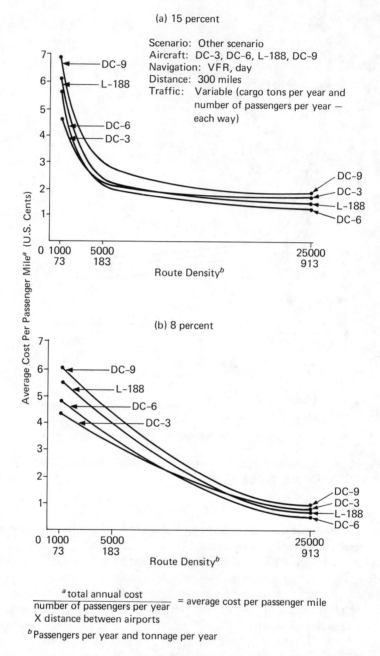

Figure 9-7. Cost as a Function of Density: Other Scenario, Four Aircraft.

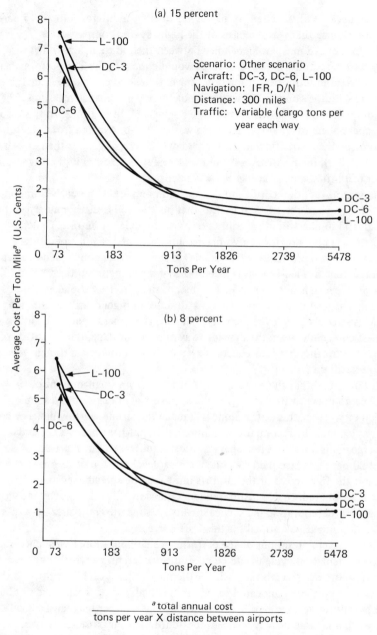

Figure 9-8. Freight Cost as a Function of Density: Other Scenario, Three Aircraft.

of course, because of the circuitry of the alignment. An interest rate of 15 percent is used, since that was the basis of the highway–rail comparison.

The first question is, given a choice between the old road, a new highway, and the air operation, what commodities would choose each? The performance of the old road in terms of waiting time, travel time and cost, is given in Table 9-5, along with the commodity weighting of these performance measures. The same computation is repeated for the new highway and the airline. In this case, the cheapest plane for the traffic volume was the DC-6, selected from Figure 9-3(a). While the traffic flow of 100 tons/day each way is greater than any shown in Figure 9-3(a), the cost curves become essentially horizontal in that figure, so cost per ton is the same as at higher traffic density.

Comparing the total cost, both market and nonmarket, for each commodity on the old road and the DC-6, it is clear that bulk would overwhelmingly prefer the road, and in fact would probably not move at all at the air rate. General prefers the road by a factor of two in cost, but presumably some percentage of this commodity, representing high value, or a special-order good (such as a repair part or machine needed to restore operations of a production process), would choose air. Special is not even evaluated by air, since no tanker planes were considered and special is less likely than bulk to move at higher tariffs. Common passengers strongly prefer the highway, but for private passengers, the air is a clear first choice. Between the new highway and the airplane, the advantage of the highway for the first four classes is even more pronounced, although private passengers still prefer to fly.

Having found that the air service will attract only a small amount of the general cargo plus private passengers, the air investment decision is a simple question of whether this traffic alone will make the airline worthwhile. The cost of air service must be recomputed, eliminating all but passenger traffic and a little cargo. This does not alter operating cost significantly since private passengers, at 20 per day place the DC-6 on an almost level portion of its operating cost curve, but the fixed costs of the airports must then be spread over much less traffic. It would reduce departure frequency substantially and thereby increase waiting time, deteriorating the service quality. Also, a different aircraft–airport combination might be optimal for this traffic level.

Clearly several iterations of the performance computation, modal choice, and total cost calculation cycle would be necessary to determine whether the savings of air transport were worth the cost. Furthermore, these will be sensitive to the portion of airport costs allocated to this link. If high airport costs need not be borne by this service, perhaps because one city has a rather inexpensive facility and the other is more heavily utilized, the addition of air passenger service would be economically justifiable. It seems unlikely, however, that air service could substitute for all ground transport without seriously curtailing many cargo shipments.

The results found in this example are probably typical in showing that air travel can attract a small percentage of all passengers (here it is 10 percent) and a

Table 9-5
Shippers Highway–Air Modal Choice Data
(Base Scenario, Hilly Terrain, Balanced Flow, 100 Tons/Day Each Way, 300 Miles, 15 Percent Interest, VFR, Day)

	Performance			Commodity Weightings of Performance			Total Commodity Perceived Costs/Ton
	WT^a	TT^b	CST^c	WWT^d	WTT^e	$WCST^f$	
Old Road							
Bulk	2.37	30.39	18.69	.049	0.041	1.0	$ 20.05
General	1.95	30.39	24.19	.514	0.362	1.0	36.19
Special	4.95	30.39	23.07	.00154	0.00205	1.0	23.14
Common passengers	3.11	30.39	30.72	1.0	1.0	1.0	64.22
Private passengers	0.67	30.39	794.82	5.0	5.0	1.0	950.12
New Highway							
Bulk	2.37	15.15	8.51	.049	.041	1.0	$ 9.25
General	1.95	15.75	11.03	.514	.362	1.0	17.73
Special	4.95	16.74	11.37	.00154	.00205	1.0	11.41
Common passengers	3.11	14.91	14.31	1.0	1.0	1.0	32.33
Private passengers	0.67	10.59	297.15	5.0	5.0	1.0	353.45
Airline (DC-6)							
Bulk	9.48	1.64	109	0.049	0.041	1.0	$109.53
General	9.48	1.64	109	0.514	0.362	1.0	114.47
Special	–	–	–	–	–	–	–
Common passengers	9.48	1.64	90	1.0	1.0	1.0	101.12
Private passengers	9.48	1.64	127	5.0	5.0	1.0	182.6

^{a}WT = Average waiting time (hours).
^{b}TT = Average travel time (hours).
^{c}CST = Average cost of travel (dollars).
^{d}WWT = Weight assigned to waiting time (dollars/hour).
^{e}WTT = Weight assigned to travel time (dollars/hour).
^{f}WCST = Weight assigned to cost (usually 1.0) (dollars/dollar).

smaller percentage of all cargo traffic away from a highway. This diversion of surface traffic is small enough so that it will not substantially affect congestion on the surface routes. Thus, ground performance and costs for remaining traffic will be little affected by the presence or absence of a competing air link, although the link is very important to those who use it.

This analysis can be taken one step further to see the impact of the air link on the decision whether or not to build the new highway. Assume that the DC-6 service is instituted, and does attract all private passengers. In Chapter 7 it was shown that the total cost of building and using the new highway for low volume in hilly terrain was slightly less than the cost of continued use of the old road: $7,559,000 for the old road and $7,408,000 for the new. Thus the new highway was the preferred alternative. Those cost calculations can be repeated with the private passengers omitted, since they will use the airline in any event. Now the total cost for using the old road is $5,972,000; the new road costs $6,776,000, slightly greater than 10 percent more. With private passengers off the road system entirely, the new highway is no longer justifiable, since a substantial part of the benefits of that highway came from better service to these passengers. The presence of an air link, even though it attracts relatively little traffic, may therefore still alter the benefits of new construction to change the ultimate project choice among surface alternatives.

One other question of interest is what type of commodity would choose air under the cost and performance conditions originally computed. If we assume that commodity weighting of performance occurs in the manner described in Chapter 5, the primary factor influencing that choice will be the value of the goods. Referring to Table 9-5, it is clear that travel time is much less by air, so if commodity weighting of travel and waiting time is increased, total road cost will rise faster than air. Suppose that these two commodity preference elements were increased by a factor of 10. The total cost for general goods by the old road would then be $144.22 and by air $163.65. At a factor of 13 they would be about equal. Thus, a commodity whose value was about 13 times the average for the general goods would be presented with an even choice between air and highway in this case. Such commodities do exist, but they are a relatively small portion of the general category. The points should be stressed again that the conclusion reached here is a result of the particular facts studied here, and would be changed by different pricing policies, terrain, traffic, distance and so forth.

If the terrain is more rugged or the old road is worse, the relative position of the air service will be improved. Also, an increase in the distance will favor air operation since ground costs are nearly linear with distance while air costs encounter substantial economies with distance; conversely, a reduction in distance will favor surface travel, and at some minimum distance, no goods or passengers would find air travel advantageous. Finally, if traffic volume increases, it will increase the frequency of aircraft departure, improving service, at the same time spreading terminal costs over more traffic. This would increase the attractiveness of the air alternative. Large changes in any of these conditions would thus radically alter the modal choice and project selection.

Concluding Observations

The air model provides a flexible procedure for computing the cost of a large variety of aircraft technologies. The detail in which the model represents alternative technologies is such that input requirements are considerable, but so are the benefits. The model can be employed to test a wide range of alternative factor prices and operating characteristics occurring in developing countries. The simulation results suggest that the structure of comparative costs of alternative technologies does depend to a very considerable extent on factor prices and input productivity. High capital and foreign exchange costs penalize jet technology relative to older piston aircraft. The trade-offs are complex, with the optimal technological choice dependent on factor prices, scheduling, the level of demand, and available financing arrangements.

It must be emphasized that the quantitative results obtained in this study depend upon the particular data and assumptions used, and should not be applied to actual situations without first determining whether the data and assumptions are valid there, and adjusting the results if they are not. Subject to this limitation, the findings can be briefly summarized.

Higher rates of interest, lower utilization, shorter stage lengths, and lower traffic densities all tend to favor inexpensive piston planes such as the DC-3 and DC-6, while the opposite conditions tend to favor larger jets like the DC-9. Thus, in some countries and under certain conditions the DC-3 may still be the optimal aircraft, while in other countries or the same country with different traffic and link conditions, the L-100 or DC-9 may be best. Higher wage rates shift all choices toward the more capital intensive technology — the larger newer jets. Because all these factors are closely related, no one simple cutoff point can be established for switching from one aircraft to another without specifying values for all variables. The model can also be used to estimate the amount of traffic that could be attracted away from existing or projected surface modes of transportation, and to determine whether instituting a particular service is justifiable economically.

A comparison of air service with surface transportation shows that aircraft may be an important part of a transport system even in developing countries with relatively low income levels. The percentage of total traffic between any pair of cities that can be diverted from surface carriers will be quite small under any circumstances, because air will be more expensive under any but the most unusual conditions. Still, by providing an alternative for shippers or passengers to whom speed and quality of service are important, air can sometimes greatly improve the access between cities at a relatively low capital cost. By providing this service, air can also relieve the pressure for improving surface facilities, thus postponing major expenditures. As the distance between cities increases or the intervening terrain becomes more rugged, the benefits from an air alternative rise rapidly.

10

Objective Measures and Project Evaluation

Two major purposes of this study have been to develop analytical procedures for determining when one transportation investment is better than another, and to illustrate the computation of numerical measures of the desirability of different projects in some specific situations. As an intermediate step, it was necessary to devise a procedure for selecting what we chose to call the best design for a proposed transportation facility of a particular type. The computational procedures developed for achieving these ends are described in detail earlier in this report. So far, however, the crucial issue of what constitutes "best" has received attention only on a few major issues, such as the evaluation of nonmarket performance or cost, but it has not been dealt with comprehensively. In general, it has been implied that the best project was the one that minimized total cost. Several issues of what are properly to be included as costs have been left open and many problems of computing costs have been mentioned but not resolved.

This chapter will consider the issue of an appropriate objective function in transportation investment decisions and how such objective functions can be incorporated into the analytical methods used here. It will also deal with the problems of how to evaluate the costs in that objective function. It is important to remember, particularly where sophisticated computational machinery has been employed, that although careful computation can yield seemingly precise numerical answers, when the definitions of the variables used are not themselves precise, or when there is no agreement on how they are to be measured, then the numerical answers do not give the unqualified guidance for policy making that their apparent precision suggests. The assumptions made in this study, many of which are frequently made in transportation investment analyses, do not avoid the problems that have been mentioned above. The problems that are raised here are not a complication that has been somehow added by the method of analysis used. Rather they represent problems that inevitably occur in all project analyses, whatever methods are used. The discussion here is simply a reflection of the fact that each has been considered, and a conscious position taken with regard to its resolution.

The Role of Viewpoint

The items to be included in a project analysis depend upon the person for whom it is prepared and the use to which that analysis will be put. Assuming

165

that economic units usually operate in their own self-interest, different units will view the economic consequences of a project individually and will not want to have them confused with other economic entities. In the highway–rail analysis four primary interest groups have been identified. Their viewpoints will be briefly explored here.

Truck Operators

The conclusion was easily reached in Chapter 2 that truck operators would prefer the new highway as the best of the four alternatives and would definitely not want to see the competing railroad built. In the example problem, at medium volume levels the truck operators saved $27.8 million over the useful life of the facility when operating over the new highway as compared to carrying the same traffic over the old road. If the new highway is financed from general government revenues or from a general gasoline tax, the truck operators get the benefits of the new facility without a direct increase in cost to themselves for its construction. Even where the new highway is to be financed by direct user tolls, the truckers may still prefer its construction if sufficiently large savings can be made in operating costs. In the example problem of Chapter 2 the highway gas tax level was unaffected by the construction of the new road and taxes paid by users amounted to less than the cost of the facility so that vehicle operators on the whole received more from the new construction than they paid out.

Taxes have little effect on the total value of a project from a social point of view, because they represent only a transfer payment. It is clear however, that taxes have a substantial impact upon the project as viewed by truck operators. To the extent that changes in tax level affect total truck operating cost and truck prices they alter the total traffic volume that will use the new facility and thereby change the total benefits that are derived from the project.

The perceptions of truck operators will also be affected by competition in the trucking industry. If perfect competition prevails the same profit rate should ultimately be reached after the construction of a new highway as occurred before. However, if the trucking industry is characterized by strong oligopoly or monopoly it may be possible to continue charging the same tariff after the new construction as before so that the lower operating costs will greatly increase truck profits. It is clear that the same project will appear more advantageous to truckers in an oligopoly or monopoly situation. It can be seen, then, that computations involving the point of view of truckers should incorporate pricing mechanisms that reflect the existing competitive situation. It is also obvious that a social welfare cost–benefit analysis of the new facility may produce different results from an analysis based on the point of view of users who do not pay tolls to finance construction of the facility.

Railroads

The objectives of the railroad are likely to be analogous to those of trucking operators in that they will tend to prefer construction of facilities supporting their mode while rejecting construction for other modes. This is particularly true of publicly owned railroads, since they frequently receive capital funds for new construction from general government revenues while meeting operating expenses out of their own revenues. In such a situation, the railroad will want to have the new facility constructed as long as operating revenues exceed operating costs, even if the construction costs can never be recovered. Thus, like highway users who do not pay for a specific facility with specific revenues, the railroad, by not viewing total costs, will tend to ask for far more railroad construction than would be advocated by a social welfare cost–benefit analysis. If the railroad is required to finance the construction itself, it will be much less eager to build a line, unless it appears that revenues will cover both operating expenses and debt service for construction. Railroads frequently have a monopoly on rail facilities, so that they enjoy greater pricing freedom than competitive truckers. However, political pressures on a publicly owned railroad generally more than offset this freedom. It should be recognized that a publicly owned railroad may not have an explicitly stated objective, such as maximizing profits but may instead be seeking to maximize total traffic or even to maximize size of physical plant, subject to profit or deficit constraints. Where this is the case, an analysis performed for the railroad will differ greatly from one performed for a profit-maximizing organization.

Shippers

The viewpoint of shippers is more difficult to characterize than that of the carriers. Some shippers would prefer the construction of a highway while others will want to have the new rail facility. Even where modal preferences are quite strong, however, it would not be surprising to find that all shippers worked enthusiastically for any new transportation facility. For example, shippers who preferred to use trucks might still wish to have a parallel railroad constructed because that would tend to place a ceiling on the rates truckers could charge and provide an alternative means of transportation in case of failure in the trucking operation.

Shippers in different cities may compete in national markets, so that each will want the best possible transportation from this location to the rest of the country. Thus, shippers can be expected to favor construction of as many transportation links as possible near their base of operations, and to have these financed from general government revenues. Most transportation projects tend to lower the cost of movement. Shippers, therefore, will tend to press for unlimited amounts of construction since to do so ordinarily costs them nothing.

Government

A local government will probably react somewhat like a group of shippers in advocating the maximum possible construction so long as someone else (preferably the central government) pays for it. A central government, however, is likely to take a rather broad view of the transportation investment priorities. Because revenues are rarely associated with a single transportation project, the central government is likely to indicate some sort of cost–benefit analysis to determine the order in which projects should be undertaken. Since this analysis alone among the four that have been mentioned is not based upon cash revenues and expenditures, it is the one most likely to raise difficult quesitons of definition and evaluation. Instead of looking at revenues and expenditures for a single shipper, the government should evaluate costs and benefits to all affected entities in the economy. It is here that it must consider equity and deal with questions of interpersonal comparisons of utility. Costs and benefits cannot be evaluated without deciding whose costs and benefits should be included and what weight should be attached to costs and benefits incident to the different entities. Thus, it becomes useful to describe a social welfare function which will provide answers to the questions of interpretation and analysis that arise.

Elements of an Objective Function

A very simple objective function is the minimization of total costs or their present discounted values, where benefits are perceived as reductions in cost. This procedure has been used throughout this study. The simple statement of this function, however, conceals the substantial difficulties that are involved in practical application. A number of the more important problems that arose in the course of this study are discussed below, and should be considered by anyone who wishes to use the project analysis techniques.

Allocation of Costs and Benefits
Among Different Groups

A first issue in the analysis is the relative evaluation of costs or benefits incident to different groups. Many government functions involve taxing one group of people to pay for services provided to another. This suggests that the government's objectives recognize that there is some greater value for the money or services in the hands of the recipient than in the hands of the donor. It is inconsistent, therefore, for the government to weigh benefits to these two groups equally when planning transportation, when they are weighed differently for other purposes. If economic development of a particular region or industry is being encouraged, it would be reasonable to value benefits to that region or industry more highly than benefits to other industries or other regions. It would probably be impractical to compile a comprehensive list of different weightings for all groups in a country, but for a *particular* transportation project it might be possible to identify two or three *particular* groups for special consideration. Because the present study is a general one, no such distinctions have been made here.

Shadow Pricing

A second issue is that of price adjustment to reflect actual opportunity cost of resources used. This was discussed in Chapter 3, where it was suggested that because of imperfections in the price system, market prices may not represent true social cost. For example, if workers engaged in constructing or operating a project would otherwise have been unemployed, the real cost to the economy of their employment may be very small although total wages paid out could be substantial. Conversely, if a project utilized resources or skills that were very scarce in the country, the value of the resources consumed by the project could be much greater than the actual wages paid. This problem of price adjustment arises most frequently with skilled workers, with unemployed labor, with goods produced by subsidized industries, and with imported or exported goods. Foreign exchange is a special case of price adjustment where expenditures in foreign currencies are weighed more heavily than the official foreign exchange rate would indicate, reflecting the scarcity of foreign capital resulting from an unfavorable balance of payments.

Double Counting

A third issue to be considered is the avoidance of double counting of either costs or benefits. This is likely to arise in the case of construction costs for a highway, for example, which are accounted for directly in the construction cost and the indirectly in the tax revenues collected from users. Although the different evaluation of the groups who are taxed and who benefit has its own impact, taxes represent a transfer rather than a use of resource and should not be included in a computation of total costs or total benefits. In the analysis performed for this study, results are given as total costs and, separately, as adjusted total cost. The adjusted total cost deletes all tax payments and adjusts foreign exchange to account for its real cost.

Nonmonetary Effects

A fourth item addressed in this study is the evaluation of nonmonetary benefits or costs. Chapter 5 on nonmarket costs is devoted to the determination of
the dollar value of improvements in service brought about by making changes to
the transportation link. Output of the project analysis computer routines indicate market costs and nonmarket costs of each alternative separately, so that it is
possible to consider them either separately or together. Although the flexibility
to ignore nonmonetary benefits has been provided, it would be a serious error to
neglect them.

In addition to the nonmarket performance measures considered here, there
are others that could be evaluated. The externalities of transportation have long
been alluded to as important factors for consideraton, although this is probably
more true within urban areas than for intercity travel, especially at light traffic
densities. Still, to the extent that it is possible to quantify the harmful effects of
the noise pollution and accidents of transportation activities, these should be considered in a complete analysis.

Impact on the Economy

A separate but related issue is the indirect effect of changes in the transportation system on the economy. Throughout this study, it has been assumed that the
initial impact on the economy of a change in the transportation system is limited
to the magnitude of the cost savings where both market and nonmarket costs are
included. Frequently, transportation investments are undertaken with the specific
intent of promoting economic development, thus implying that there is a value
to be derived from its effect on the economy beyond the initial cost savings.
Most frequently, projects of this type are expected to contribute to the growth of
gross national product or benefit of a particular industry or region.

Where these effects are important, a project analysis such as that performed
here is really not the appropriate way to measure the value of the improvement.
What is needed instead is a full-scale systems analysis that studies both the economy and the transportation system with a strong linkage between them to reflect
the impact of transportation improvements on the economy. It would be difficult
to perform such an evaluation using a project analyzer, as one cannot follow a
particular effect through from the transportation improvement to a particular
industry or to the economy as a whole. Also, the chances are great that other
equally important effects would be ignored. This, or any other project analysis,
should be used with a clear understanding of its limited usefulness and of the
assumptions implied about the remainder of the economy.

This study has not dealt with the concept of consumer surplus because, as
volumes are assumed to be the same for all projects, there is no consumer surplus

to be measured. In fact, it can be argued that if the impact of a project on the volume of goods flowing is large enough to permit computation of surplus, then it is probable that there are other important changes in the economy beside the change in the particular volume under study. Thus, in those cases where a consumer surplus evaluation can be made, it is probably more appropriate to engage in a systems analysis of the entire economy using simulation to reflect changes in the level of economic activity.

Uncertainty in Transportation Planning

A sixth issue that has not been dealt with in this report is the treatment of uncertainty in transportation planning. Clearly, the projection of future traffic volumes and mixes as well as the costs, prices, and revenues to be earned are all subject to a substantial amount of uncertainty. For some of these, a probability distribution might be estimated, while for others, too little information would be available to do much more than estimate the mean of the distribution. The effect of this uncertainty on the construction of facilities may depend upon a number of factors, including whether or not the government is risk-averse. For example, in the problem of Chapter 2, the combined alternative appears to be slightly better than the new highway alone. However, a government might rationally decide to build just the highway, reasoning that the traffic volume and other projections are subject to considerable uncertainty, and if the highway alone were built then the traffic volumes could greatly exceed those projected and costs per year would still be about the same as for the combined project. If, however, the traffic volumes were less than those predicted, the combined project would be much worse than just the highway as the addition of the railroad depends upon a substantial traffic volume. The project analyzer does not presently incorporate specific mechanisms for dealing with uncertainties, but the user can make his own adjustments for them in considering the final results of the project analysis.

Qualitative Considerations

Finally, a number of factors may enter into transportation planning decisions that cannot really be represented in a model such as this one. Massive public works projects are sometimes defended not because of a favorable cost–benefit analysis but rather because they are expected to have a highly beneficial effect on national pride and therefore ultimately on domestic productivity. Projects may even be undertaken to provide lasting monuments to the public-spirited figures who were responsible for their initiation.

Not infrequently, developing countries must rely upon more advanced nations for aid in large-size capital investments, and may thus be subject to the aiding country's desires regarding the mode and type of facility. The latter may be governed much more by a sense of what skills are presently underutilized in its own economy rather than a perception of the needs of the developing country. Considerations such as these might be included in the analysis by attaching a bonus value to projects of a particular type, design, or location; but it is more likely that they will be ignored in the formal analysis and then weighed as an afterthought.

Even where such factors are important to the final decision, a project analysis based on more traditional economic issues can still be of value, as it will indicate what price is being paid to achieve the particular goal.

Summary

Most of the items considered in this section can be incorporated into the existing project analysis where sufficient data are available and the analysis is carefully performed. To avoid the errors which may otherwise result, these items should be used as a checklist before data are gathered. The fact that the project analyzer produces a variety of different results and records them separately, enables persons with substantially different objective functions and interests to determine their set of priorities from a single run. In the highway-rail study performed here, the difference between the total cost and adjusted total cost was quite small for highway projects, because the adjustment for tax revenues approximately cancelled the adjustment for foreign exchange expenditures. The difference was much larger for rail projects, however, with little tax revenue to counterbalance the substantial foreign exchange expenditure. Inclusion of the nonmarket costs of performance was crucial in this study, since it frequently formed almost half of the total costs.

It is, of course, most useful to consider the secondary impacts that result from making a transport improvement. A number of possible consequences could occur. The next section reviews these possible consequences and the nature of their possible impact on the economy.

Effect of Transportation Cost Savings
on the Economy

Project evaluations, either feasibility or cost–benefit studies, generally assume that all costs saved in the transportation sector as a result of the project are direct benefits that can be summed to produce total benefits. In many cases this may be appropriate; but it is interesting to consider those cases where this may be misleading, if not entirely erroneous. This can be done by tracing the impact of a transportation cost saving through a portion of the economy. Consider a hypothetical developing country in which a transportation investment is undertaken. Assume that the economy is operating essentially at full capacity, there is little or no unemployment, and all industries are fully utilizing their plant and labor. Now assume that an old winding and unpaved road is replaced by a new highway with lower grades, hard pavement, and a substantially shorter distance. Trucks operating over the new highway will find that they use less gasoline, less tires, less maintenance, and require less time for the trip, saving both driver wages and depreciation. If total traffic is unchanged by the improvement, there will be net savings to the economy of the above factors and including tires, fuel, and labor. Because the economy is running at full capacity, these factors can easily be diverted to other users in similar industries such as light manufacturing or construction. Another, and somewhat more probable situation is that the savings in trucking costs will be used to expand capacity within the transport industry, perhaps allowing a slight general increase in truck transportation throughout the country. In this simple case the value to the economy of the transportation improvement can be measured by the price of the resources saved as a result of its introduction.

Even so, it should be noted that there are distributional effects from the project that should be considered. For instance, if the truckers do not lower their tariffs along with their reduction in operating costs, their profits will increase substantially in which case they will retain directly most of the monetary benefits that the project has created. The truckers may decide to reduce tariffs, however, to induce more or further shipment. To the extent that the benefits take the form of better or faster service they are almost certain to be passed on to the shippers and receivers of goods traveling over the highway. These shippers and receivers may lower their prices in response to the savings realized or they could maintain previous prices thus retaining for themselves the portion of the benefits that were initially theirs. If the project is a local one, industries and consumers in the local area will benefit more than those elsewhere in the country, and these benefits may or may not be passed on. If the public decision maker has reason to hold different feelings about the worthiness of trucking companies, shippers, and consumers, it may be important to him to decide which benefits will be retained and which passed on. Thus, although the computed benefits may accurately measure savings to the economy, the incidence of these benefits may require a revaluation or recounting according to some social welfare or objective function.

Now let us consider a more complicated example. Suppose that the economy is depressed so that unemployment is generally high. Many industries are working at less than full capacity. Let us postulate the same highway project with the same saving in both operating cost and service performance.

One result of the improvement will be that truckers use less gasoline to perform the same transportation service. If the petroleum industry is operating at substantially less than capacity, then the gasoline that is no longer used for operating over this road will not be resold elsewhere in the country. Thus the cost saving to the trucking companies is a loss of income to gasoline companies, and may appear as a reduction in the total gross national product. A further result of the project is that fewer drivers are needed to move the same number of ton-miles of traffic. If there is substantial unemployment in the trucking industry, these truck drivers will not be reemployed on other routes, but will be added to the pool of unemployed labor. Here the cost saving to the trucking company is reflected by a loss of income to truck drivers, and may therefore also contribute to a decline in total gross national product. Similar analyses may be made for tires, repair parts, and other factors saved as a result of the transportation improvement.

This demonstrates the result, which some may find startling, that cost savings in an economy operating at substantially less than capacity may be of little benefit to the economy as a whole, and can in fact reduce aggregate measures of economic activity. This is merely a reflection of the simple economic fact that for every buyer there must be a seller, so that every reduction in the purchase of inputs used to produce one output means a reduction in sales by some other member of the ecnomy. If there are alternatives for which that input will be used, then these alternatives measure the value of saving the input. If there are no alternative uses, as may frequently be the case in a slowly growing or stagnant economy, there may be little value in saving the resource. Chapter 3 of this report discusses how factor prices used in the models might be adjusted downward where it was apparent that there were few or no alternative uses for that factor. This adjustment will change the total present value of the project, and is at least a partial step toward recognizing the effects that can be shown by a full systems simulation.

In the case of the underemployed economy, just as in that of full employment economy, it is important to consider not only the aggregate value of the benefits to the economy but also the incidence of those benefits. Once again we must ask whether those who initially receive the benefits from the improvement will be able to retain them for themselves or whether they will be passed on to other sectors of the economy. The answers will come only from an examination of the market structure of the various firms and industries affected and a prediction of their probable reactions. This would have to be done in any event if the sort of multiviewpoint evaluation of results suggested above is to be performed. Here, however, rather than seeing how individual groups will react to the project, we are determining how the impact of the project on those groups should be valued by the decision maker, or by society.

The complexities suggested by the above discussion should not be taken as a sign that nothing can be done without a full-scale systems analysis. These comments apply to any project analysis whether done by traditional methods or by those employed here. This discussion was intended to suggest the sort of items that should properly be considered to some degree in any project evaluation. The programs and methods described in this report, far from increasing the difficulty of analysis, facilitate it by providing a variety of detailed outputs that can be used to evaluate some of the factors suggested here. Thus, these complexities can probably be treated more easily by the new methods than by traditional ones.

There is no way to avoid a specific decision on them; a decision not to consider them at all simply decides each in a particular way. Consideration of all of the above problems clearly makes the project analysis more time consuming than it would otherwise be, since it involves the construction of some sort of objective function and adjusting the data where necessary. The result, however, is much more useful to policy makers than one based upon raw data, since such an answer must then be adjusted in an informal *ad hoc* manner to compensate for omissions from the formal anslysis.

Conclusion

This chapter has attempted to recognize the fact that project selection, in the field of transportation as in other public investments, cannot be based upon a simple mechanical addition of costs and benefits. Even when the viewpoint to be taken is well defined, it is usually necessary to make judgments about many of the elements of the analysis that will often have a substantial impact upon the final result. We have tried to emphasize here the points at which these judgments must be made and the way in which they might vary with different viewpoints or objective functions, along with the way in which they were resolved for this study.

A central matter upon which careful judgment must be made is the adjustment of costs incurred in various projects by shadow prices that differ from actual market prices paid. Frequently these adjustments will be different, for a given project, depending upon the viewpoint and objectives functions of the person doing the analysis. A closely related matter for consideration is the weighting of benefits to different groups; this will be even more dependent upon viewpoint and objective than was shadow pricing. In addition it is necessary to decide what values should be attached to nonmarket aspects of performance of the projects. Finally some thought must be given to the impact of the project on the local and national economy, and whether this has been adequately reflected in the adjustments already made.

It is sometimes said that economic analysis of transport projects is a waste of effort, since the ultimate decision must be a political one anyway. This opinion, however, is based upon an erroneous conception of the purpose of economic analysis. Even where a decision is in fact a political one, the economic analysis will still show what the impact of the project will be and thus provide important input information for the political decision-making process. Rarely would even the most political decision be made without some consideration of the cost of the project and its effect on various groups. And as has been shown above, many elements of the political process of evaluation can be formally included in the project analysis, by the use of shadow prices, weighting of benefits, analysis of different viewpoints.

It is our hope that the methodology described here, and its supporting computer programs, will be useful to project analysts and will enable them to improve their analyses. The example problems of this report were designed to give guidance in use of the Project Analyzer and to point up some of the questions that demand answers in project selection in developing countries. The purpose of the study will have been fulfilled if these two goals have been met.

Appendix A: Scenario Factor
Price Data and Definitions

General

Prices given here are in accordance with the conditions in the particular scenario chosen and the modal technology, described in Appendix C.

For less developed nations, the opportunity cost of capital is usually relatively high and a 15 percent rate of interest was therefore used for all scenarios. An exception was made for private car owners for whom a 20 percent interest rate was used, since the interest rate charged private operators is usually higher than for commercial truckers.

All prices are expressed in equivalent U.S. dollars according to the official exchange rate. The prices represent purchase costs, and the tax and foreign exchange components for each item are given in the following sections.

The *FORTRAN* variable names are used throughout with the following indices: *ICLAS, ISURF,* and *LT. ICLAS* represents the five commodity classes: *BULK, GENERAL, SPECIAL, COMMON,* and *PRIVATE.* Each class has a representative vehicle or rail car with the exception of a private rail car. If traffic is assigned to *PRIVATE* on a railroad, it is treated as *COMMON. ISURF* represent three surface types for highways: *PAVED, GRAVEL,* and *DIRT.*

LT represents three line-haul locomotive types: 1, 2, and 3. Type 1 is assigned to the most powered locomotive and Type 3 to the least powerful one.

Base Scenario – Definitions and Data

Highway

Sources of Data.
Ingetec, Ltds., "Evaluaccion de Proyectos de Carretera," Bogota, 1966.
Integral, Ltda., "Medellin Bogota Highway Feasibility Report," Medellin, 1966.
Enrique Ordonez R., "Aspectos Diversos del Transporte en Colombia," Banco de la Republica, Dept. de Investigaciones Economicas, Bogota, 1966.

Vehicle Cost.

COST(ICLAS)	=	Initial vehicle cost by class
COST(BULK)	=	16,400 $/vehicle
COST(GENERAL)	=	13,300 $/vehicle
COST(SPECIAL)	=	15,200 $/vehicle

177

COST(COMMON)   = 13,600 $/vehicle
COST(PRIVATE)   =   8,100 $/vehicle

Tire Cost.
TC(ICLAS)   = Cost of new tire by class
TC(BULK)   = 140$/tire
TC(GENERAL)   = 101$/tire
TC(SPECIAL)   = 101 $/tire
TC(COMMON)   =   87 $/tire
TC(PRIVATE)   =   27 $/tire

Crew Wages.
UDT(ICLAS)   = Crew wages per hour per man by class
UDT(BULK)   = 0.33 $/man-hour
UDT(GENERAL)   = 0.33 $/man-hour
UDT(SPECIAL)   = 0.33 $/man-hour
UDT(COMMON)   = 0.33 $/man-hour
UDT(PRIVATE)   = 0.20 $/man-hour

Fuel Cost.
FC(ICLAS)   = Fuel cost per gallon by class
FC(BULK)   = 0.154 $/U.S. gallon
FC(GENERAL)   = 0.154 $/U.S. gallon
FC(SPECIAL)   = 0.154 $/U.S. gallon
FC(COMMON)   = 0.154 $/U.S. gallon
FC(PRIVATE)   = 0.154 $/U.S. gallon

Oil Cost.
OILC   = Oil cost per quart
OILC   = 0.233 $/quart

Mechanics Wages.
WAGEM   = Mechanics wages per hour per man
WAGEM   = 0.40 $/man-hour

Way Maintenance.
CK8(ISURF)   = Fixed way maintenance cost per mile per year by surface
                    type
CK9(ISURF)   = Variable way maintenance cost per vehicle per year by
                    surface type
CK8(PAVED)   = 180 $/mile/year
CK8(GRAVEL)   =   90 $/mile/year

$CK8(EARTH)$ = 26.7 \$/mile-year
$CK9(PAVED)$ = 0.08 \$/vehicle-mile/year
$CK9(GRAVEL)$ = 0.38 \$/vehicle-mile/year
$CK9(EARTH)$ = 1.14 \$/vehicle-mile/year

Railroad

Sources of Data.
Parsons, Brinkerhoff, Quade & Douglas, "Plan for Improvements in National Transportation," Report to the Ministry of Public Work of Colombia, 1961.

Colombia National Railroads, "Boletin Estadistica," 1963, and later.

Madigan-Hyland De la Cruz & Co., Ltd., "Economic Feasibility of a Railroad Extension to Barranquilla and Cartangena," Report to the Colombia National Railroads, 1965.

Madigan-Hyland South American Corporation, "Completion of Atlantic Railroad and Review of Financial Problems," Report to the Colombia National Railroads, 1959.

Madigan-Hyland South American Corporation, "Rehabilitation of National Railroads," Report to the Colombia National Railroads, 1956.

Locomotive Cost.
$CSTLOC(LT)$ = Initial locomotive cost by locomotive type
$CSTLOC(1)$ = 250,000 \$/locomotive
$CSTLOC(2)$ = 220,000 \$/locomotive
$CSTLOC(3)$ = 150,000 \$/locomotive

Car Cost.
$CARCST(ICLAS)$ = Initial car cost by class
$CARCST(BULK)$ = 8,050 \$/car
$CARCST(GENERAL)$ = 8,050 \$/car
$CARCST(SPECIAL)$ = 12,000 \$/car
$CARCST(COMMON)$ = 45,000 \$/car

Cars and Other Rolling-Stock Maintenance.
$A1$ = Fixed maintenance cost for cars and other rolling stock per car per year
$B1$ = Variable maintenance cost for cars and other rolling stock per car-mile
$A1$ = 75.0 \$/car-year
$B1$ = 0.007 \$/car-mile

Locomotive Maintenance.
$A2$ = Fixed maintenance cost for locomotives per locomotive per year

$B2$ = Variable maintenance cost for locomotives per locomotive-mile
$A2$ = 1500 \$/locomotive-year
$B2$ = 0.1149 \$/locomotive-mile

Way Maintenance.
$A3$ = Fixed way-maintenance cost per mile per year
$B3$ = Variable way-maintenance cost per gross ton-mile
$A3$ = 4000 \$/mile-year
$B3$ = 0.0016 \$/gross ton-mile

Crew Cost.
$B4$ = Crew cost per train-mile
$B4$ = 0.33 \$/train-mile

Fuel Cost
$B5$ = Fuel cost per gallon
$B5$ = 0.167 \$/U.S. gallon

Oil Cost.
$B6$ = Lubricating oils cost per gallon
$B6$ = 0.9 \$/U.S. gallon

Taxes

The tax input includes 15 items which specify the amount of tax on a given item. The first 10 are expressed as fractions of the cost before tax and the last 5 are fixed dollar amounts.

$TAX(1)$ = Import tax on autos and trucks
$TAX(1)$ = 0.9
$TAX(2)$ = Import tax on tires for autos and trucks
$TAX(2)$ = 0
$TAX(3)$ = Import tax on parts for repairs
$TAX(3)$ = 0.25
$TAX(4)$ = Import tax on locomotives
$TAX(4)$ = 0
$TAX(5)$ = Import tax on rail cars
$TAX(5)$ = 0
$TAX(6)$ = Import tax on dock equipment
$TAX(6)$ = 0.2
$TAX(7)$ = Highway fuel tax
$TAX(7)$ = 0.8

$TAX(8)$	=	Railroad fuel tax
$TAX(8)$	=	0
$TAX(9)$	=	Lube oil tax
$TAX(9)$	=	0.05
$TAX(10)$	=	Income tax (average on wages)
$TAX(10)$	=	0.2
$TAX(11)$	=	Registration fee on highway vehicles class *BULK*
$TAX(11)$	=	3.0 $/vehicle-year
$TAX(12)$	=	Registration fee on highway vehicles class *GENERAL*
$TAX(12)$	=	1.7 $/vehicle-year
$TAX(13)$	=	Registration fee on highway vehicles class *SPECIAL*
$TAX(13)$	=	5.0 $/vehicle-year
$TAX(14)$	=	Registration fee on highway vehicles class *COMMON*
$TAX(15)$	=	1.0 $/vehicle-year
$TAX(15)$	=	Registration fee on highway vehicles class *PRIVATE*
$TAX(15)$	=	2.0 $/vehicle-year

Foreign Exchange

The foreign exchange input includes nine items expressed as fractions of the cost before tax and another variable to express the shadow price of foreign exchange that exists in most less developed nations because of a deficit in the balance of payments, expressed as a fraction of actual foreign exchange.

$FRNEXC(1)$	=	Foreign exchange on purchase of autos and trucks
$FRNEXC(1)$	=	1.0
$FRNEXC(2)$	=	Foreign exchange on purchase of tires for autos and trucks
$FRNEXC(2)$	=	0.2
$FRNEXC(3)$	=	Foreign exchange on purchase of parts for repair
$FRNEXC(3)$	=	0.9
$FRNEXC(4)$	=	Foreign exchange on purchase of locomotives
$FRNEXC(4)$	=	1.0
$FRNEXC(5)$	=	Foreign exchange on purchase of rail cars
$FRNEXC(5)$	=	0.95
$FRNEXC(6)$	=	Foreign exchange on purchase of dock equipment
$FRNEXC(6)$	=	1.0
$FRNEXC(7)$	=	Foreign exchange on purchase of highway fuel
$FRNEXC(7)$	=	0.33
$FRNEXC(8)$	=	Foreign exchange on purchase of railroad fuel
$FRNEXC(8)$	=	0.33
$FRNEXC(9)$	=	Foreign exchange on purchase of lube oil
$FRNEXC(9)$	=	0.33

SHDPRF   =   Shadow price of foreign exchange factor (fraction of the expenditures added again as a surcharge)

SHDPRF   =   1.0

Other Scenario — Data
(See base scenario for definitions.)

Highway

Source of Data.

Cartier-Cote-Piette-Boulva-Wesmenlinger & Associates, Philippe Ewart & Associates, "The Ayalon Project, Feasibility Study and Engineering Report," prepared for Netivey Ayalon Limited, Tel-Aviv, 1968.

BCEOM, SETEC, "Economic Transportation Survey, I-Report," prepared for the Government of Israel, Ministry of Labour, 1966.

Government of Israel, Ministry of Transport, unpublished notes, received 1969.

Vehicle Cost.

COST(BULK)	=	12,600 $/vehicle
COST(GENERAL)	=	10,400 $/vehicle
COST(SPECIAL)	=	5,750 $/vehicle
COST(COMMON)	=	5,550 $/vehicle
COST(PRIVATE)	=	7,700 $/vehicle

Tire Cost.

TC(BULK)	=	100 $/tire
TC(GENERAL)	=	90 $/tire
TC(SPECIAL)	=	95 $/tire
TC(COMMON)	=	95 $/tire
TC(PRIVATE)	=	22 $/tire

Crew Wages.

UDT(BULK)	=	1.50 $/man-hour
UDT(GENERAL)	=	1.50 $/man-hour
UDT(SPECIAL)	=	1.50 $/man-hour
UDT(COMMON)	=	1.50 $/man-hour
UDT(PRIVATE)	=	0.90 $/man-hour

Fuel Cost.

FC(BULK)	=	0.108 $/U.S. gallon

FC(GENERAL)	=	0.108 $/U.S. gallon
FC(SPECIAL)	=	0.108 $/U.S. gallon
FC(COMMON)	=	0.108 $/U.S. gallon
FC(PRIVATE)	=	0.715 $/U.S. gallon

Oil Cost.

OILC	=	0.491 $/quart

Mechanics Wages.

WAGEM	=	1.80 $/man-hour

Way Maintenance.

CK8(PAVED)	=	685 $/mile/year
CK8(GRAVEL)	=	342 $/mile/year
CK8(EARTH)	=	101 $/mile/year
CK9(PAVED)	=	0.304 $/vehicle-mile/year
CK9(GRAVEL)	=	1.44 $/vehicle-mile/year
CK9(EARTH)	=	4.35 $/vehicle-mile/year

Railroad

Sources of Data.

BCEOM, SETEC, "Economic Transportation Survey, I-Report," prepared for the Government of Israel, Ministry of Labour, 1966.

Government of Israel, Ministry of Transport, unpublished notes, received 1969.

Locomotive Cost.

CSTLOC(1)	=	220,000 $/locomotive
CSTLOC(2)	=	185,000 $/locomotive
CSTLOC(3)	=	150,000 $/locomotive

Car Cost.

CARCST(BULK)	=	6,700 $/car
CARCST(GENERAL)	=	6,700 $/car
CARCST(SPECIAL)	=	8,700 $/car
CARCST(COMMON)	=	40,000 $/car

Cars and Other Rolling-Stock Maintenance.

*A*1	=	245 $/car-year
*B*1	=	0.023 $/car-mile

Locomotive Maintenance.
$A2$ = 4920 \$/locomotive-year
$B2$ = 0.376 \$/locomotive-mile

Way Maintenance.
$A3$ = 12,000 \$/mile-year
$B3$ = 0.0048 \$/gross ton-mile

Crew Cost.
$B4$ = 1.50 \$/train-mile

Fuel Cost.
$B5$ = 0.108 \$/U.S. gallon

Oil Cost.
$B6$ = 2 \$/U.S. gallon

Taxes

$TAX(1)$ = 0.1
$TAX(2)$ = 0.085
$TAX(3)$ = 0.25
$TAX(4)$ = 0
$TAX(5)$ = 0
$TAX(6)$ = 0
$TAX(7)$ = 0
$TAX(8)$ = 0
$TAX(9)$ = 0.1
$TAX(10)$ = 0.2
$TAX(11)$ = 500 \$/vehicle-year
$TAX(12)$ = 500 \$/vehicle-year
$TAX(13)$ = 500 \$/vehicle-year
$TAX(14)$ = 500 \$/vehicle-year
$TAX(15)$ = 181 \$/vehicle-year

Foreign Exchange

$FRNEXC(1)$ = 0.50
$FRNEXC(2)$ = 0.40
$FRNEXC(3)$ = 0.90

$FRNEXC(4)$ = 1.0
$FRNEXC(5)$ = 0.95
$FRNEXC(6)$ = 1.0
$FRNEXC(7)$ = 1.0
$FRNEXC(8)$ = 1.0
$FRNEXC(9)$ = 0.131
$SHDPRF$ = 0.3

Appendix B: Scenario Construction Cost Data and Definitions

General

The construction routine as described in Chapter 6 required two cost items to compute the construction cost of a road or a railroad. The first item is the unit surface cost and the second is the unit cost of earth movement. This appendix will explain the preparation of the cost items. Prices are in accordance with the conditions in the particular scenario and are expressed in equivalent U.S. dollars computed with the official exchange rate. The *FORTRAN* variable names are used for the input items with the index *ISURF* to identify the three surface types: *PAVED, GRAVEL*, and *EARTH*. Cross-section designs are based on engineering experience for average soil conditions and are assumed to be identical in all types of terrains considered in this project.

Base Scenario Definitions and Data

Highway

Design Features and Data Sources.
The roadway cross section is assumed to be built on a subgrade with adequate strength and good drainage. Dimensions of the roadbed, base, and pavement are shown in Figure B-1.

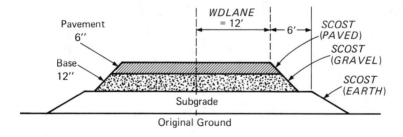

SCOST (PAVED) = 16700 $/lane mile
SCOST (GRAVEL) = 7700 $/lane mile
SCOST (EARTH) = 2700 $/lane mile
EWCOST = 0.3 $/cubic yard

Figure B-1. Physical Dimensions and Cost Data for the Highway Cross-Section.

Cost figures taken from unpublished engineers' notes of the Ministry of Public Works of Colombia (M.O.P.), 1966.

Surface.

$$\text{Cost/mile} = \frac{\text{depth} \times \text{width} \times \text{length}}{\text{ft.}^3/\text{yd.}^3} \times \text{cost/yd.}^3$$

Cost/cubic yard = 7.7 \$/yd.^{3}

$$\text{Cost/mile} = \frac{0.5 \text{ ft.} \times 12 \text{ ft./lane} \times 5280 \text{ ft./mi.}}{27 \text{ ft.}^3/\text{yd.}^3} \times 7.7 \text{ \$/yd.}^3 = 9035 \text{ \$/lane-mile}$$

Taken as 9000 \$/lane-mile.

Base.

$$\text{Cost/mile} = \frac{\text{depth} \times \text{width} \times \text{length}}{\text{ft.}^3/\text{yd.}^3} \times \text{cost/yd.}^3$$

Cost/cubic yard = 2.15 \$/yd.^{3}

$$\text{Cost/mile} = \frac{1 \text{ ft.} \times 12 \text{ ft./lane} \times 5280 \text{ ft./mi.}}{27 \text{ ft.}^3/\text{yd.}^3} \times 2.15 \text{ \$/yd.}^3 = 5045 \text{ \$/lane-mile.}$$

Taken as 5000 \$/lane-mile.

Subgrade Preparation.

$$\text{Cost/mile} = \frac{\text{width} \times \text{length}}{\text{ft.}^2/\text{yd.}^2} \times \text{cost/yd.}^2$$

Cost/square yard = 0.38 \$/yd.^{2}

$$\text{Cost/mile} = \frac{12 \text{ ft./lane} \times 5280 \text{ ft./mi.}}{9 \text{ ft.}^2/\text{yd.}^2} \times 0.38 \text{ \$/yd.}^2 = 2675 \text{ \$/lane-mile}$$

Taken as 2700 \$/lane-mile.

Excavation.
Cost/cubic yard = 0.3 \$/yd.^{2}

Summary.

SCOST(ISURF) = cost of surface per lane-mile by surface type

EWCOST = cost of earth work per cubic yard

SCOST(PAVED) = surface + base + subgrade preparation = 9000 + 5000 + 2700 = 16700 \$/lane-mile

SCOST(GRAVEL) = base + subgrade preparation = 5000 + 2700 = 7700 \$/lane-mile

SCOST(EARTH) = subgrade preparation = 2700 \$/lane-mile
EWCOST = 0.3 \$/yd.^{3}

Railroad

Design Features and Data Sources.

The rail cross-section is assumed to be built on a subgrade with adequate strength and good drainage. Dimensions of the roadbed, ballast, and track are shown in Figure B–2. Railroad standards are from Walter Lohring Webb, *Railroad Construction Theory and Practice,* New York, Wiley, 1922.

Cost figures are taken from "Economic Feasibility of a Railroad Extension to Barranquilla and Cartagena," prepared for the Colombia National Railroads by Madigan-Hyland, De la Cruz, 1965. Also from unpublished working papers of the Colombian National Railroads and interviews with their consultants and staff.

Rail.

Assume narrow-gauge (one meter) rail as exists in Colombia at 75 pounds per yard.

$$\text{Cost/mile} = \text{steel cost/ton} \ \frac{\text{No. of tracks} \times \text{length}}{\text{ft./yd.} \times \text{lbs./ton}} \ \text{rail weight/yd.}$$

$$\text{steel cost/ton} = 200 \ \$/\text{ton}$$

$$\text{Cost/mile} = \$200 \times \frac{2 \text{ tracks} \times 5280 \text{ ft./mi.}}{3 \text{ ft./yd.} \times 2240 \text{ lb./ton}} \times 75 \text{ lb./yd.} = 23{,}600 \ \$/\text{mile}$$

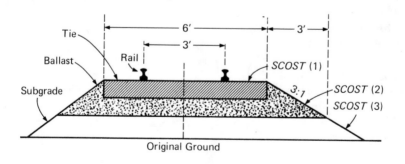

$SCOST$ (1) = 23,850 \$/½ track mile
$SCOST$ (2) = 3,850 \$/½ track mile
$SCOST$ (3) = 1,350 \$½ track mile
$EWCOST$ = 0.3 \$/cubic yard

Figure B–2. Physical Dimensions and Cost Data for the Rail Cross-Section.

Ties.
Assume tie spacing of 30 inches (2000 ties/mile).

Cost/tie   = 1.00 $/tie
Cost/mile = ties/mile × cost/tie
Cost/mile = 2000 ties/mile × 1.00 $/tie = 2000 $/mile

Other Track Material (OTM).
Assume OTM is 20 percent of rail cost.

Cost/mile = 0.2 × rail cost/mile
Cost/mile = 0.2 × 23,600 $/mile = 4,720 $/mile
Taken as 4,700 $/mile.

Ballast.
Assume 6′ ballast under ties and ignore volume of ties.

$$\text{Cost/mile} = [(\text{width} \times \text{depth}) + 2(\tfrac{1}{2}\text{depth} \times \text{slope})] \times \frac{\text{length}}{\text{ft.}^3/\text{yd.}^3} \times \frac{\text{cost}}{\text{yd.}^3}$$

Cost/cubic yard = 2.85 $/cubic yard

Cost/mile = [(6 ft. × 1 ft.) + 2 × (½ × 1 ft. × 3 ft.)]

$$\times \frac{5280 \text{ ft./mi.}}{27 \text{ ft.}^3/\text{yd.}^3} \times 2.85 \text{ \$/yd.}^3$$

$$= 5016 \text{ \$/mile}$$

Taken as 5000 $/mile.

Construction.
Cost/mile = 9700 $/mile

Subgrade Preparation.
Assume cost equal to that of subgrade preparation for one highway lane because of narrow overall width.

Cost/mile = 2700 $/mile

Summary.
$SCOST(1)$ = 1/2 rail + 1/2 ties + 1/2 OTM + 1/2 ballast + 1/2 construction

                + 1/2 subgrade preparation

            = 11,800 + 1,000 + 2,350 + 2,500 + 4,850 + 1,350

            = 23,850 $/½track-mile

$SCOST(2)$ = 1/2 ballast + 1/2 subgrade preparation

$$= \quad 2,500 + 1,350$$

$$= \quad 3,850 \text{ \$/½track mile}$$

$$SCOST(3) = \quad 1/2 \text{ subgrade preparation}$$

$$= \quad 1,350 \text{ \$/½track-mile.}$$

$$EWCOST = \quad 0.3 \text{ \$/cubic yard}$$

Other Scenario

Highway

Source of Data.
Cost figures are taken from Carteir Cote, et al., "The Ayalon Project Feasibility Study and Engineering Report," Tel-Aviv, 1968.

Surface.
Cost/cubic yard = 20.2 $/cubic yard
Cost/mile = 23,700 $/lane-mile

Base.
Cost/cubic yard = 7.2 $/cubic yard
Cost/mile = 16,900 $/lane-mile

Subgrade Preparation.
Cost/square yard = 0.7 $/square yard
Cost/mile = 4900 $/lane-mile

Excavation.
Cost/cubic yard = 0.54 $/cubic yard

Summary.

SCOST(PAVED)	=	23,700 + 16,900 + 4,900 = 45,000 $/lane-mile
SCOST(GRAVEL)	=	16,900 + 4,900 = 21,800 $/lane-mile
SCOST(EARTH)	=	4,900 $/lane-mile
EWCOST	=	0.54 $/cubic yard

Railroad

Source of Data.
Cost figures are taken from "Government of Israel — Economic Transportation Survey, I-Report," BCEOM-SETEC, 1966.

Rail.
Cost/mile = 18,750 $/mile

Ties.
Cost/tie = 10 $/tie
Cost/mile = 20,000 $/mile

Other Track Material (OTM).
Cost/mile = 0.2 × 18,750 $/mile = 3,750 $/mile

Ballast.
Cost/cubic yard = 8.0 $/cubic yard
Cost/mile = 14,000 $/mile

Construction.
Cost/mile = 14,000 $/mile

Subgrade Preparation.
Cost/mile = 4,900 $/mile

Summary.
$SCOST(1)$ = 9,375 + 10,000 + 1,875 + 7,000 + 7,000 + 2,450
          = 37,700 $/½track-mile
$SCOST(2)$ = 7,000 + 2,450
          = 9,450 $/½track-mile
$SCOST(3)$ = 2,450 $/½track-mile
$EWCOST$ = 0.54 $/cubic yard

Appendix C: Modal Technology Data and Definitions

General

It was assumed that vehicle characteristics and vehicle types in use for the various commodities change very little from country to country. This assumption is particularly justified for less developed nations. Following this assumption the modal technology data described in this appendix was used for all scenarios. The data is primarily based on the base scenario conditions and proved to be satisfactory when considered for the other scenario.

A typical vehicle or car is selected to represent average vehicle characteristics within each commodity class. For purposes of demonstration, consider the truck assigned to the commodity class *BULK*. This truck is specified here by its weight, payload, rated horsepower, and number of tires. In the base scenario a U.S.-made truck is used and its price was given to the variable *COST(BULK)* for the base scenario in Appendix A. In the other scenario an English-made truck with the same characteristics is used and the different price is assigned to *COST(BULK)* for other scenario.

The *FORTRAN* variable names are used throughout and the indices are the same as in Appendix A.

Highway

Vehicle Characteristics

W(ICLAS)	= vehicle weight by class
W(BULK)	= 9,000 pounds/vehicle
W(GENERAL)	= 8,000 pounds/vehicle
W(SPECIAL)	= 10,000 pounds/vehicle
W(COMMON)	= 9,000 pounds/vehicle
W(PRIVATE)	= 3,600 pounds/vehicle
PAYLOD(ICLAS)	= vehicle payload by class
PAYLOD(BULK)	= 10.30 tons/vehicle
PAYLOD(GENERAL)	= 7.16 tons/vehicle
PAYLOD(SPECIAL)	= 5.00 tons/vehicle
PAYLOD(COMMON)	= 3.57 tons/vehicle
PAYLOD(PRIVATE)	= 0.35 tons/vehicle

HP(ICLAS)	=	vehicle rated horsepower by class
HP(BULK)	=	275 HP/vehicle
HP(GENERAL)	=	195 HP/vehicle
HP(SPECIAL)	=	170 HP/vehicle
HP(COMMON)	=	170 HP/vehicle
HP(PRIVATE)	=	150 HP/vehicle
TIRES(ICLAS)	=	number of tires per vehicle by class
TIRES(BULK)	=	6 tires/vehicle
TIRES(GENERAL)	=	6 tires/vehicle
TIRES(SPECIAL)	=	6 tires/vehicle
TIRES(COMMON)	=	6 tires/vehicle
TIRES(PRIVATE)	=	4 tires/vehicle
TOTMIL(ICLAS)	=	lifetime vehicle mileage on paved roads by class
TOTMIL(BULK)	=	350,000 miles/vehicle
TOTMIL(GENERAL)	=	186,000 miles/vehicle
TOTMIL(SPECIAL)	=	186,000 miles/vehicle
TOTMIL(COMMON)	=	186,000 miles/vehicle
TOTMIL(PRIVATE)	=	70,000 miles/vehicle
AVEMI(ICLAS)	=	average vehicle mileage per year by class
AVEMI(BULK)	=	28,000 miles/year
AVEMI(GENERAL)	=	18,600 miles/year
AVEMI(SPECIAL)	=	18,600 miles/year
AVEMI(COMMON)	=	31,000 miles/year
AVEMI(PRIVATE)	=	10,000 miles/year
TIRLIF(ICLAS)	=	average tire life mileage per tire by class
TIRLIF(BULK)	=	30,000 miles/tire
TIRLIF(GENERAL)	=	30,000 miles/tire
TIRLIF(SPECIAL)	=	30,000 miles/tire
TIRLIF(COMMON)	=	30,000 miles/tire
TIRLIF(PRIVATE)	=	30,000 miles/tire
CREW(ICLAS)	=	average crew size in man per vehicle by class
CREW(BULK)	=	1.2 man/vehicle
CREW(GENERAL)	=	1.2 man/vehicle
CREW(SPECIAL)	=	1.2 man/vehicle
CREW(COMMON)	=	1.0 man/vehicle

CREW(PRIVATE)   =   1.0 man/vehicle

UMC(ICLAS)   =   maintenance cost for parts per vehicle-mile, as a percentage of initial vehicle cost by class

UMC(BULK)   = 7.5×10^{-7}
UMC(GENERAL)   = 1.22×10^{-6}
UMC(SPECIAL)   = 5.0×10^{-7}
UMC(COMMON)   = 7.6×10^{-7}
UMC(PRIVATE)   = 1.12×10^{-6}

ULT(ICLAS)   =   maintenance requirement for labor in hours per vehicle-mile by class

ULT(BULK)   =   0.005 hours/vehicle-mile
ULT(GENERAL)   =   0.008 hours/vehicle-mile
ULT(SPECIAL)   =   0.004 hours/vehicle-mile
ULT(COMMON)   =   0.003 hours/vehicle-mile
ULT(PRIVATE)   =   0.001 hours/vehicle-mile

OC(ICLAS)   =   oil consumption in quarts per mile on paved roads by class

OC(BULK)   =   0.0045 quarts/mile
OC(GENERAL)   =   0.006 quarts/mile
OC(SPECIAL)   =   0.005 quarts/mile
OC(COMMON)   =   0.006 quarts/mile
OC(PRIVATE)   =   0.005 quarts/mile

Road Characteristics

SCPWP   =   standard capacity per unit lane width for a paved surface in *PRIVATE* vehicles per hour
SCPWP   =   120 *PRIVATE* vehicles/hour/foot

Railroad

Locomotive Characteristics

HP(LT)   =   locomotive rated horsepower by locomotive type

HP(1)   =   1,500 HP/locomotive
HP(2)   =   1,200 HP/locomotive
HP(3)   =   800 HP/locomotive

WL(LT)   = locomotive weight by locomotive type

WL(1)   = 100 tons/locomotive
WL(2)   =   90 tons/locomotive
WL(3)   =   80 tons/locomotive

A(LT)   = locomotive frontal area by locomotive type

A(1)   = 100 square feet
A(2)   = 100 square feet
A(3)   =   90 square feet

AXLES(LT)   = number of driving axles on each locomotive

AXLES(1)   = 6 axles/locomotive
AXLES(2)   = 6 axles/locomotive
AXLES(3)   = 6 axles/locomotive

FUEL(LT)   = fuel-consumption rate in gallons per rated HP-hour by locomotive type

FUEL(1)   = 0.025 U.S. gallon/HP-hour
FUEL(2)   = 0.025 U.S. gallon/HP-hour
FUEL(3)   = 0.025 U.S. gallon/HP-hour

OR   = oil ratio in gallons of fuel oil per gallon of lubricating oil

OR   = 32

SLOCLF(LT)   = standard locomotive life by locomotive type

SLOCLF(1)   = 15 years
SLOCLF(2)   = 15 years
SLOCLF(3)   = 15 years

RFLOC(LT)   = locomotive reserve factor, expressed as a fraction of the number of locomotives, by locomotive type

RFLOC(1)   = 0.40
RFLOC(2)   = 0.40
RFLOC(3)   = 0.40

YTL(LT)   = typical locomotives yard time by locomotive type

YTL(1)   = 4 hours
YTL(2)   = 4 hours
YTL(3)   = 4 hours

Car Characteristics

W(ICLAS)	= car weight by class
W(BULK)	= 13 tons/car
W(GENERAL)	= 13 tons/car
W(SPECIAL)	= 13 tons/car
W(COMMON)	= 20 tons/car
PAYLOD(ICLAS)	= car payload by class
PAYLOD(BULK)	= 30 tons/car
PAYLOD(GENERAL)	= 30 tons/car
PAYLOD(SPECIAL)	= 20 tons/car
PAYLOD(COMMON)	= 6 tons/car
CARLIF(ICLAS)	= typical car life by class
CARLIF(BULK)	= 35 years
CARLIF(GENERAL)	= 35 years
CARLIF(SPECIAL)	= 35 years
CARLIF(COMMON)	= 35 years
CARRF(ICLAS)	= car reserve factor, expressed as a fraction of the number of cars, by class
CARRF(BULK)	= 0.12
CARRF(GENRAL)	= 0.12
CARRF(SPECIAL)	= 0.10
CARRF(COMMON)	= 0.15
YTC(ICLAS)	= typical car yard time by class
YTC(BULK)	= 5 hours
YTC(GENERAL)	= 5 hours
YTC(SPECIAL)	= 5 hours
YTC(COMMON)	= 4 hours
THAND(ICLAS)	= average handling time per car by class
THAND(BULK)	= 0.1 hours/car
THAND(GENERAL)	= 0.2 hours/car
THAND(SPECIAL)	= 0.2 hours/car
THAND(COMMON)	= 0.1 hours/car

Appendix D: Results

The barest summary of the voluminous results generated by this study have been brought together in this appendix. Tables D-1 to D-4 contain results of project analysis. Table D-5 contains the sensitivity analysis results. The highway-railroad project analysis was performed completely for the base scenario and for the other scenario, results from the former appearing in Tables in D-1, D-2, and the latter in D-3, D-4. Each analysis covered a 20-year period, and future costs were discounted to the present at a 15 percent discount rate. Each box in a table shows the present discounted value of forecast components, their total, and an adjusted total for a single project condition. The adjusted total has excluded taxes and applied a shadow price to foreign exchange costs. Three different terrains are covered, three volume levels, and three commodity mixes are considered for each facility. (See Chapter 3.) Note that the designs of a given facility will be different in each terrain and may be different for each volume level. (See Chapter 6.) Projects may be compared by selecting a terrain, a volume level, and a commodity mix, then seeing which of the three possible projects has the lowest total or adjusted total cost. Tables D-1 and D-3 include market plus nonmarket costs, while Tables D-2 and D-4 include market costs only, and show only the total and adjusted total costs. (See Chapter 5.)

Table D-5 contains the results of the sensitivity analysis study. (See Chapter 8.) It examines the sensitivity of costs to various 10-percent changes in factor prices at three volume levels for three facilities. The original costs are shown in the bottom set of boxes, and will be seen to be identical with the costs of Table D-1 for hilly terrain and balanced traffic (fourth row of boxes in D-1). The first row of boxes shows the costs incurred when the interest rate is raised 10 percent. The second row of boxes shows the costs when interest is at its initial value but fuel and oil prices are raised 10 percent and so forth. All costs are present discounted values, in thousands of dollars.

Table D-1
Results of Project Analysis; Costs of Alternative Projects, Market Plus Nonmarket (Base Scenario) Present Discounted Value, Thousands of U.S. Dollars, 20 Years, 15 Percent

Terrain	Commodity Mix	Old Road 100 Tons/Day	Old Road 1000 Tons/Day	Old Road 5000 Tons/Day	New Highway 100 Tons/Day	New Highway 1000 Tons/Day	New Highway 5000 Tons/Day	New Railroad 100 Tons/Day	New Railroad 1000 Tons/Day	New Railroad 5000 Tons/Day
Flat	Balanced flow	0[a]	0	0	3,369	3,369	3,369	4,799	8,954	8,954
		225	382	1,106	269	291	393	0	0	0
		2,854	22,942	136,320	1,319	10,826	54,669	4,325	6,441	23,786
		1,905	15,890	105,709	1,004	6,506	33,407	5,196	23,519	74,080
		4,984	39,214	243,135	5,961	20,992	91,838	14,320	38,914	106,820
		5,010	39,166	239,329	5,984	21,107	91,706	14,665	39,551	111,749
	Bulk dominated	0	0	0	3,369	3,369	3,369	4,799	8,954	8,954
		226	402	1,207	269	294	407	0	0	0
		2,951	24,815	151,889	1,368	11,660	59,293	4,427	7,333	29,734
		1,680	13,889	95,915	888	5,617	29,456	4,063	19,130	65,665
		4,857	39,105	249,011	5,894	20,940	92,526	13,289	35,417	104,353
		4,878	39,033	244,535	5,917	21,063	92,271	13,640	36,413	110,884
	General dominated	0	0	0	3,369	3,369	3,369	4,799	8,954	8,954
		228	423	1,314	269	297	422	0	0	0
		3,174	27,125	174,003	1,462	12,608	64,907	4,428	7,343	29,827
		2,002	17,798	129,122	991	7,183	39,171	5,268	24,567	83,176
		5,404	45,346	304,439	6,091	23,457	107,868	14,495	40,863	121,957
		5,440	45,409	299,585	6,121	23,647	107,728	14,846	41,869	128,572
Hilly	Balanced flow	0	0	0	3,689	7,827	11,817	9,883	15,995	15,995
		300	509	1,475	282	291	393	0	0	0
		4,596	39,238	451,211	2,012	11,454	54,669	5,166	6,813	23,786
		2,663	26,029	379,092	1,425	7,500	33,407	4,914	22,497	74,080
		7,559	65,775	831,777	7,408	27,072	100,286	19,963	45,305	113,861
		7,423	63,809	802,584	7,287	26,880	100,154	20,321	46,098	118,790
	Bulk dominated	0	0	0	3,689	7,827	11,817	9,883	15,995	15,995
		301	535	1,610	283	294	407	0	0	0
		4,752	42,825	545,838	2,075	12,295	59,293	5,287	7,603	29,734
		2,352	23,260	373,124	1,270	6,513	29,456	3,792	17,324	65,665
		7,405	66,621	920,571	7,316	26,930	100,974	18,963	40,922	111,394
		7,255	64,483	887,193	7,189	26,742	100,719	19,302	41,742	117,925

200

Mountainous

Category	Item									
General dominated	Construction	0	0	0	3,689	7,827	11,817	9,883	15,995	15,995
	Maintenance of way	304	564	1,753	283	297	422	0	0	0
	Market cost	5,089	47,500	726,072	2,217	13,304	64,907	5,288	7,610	29,827
	Nonmarket	2,849	30,432	573,643	1,468	8,305	39,171	4,900	22,169	83,176
	Total	8,243	78,497	1,301,467	7,656	29,733	116,316	20,071	45,775	128,998
	Adjusted total	8,107	76,352	1,257,622	7,530	29,602	116,176	20,410	46,602	135,613
Balanced flow	Construction	0	0	0	4,379	4,716	11,537	9,118	14,695	58,148
	Maintenance of way	375	636	1,843	350	407	510	0	0	0
	Market cost	7,118	63,995	1,070,009	2,251	18,144	93,416	8,913	20,254	84,163
	Nonmarket	3,819	42,300	919,257	1,521	11,444	63,920	5,026	39,630	134,049
	Total	11,312	106,931	1,991,109	8,501	34,712	169,383	23,056	74,579	276,361
	Adjusted total	10,908	102,039	1,917,547	8,402	33,940	164,563	24,041	81,099	307,313
Bulk dominated	Construction	0	0	0	4,379	4,716	11,537	9,118	14,695	58,148
	Maintenance of way	376	669	2,012	350	411	529	0	0	0
	Market cost	7,362	70,255	1,329,220	2,330	19,574	102,944	9,237	24,096	113,924
	Nonmarket	3,382	38,117	927,101	1,355	10,048	57,561	3,892	32,925	124,636
	Total	11,120	109,041	2,258,332	8,413	34,749	172,570	22,247	71,716	296,708
	Adjusted total	10,690	103,797	2,173,426	8,308	33,932	167,312	23,164	80,045	340,951
General dominated	Construction	0	0	0	4,379	4,716	11,537	9,118	14,695	58,148
	Maintenance of way	380	705	2,191	350	415	548	0	0	0
	Market cost	7,873	78,355	1,753,074	2,487	21,224	115,232	9,238	24,114	114,169
	Nonmarket	4,136	49,860	1,402,479	1,576	12,748	76,234	5,018	42,522	155,169
	Total	12,389	128,920	3,157,743	8,793	39,103	203,551	23,373	81,330	327,486
	Adjusted total	11,965	123,462	3,045,467	8,691	38,344	198,098	24,291	89,676	371,955

[a] Legend:
Construction
Maintenance of way
Market cost
Nonmarket
Total
Adjusted total

Table D-2
Results of Project Analysis; Costs of Alternative Projects, Market Only (Base Scenario)
Present Discounted Value, Thousands of U.S. Dollars, 20 Years, 15 Percent

Terrain	Commodity Mix		Old Road			New Highway			New Railroad		
			100 Tons/Day	1000 Tons/Day	5000 Tons/Day	100 Tons/Day	1000 Tons/Day	5000 Tons/Day	100 Tons/Day	1000 Tons/Day	5000 Tons/Day
Flat	Balanced flow	Total	3,079[a]	23,324	137,426	4,957	14,486	58,431	9,124	15,395	32,740
		Adjusted	3,105	23,276	133,621	4,980	14,601	58,300	9,469	16,033	37,669
	Bulk dominated	Total	3,177	25,216	153,096	5,006	15,323	63,069	9,226	16,287	38,688
		Adjusted	3,199	25,145	148,620	5,029	15,445	62,814	9,577	17,283	45,219
	General dominated	Total	3,401	27,548	175,317	5,100	16,273	68,698	9,227	16,297	38,781
		Adjusted	3,438	27,611	170,463	5,130	16,463	68,557	9,578	17,302	45,397
Hilly	Balanced flow	Total	4,896	39,747	452,686	5,983	19,572	66,879	15,049	22,808	39,781
		Adjusted	4,760	37,780	423,492	5,862	19,381	66,748	15,407	23,601	44,710
	Bulk dominated	Total	5,053	43,361	547,448	6,046	20,416	71,517	15,170	23,598	45,729
		Adjusted	4,903	41,222	514,070	5,919	20,228	71,262	15,509	24,419	52,260
	General dominated	Total	5,393	48,064	727,825	6,188	21,428	77,146	15,171	23,605	45,822
		Adjusted	5,258	45,920	683,980	6,062	21,296	77,005	15,510	24,433	52,438
Mountainous	Balanced flow	Total	7,493	64,631	1,071,852	6,980	23,268	105,463	18,031	34,949	142,311
		Adjusted	7,089	59,739	998,291	6,881	22,496	100,642	19,015	41,469	173,263
	Bulk dominated	Total	7,739	70,924	1,331,231	7,058	24,701	115,009	18,355	38,791	172,072
		Adjusted	7,309	65,680	1,246,325	6,952	23,884	109,751	19,273	47,121	216,315
	General dominated	Total	8,253	79,060	1,755,264	7,217	26,355	127,317	18,356	38,809	172,317
		Adjusted	7,829	73,602	1,642,988	7,115	25,597	121,864	19,273	47,155	216,785

[a] Legend:
Total
Adjusted total

203

Table D-3
Results of Project Analysis; Costs of Alternative Projects, Market Plus Nonmarket (Other Scenario) Present Discounted Value, Thousands of U.S. Dollars, 20 Years, 15 Percent

Terrain	Commodity Mix	Old Road			New Highway			New Railroad		
		100 Tons/Day	1000 Tons/Day	5000 Tons/Day	100 Tons/Day	1000 Tons/Day	5000 Tons/Day	100 Tons/Day	1000 Tons/Day	5000 Tons/Day
Flat	Balanced flow	0[a]	0	0	9,152	9,152	9,152	7,592	15,070	15,070
		854	1,449	4,193	1,023	1,107	1,493	0	0	0
		4,894	37,562	254,358	2,046	15,370	83,204	12,395	18,235	53,756
		1,905	15,890	105,709	1,004	6,506	33,407	5,196	23,519	74,080
		7,653	54,901	364,261	13,226	32,135	126,256	25,183	56,824	142,907
		7,384	51,765	334,836	13,196	31,481	121,459	25,156	56,747	143,567
	Bulk dominated	0	0	0	9,152	9,152	9,152	7,592	15,070	15,070
		858	1,524	4,577	1,024	1,118	1,547	0	0	0
		4,984	40,401	282,944	2,085	16,527	89,773	12,684	20,048	64,076
		1,680	13,889	95,915	888	5,617	29,456	4,063	19,130	65,665
		7,521	55,813	383,436	13,149	32,414	129,928	24,338	54,248	144,811
		7,244	52,596	351,025	13,119	31,793	124,928	24,269	54,168	145,587
	General dominated	0	0	0	9,152	9,152	9,152	7,592	15,070	15,070
		866	1,605	4,983	1,025	1,129	1,605	0	0	0
		5,459	45,433	336,867	2,277	18,475	102,604	12,684	20,056	64,168
		2,002	17,798	129,122	991	7,183	39,171	5,268	24,567	83,176
		8,327	64,836	470,972	13,445	35,939	152,531	25,544	59,693	162,414
		7,989	60,946	429,529	13,394	35,110	145,763	25,475	59,615	163,210
Hilly	Balanced flow	0	0	0	9,883	17,177	24,358	16,535	27,745	27,745
		1,139	1,931	5,591	1,075	1,107	1,493	0	0	0
		7,871	66,511	980,011	3,487	17,524	82,204	14,940	19,157	53,756
		2,663	26,029	379,092	1,425	7,500	33,407	4,914	22,495	74,080
		11,674	94,471	1,364,692	15,869	43,308	141,462	36,389	69,399	155,582
		11,255	88,651	1,215,815	15,711	42,217	136,665	36,335	69,333	156,242
	Bulk dominated	0	0	0	9,883	17,177	24,358	16,535	27,745	27,745
		1,143	2,032	6,102	1,075	1,118	1,547	0	0	0
		8,030	72,604	1,171,304	3,537	18,657	89,773	15,347	21,384	64,076
		2,352	23,260	373,122	1,270	6,513	29,456	3,792	17,324	65,665
		11,525	97,896	1,550,528	15,765	43,465	145,134	35,675	66,452	157,486
		11,093	91,638	1,371,903	15,606	42,406	140,134	35,556	66,242	158,262

204

Table (rotated on page). Row group: **Mountainous**. Row items per legend: Construction, Maintenance of way, Market cost, Nonmarket, Total, Adjusted total.

Group	Item									
General dominated	Construction	27,745	27,745	16,535	24,358	17,177	9,883	0	0	0
	Maintenance of way	0	0	0	1,605	1,129	1,076	6,644	2,140	1,154
	Market cost	64,168	21,390	15,348	102,604	20,815	3,850	1,623,400	83,592	8,764
	Nonmarket	83,176	22,169	4,900	39,171	8,305	1,468	573,641	30,432	2,849
	Total	175,089	71,304	36,783	167,737	47,427	16,277	2,203,685	116,164	12,767
	Adjusted total	175,885	71,095	36,663	160,969	46,106	16,075	1,943,441	108,174	12,235
Balanced flow	Construction	102,888	24,360	14,599	24,781	12,826	12,006	0	0	0
	Maintenance of way	0	0	0	1,941	1,550	1,331	6,988	2,414	1,424
	Market cost	136,178	44,341	24,994	164,014	29,258	3,869	2,423,737	113,468	12,536
	Nonmarket	134,050	39,630	5,026	63,921	11,444	1,521	919,259	42,300	3,819
	Total	373,116	108,330	44,619	254,657	55,078	18,762	3,349,984	158,182	17,779
	Adjusted total	381,364	109,636	44,610	238,593	52,908	18,539	2,957,921	147,344	17,091
Bulk dominated	Construction	102,888	24,360	14,599	24,781	12,826	12,006	0	0	0
	Maintenance of way	0	0	0	2,012	1,565	1,331	7,628	2,539	1,429
	Market cost	172,438	50,319	26,059	180,750	31,448	3,958	2,956,396	124,441	12,806
	Nonmarket	124,636	32,924	3,892	57,561	10,048	1,355	927,108	38,117	3,382
	Total	399,963	107,603	44,550	265,104	55,887	18,650	3,891,131	165,097	17,617
	Adjusted total	411,719	109,214	44,393	247,586	53,659	18,455	3,412,630	153,361	16,903
General dominated	Construction	102,888	24,360	14,599	24,781	12,826	12,006	0	0	0
	Maintenance of way	0	0	0	2,086	1,581	1,333	8,305	2,675	1,443
	Market cost	172,665	50,333	26,060	210,324	35,075	4,299	4,034,872	143,799	13,937
	Nonmarket	155,170	45,522	5,018	76,234	12,748	1,576	1,402,492	49,860	4,136
	Total	430,722	117,215	45,676	313,426	62,229	19,214	5,445,669	196,334	19,516
	Adjusted total	442,535	118,833	45,520	291,094	59,506	18,973	4,770,603	181,429	18,640

[a] Legend:
Construction
Maintenance of way
Market cost
Nonmarket
Total
Adjusted total

Table D-4

Results of Project Analysis; Costs of Alternative Projects, Market Only (Other Scenario) Present Discounted Value, Thousands of U.S. Dollars, 20 Years, 15 Percent

Terrain	Commodity Mix		Old Road			New Highway			New Railroad		
			100 Tons/Day	1000 Tons/Day	5000 Tons/Day	100 Tons/Day	1000 Tons/Day	5000 Tons/Day	100 Tons/Day	1000 Tons/Day	5000 Tons/Day
Flat	Balanced flow	Total	5,748[a]	39,011	258,551	12,222	25,630	92,850	19,987	33,305	68,826
		Adjusted	5,479	35,875	229,127	12,192	24,975	88,052	19,960	33,229	69,487
	Bulk dominated	Total	5,842	41,924	287,521	12,261	26,797	100,472	20,276	35,118	79,146
		Adjusted	5,564	38,708	255,109	12,230	26,176	95,471	20,206	35,038	79,922
	General dominated	Total	6,325	47,038	341,850	12,454	28,756	113,360	20,276	35,126	79,238
		Adjusted	5,987	43,148	300,407	12,403	27,927	106,592	20,207	35,048	80,035
Hilly	Balanced flow	Total	9,010	68,443	985,601	14,444	35,808	108,056	31,475	46,902	81,501
		Adjusted	8,592	62,623	836,725	14,286	34,717	103,258	31,421	46,836	82,162
	Bulk dominated	Total	9,173	74,635	1,177,406	14,496	36,951	115,678	31,882	49,129	91,821
		Adjusted	8,741	68,378	998,782	14,336	35,892	110,677	31,763	48,918	92,597
	General dominated	Total	9,918	85,731	1,630,044	14,809	39,122	128,566	31,883	49,135	91,913
		Adjusted	9,385	77,742	1,369,800	14,607	37,800	121,798	31,763	48,925	92,710
Mountainous	Balanced flow	Total	13,960	115,882	2,430,725	17,205	43,634	190,737	39,593	68,701	239,066
		Adjusted	13,272	105,044	2,038,662	17,018	41,464	174,672	39,585	70,006	247,314
	Bulk dominated	Total	14,235	126,980	2,964,023	17,295	45,838	207,543	40,658	74,679	275,326
		Adjusted	13,521	115,244	2,485,522	17,100	43,610	190,025	40,502	76,293	287,083
	General dominated	Total	15,380	146,474	4,043,177	17,638	49,482	237,191	40,659	74,693	275,553
		Adjusted	14,504	131,569	3,368,111	17,397	46,758	214,859	40,502	76,312	287,365

[a] Legend:
Total
Adjusted total

207

Table D-5
Results of Sensitivity Analysis: Costs Resulting From Specified Factor Price Changes (Base Scenario, Hilly Terrain, Balanced Flow) Present Discounted Value, Thousands of U.S. Dollars, 20 Years, 15 Percent

Factor Price Change	Old Road			New Highway			New Railroad		
	100 Tons/Day	1000 Tons/Day	5000 Tons/Day	100 Tons/Day	1000 Tons/Day	5000 Tons/Day	100 Tons/Day	1000 Tons/Day	5000 Tons/Day
Interest rate (+10%)	0[a]	0	0	3,689	7,827	11,817	9,883	15,995	15,995
	277	470	1,360	261	268	362	0	0	0
	4,310	36,756	426,782	1,886	10,690	50,995	4,797	6,352	22,222
	2,457	24,014	349,750	1,315	6,919	30,821	4,534	20,756	68,346
	7,044	61,240	777,892	7,150	25,705	93,996	19,213	43,103	106,563
	6,922	59,455	751,511	7,039	25,534	93,904	19,574	43,999	111,377
Fuel and Oil (+10%)	0	0	0	3,699	7,858	11,868	9,918	16,063	16,063
	300	509	1,475	282	291	393	0	0	0
	4,737	40,515	457,587	2,084	11,832	56,383	5,171	6,845	24,483
	2,663	26,029	379,092	1,425	7,500	33,407	4,914	22,497	74,080
	7,700	67,053	838,154	7,491	27,481	102,051	20,003	45,405	114,626
	7,530	64,769	807,377	7,351	27,197	101,504	20,363	46,206	119,738
Aggregate (+10%)	0	0	0	3,777	7,911	11,900	9,941	16,043	16,043
	304	515	1,493	286	295	398	0	0	0
	4,596	39,238	451,211	2,012	11,454	54,669	5,177	6,825	23,809
	2,663	26,029	379,092	1,425	7,500	33,407	4,914	22,497	74,080
	7,563	65,782	831,796	7,500	27,160	100,374	20,032	45,365	113,932
	7,427	63,815	802,602	7,378	26,968	100,242	20,390	46,157	118,860
Wages (+10%)	0	0	0	3,817	8,057	12,146	10,130	16,395	16,395
	320	543	1,574	301	311	419	0	0	0
	4,692	40,174	468,090	2,055	11,671	55,654	5,441	7,161	24,651
	2,663	26,029	379,093	1,425	7,500	33,407	4,914	22,497	74,080
	7,676	66,746	848,757	7,598	27,539	101,626	20,485	46,053	115,126
	7,520	64,592	816,188	7,468	27,304	101,298	20,841	46,841	120,041

	Construction	Maintenance of way	Market cost	Nonmarket	Total	Adjusted total
Imports (+10%)						
	0	304	4,779	2,663	7,746	7,643
	0	517	40,668	26,029	67,214	65,500
	0	1,498	472,953	379,093	853,543	826,375
	3,799	287	2,086	1,425	7,596	7,487
	8,040	295	11,812	7,500	27,647	27,533
	12,129	398	56,352	33,407	102,287	102,537
	10,274	0	5,375	4,914	20,563	20,959
	16,514	0	7,086	22,497	46,097	46,965
	16,514	0	24,548	74,080	115,142	120,393
Base costs						
	0	300	4,596	2,663	7,559	7,423
	0	509	39,238	26,029	65,775	63,809
	0	1,475	451,211	379,092	831,777	802,584
	3,689	282	2,012	1,425	7,408	7,287
	7,827	291	11,454	7,500	27,072	26,880
	11,817	393	54,669	33,407	100,286	100,154
	9,883	0	5,166	4,914	19,963	20,321
	15,995	0	6,813	22,497	45,305	46,098
	15,995	0	23,786	74,080	113,861	118,790

a Legend:
Construction
Maintenance of way
Market cost
Nonmarket
Total
Adjusted total

Appendix E: The Air Cost Performance Model

Introduction

The air model will, with the specification of appropriate input data, develop fleet size and costs for aircraft operations and facilities that may be aggregated to obtain total annual air transport costs. Four homogeneous fleet types may be considered in the basic model, which for this study were selected as follows:

small piston: DC-3
large piston: DC-6 (A,B)
turboprop: L-188 Electra, L-100
turbojet: DC-9

For each group the aircraft type chosen is one that has in the past proven economical for short-haul service. Of course, the performance of other aircraft types may be evaluated as well, if desired.

Performance on a link is determined by three sets of basic information: (1) physical characteristics of airport location and route; (2) the volume and character of goods being carried and the resultant number of aircraft; and, (3) the performance charcteristics of the aircraft themselves. For each air link a set of vehicle performance measures is presented. Results include a breakdown showing cost components such as fuel, crew, maintenance, depreciation, etc. In addition, total foreign exchange in each of several categories will be presented. When aggregated over the entire fleet, and when nonvehicle costs are added, a single daily or yearly cost results.

Development of the Model

The development of the air model was heavily conditioned by problems of data availability. No systematic data exists on aircraft operations in the developing countries that permits statistical estimation of cost or productivity relationships between aircraft type and either the nature of the route system or traffic density. Reported costs on international operators aggregated at the firm level restricts statistical cost analyses to fairly limited models relating costs to aggregate or average measures of route system characteristics, such as average stage length or station density. Because of this level of aggregation in the data, only fairly aggregated measures of the effects on costs of choosing different aircraft or relative factor proportions can be developed statistically. Moreover, the resultant statistical estimates of the structure of costs and productivity differences among firms are most reliable in making comparisons and inferences among a subset of

211

the sample — the larger long-haul international carriers operating a relatively homogeneous aircraft fleet.[1]

Accordingly, the air model was developed in a simulation framework, much in the spirit of the other modal models. Cost and productivity equations were developed from a variety of sources. In some instances, the equations were estimated econometrically using data drawn from short-haul operations in the United States. Labor productivity and factor price variables were included in each equation in the model, to serve as a means of calibrating the model to experience in the developing countries.

Costs can be broken down into direct operating costs, indirect operating costs (excluding airport and terminal user charges), and fixed facilities costs. The first two categories usually accrue to the airlines. The third includes all airport and enroute navigation and communication equipment expenses and these costs typically accrue to various units of the federal or local government. As will be seen below, different costing procedures have been used in each case in developing equations in the model. The following outlines, in summary, fashion the basic procedure for developing each of these three portions of the model. The specific equations for each component, data sources, and the input data used in the simulation runs are described in detail in the next section of this appendix.

Direct Operating Costs

Direct operating costs denotes all expenses associated with operating the aircraft itself. The categories are as follows:

Flight crew:	pilots, copilots, and navigation costs (but excluding all cabin personnel)
Fuel and oil:	fuel and oil
Maintenance:	labor, parts, and overhead of maintenance
Depreciation:	for aircraft and spare parts
Insurance:	aircraft and passenger and cargo liability insurance

An equation is developed for each component, relating cost to the type of aircraft used and the length of haul defining the link. Most of the direct operating cost equations in the model are a modification of cost equations developed by the Air Transport Association (ATA) for estimating the costs of aircraft operations.[2] That model relates cost components by aircraft type to technological factors describing the aircraft (such as engine weight), scheduling or input utilization measures (hours between overhauls, for example), and input price variables. The ATA model has been widely accepted in the airline industry. The most recent

---

1. Mahlon Straszheim, *The International Airline Industry* (Washington, D.C.: The Brookings Institution, 1969), Chap. 4 and app. B.

2. *Standard Method for Estimating Comparative Direct Operating Costs,* Air Transport Association of America.

revision of the ATA equations, in 1967, was used as a basis for costing jet and
turboprop aircraft operations. The latest revision of ATA's piston-operating cost
equations was 1960.

Several modifications in the ATA formulas were necessary for the equations
to be useful in representing experience in the developing countries. One such
modification was the inclusion of labor productivity variables. Labor productivity
differences will occur as the result of many factors, but most importantly they
reflect the technology used in a particular operation. Experience in the United
States incorporates a highly capital intensive technology that may not be generally
appropriate for certain operations in the less developed countries. Working conditions and skill levels may also be somewhat different. In some instances, a productivity variable was added to the equation; for example, a variable defined as the
ratio of labor productivity of maintenance personnel in the country in question
to U.S. labor productivity was included as a variable in the equations determining
maintenance labor requirements. In other instances input productivity measures
are implicit in other variables; for example, in the equation for crew costs, the
variable "average pay per block hour" will reflect pilot wage rates and productivity, or how intensively pilots are utilized. There may be substantial differences in
the wages and productivity; these can easily be included in this input variable in
the model.

The direct operating cost equations also include input variables which in part
reflect management practice, and in some cases "scheduling expertise." The
most notable cases are "hours between overhauls" and "daily aircraft utilization."
The former is a critical determinant of aircraft maintenance costs. The latter is
affected by both scheduling abilities of carrier management and by the nature of
the route system.

Aircraft utilization is a particularly important variable in this model, but difficult to specify because to a considerable extent it reflects a variety of considerations that are of a "systems" character rather than having reference to a particular link. As the cost model developed here is for a single link, and average daily
utilization rate for aircraft must be included as an input variable. Conceptually
this assumption is no different than using variables that represent averages for
crew costs, productivity, or maintenance requirements as input variables in modeling costs for a single link. However, the importance of aircraft utilization on capital costs must be stressed, especially when interest rates are high. In using the
model for analysis of new air operations in less developed countries, great care
must be taken in specifying this input variable.

Scheduling, route system characteristics, weather, hours of daylight, and
available navigational aids all affect utilization. With regard to the route system,
shorter stage lengths and lower route densities aggravate scheduling problems,
especially for jets with great productive potential. The particular level of utilization feasible will depend on the nature of airline demand and the route system.
Unfortunately, models relating utilization to the nature of the route system —
either stage lengths or density of traffic on each link — are unavailable. Program-

ming models that route aircraft over networks are in their infancy. It is not possible to generalize about aircraft utilization on a given link without considering the entire route system.

The demand characteristics of the routes in question can be quite important. For example, predominantly tourist markets are more likely to accept schedules that lie in the offpeak hours. Determining the effects of different mixes of business versus tourist-oriented markets on feasible schedules is a complex marketing task.

Furthermore, achievable levels of utilization also depend heavily on the quality of airline management. The latter appears to vary widely among international operators and actual examination of smaller domestic operators in the less developed countries reinforces this conclusion. In short, no simple model of utilization seems a good substitute for careful attention to actual levels of utilization achieved by the carriers in queston. Overly optimistic utilization assumptions on short-haul systems has often led to disappointing cost results when new jet aircraft are introduced.

Finally, of course, the ATA model as modified for our purposes includes a variety of factor price variables. These are the rate of interest, labor wages, fuel costs, insurance rates, and material parts. In the case of material used in maintenance, the model includes both original prices for parts and current parts prices.

These modifications of the ATA equations provide a very flexible format for representing operating costs in a developing country under different factor price and productivity assumptions. The quality of the results of the model will, of course, depend on whether the input variables are properly specified. Calibration is thus extremely important. For example, maintenance is the most important component of piston-operating costs. These costs are likely to differ in the developing countries from the United States experience reflected in the ATA equations for maintenance. The modified equations used in the air model are capable of representing these differences. Four variables provide this capability, of which the wage rate is included in the principal ATA formulation. The other three are: maintenance labor productivity (a ratio of productivity in the country in question relative to U.S. levels); current used-engine prices relative to original prices; and current used-airframe-parts prices relative to original prices. These latter two price ratios may be significantly different from those for older piston aircraft where used or rebuilt parts are all that are available, often only at very high prices. The relevant values will depend in part on the country's location. Calibration of the equations of labor and parts expenses making up total maintenance costs is possible by adjusting all these input variables.

Indirect Operating Costs

Airline indirect costs include all of those costs that arise in running an airline that are not directly connected with aircraft operations and maintenance. Excluded, however, are costs of airport facility and costs of navigational aids such as runway, tower, and electrical equipment (or user charges for using such facilities). No model exists that relates indirect costs to aircraft type and the character of the particular link in quesiton which is equivalent to the ATA model for direct operating costs.

A largely synthetic cost model was developed. Most indirect expenses can be associated with activity at the two terminals in question. Accordingly, the model first estimates indirect operating costs on a per station or terminal basis. Two categories of inputs were considered in defining these costs — labor requirements and all nonlabor input costs. A share of these costs of operating the two terminals are then assigned to the particular link in question.

There are no satisfactory data on operations in the developing countries to estimate these cost-per-terminal relationships empirically. United States data for local-service carriers aggregated at the firm level was used. Regression analysis was used to relate terminal costs to the level and mix of cargo and passenger traffic and to summary measures of the route system such as average stage length. Since factor prices in the United States (and presumably factor proportions) are so atypical of what is of interest in this model, this regression analysis is not useful for delineating the *relative mix* of labor and nonlabor inputs that carriers in the developing countries are likely to use in indirect operations, nor the *level* of costs of either labor or nonlabor inputs. For this purpose, two additional variables are introduced, and these complete the model. The two variables are essentially means of scaling the initial estimates of labor requirements and nonlabor costs per terminal to levels appropriate for the country in question. They have been labeled the "wages" of indirect labor and the relative "price" of nonlabor inputs. This allows an adjustment for different factor prices (or productivity differences); the model user can represent a range of alternative factor costs and proportions by scaling the initial estimates based on United States experience up or down.

A brief further comment on the use of regression analysis for the U.S. local-service carriers is in order. Statistical costing procedures of this sort have been shown to be particularly useful as a means of relating common costs to the mix of passenger and freight operations.[3]

Since the estimated labor and nonlabor inputs will be scaled, as described above, these estimates provide no insight as to either factor proportions or cost levels. Rather, the empirical model of the local-service carriers is intended as a first approximation to the relative effects of *differences* in the *mix* of passenger and cargo operations on the level and mix of inputs, and the effects on these input requirements of stage length and route density characteristics which define the

---

3. John R. Meyer, "Some Methodological Aspects of Statistical Costing as Illustrated by the Determination of Rail Passenger Costs," *American Economic Review* 48 (May 1958): 209–222.

nature of the route system. The implicit assumption is that the relative amounts of labor and nonlabor inputs in indirect costs required for *different* route systems and *output mixes* is similar in the developing countries to that for the U.S. local-service carriers.

The U.S. local-service carrier data may be quite satisfactory for these purposes. The local-service carriers are operating low-density, short-haul operations in which cargo is predominantly hand stowed in passenger aircraft bellies. It seems reasonable to suppose that the type of operation, passenger-cargo mix, and fleet makeup of these carriers is a fair representation of the complexity of service to be found on domestic airlines of most developing countries. Of course, the in-direct cost equations may not do justice to the potential of higher density, more containerized all-cargo operations. Much of the potential of air cargo lies in being able to reduce cargo handling costs below the levels resulting from the extremely labor intensive process of hand loading small parcels in passenger holds. That sort of low-density operation is widespread in Latin America and elsewhere. Alter-native estimates of cargo handling costs associated with an all-cargo operation could easily be included in the air model by replacing the indirect cost equations for "Aircraft and Traffic Servicing" and "Promotion and Sales."

The statistical cost model for the local-service carrier operations can be easily described. The model first relates labor requirements and nonlabor costs per station for each of several cost categories to independent variables describing the route system and the mix and level of cargo and passenger operations. Since indirect expenses are largely labor, the labor requirements equations are quite important. The equations are of the following general form:

$$\frac{L_j}{n} = \alpha_1 P + \alpha_2 T + \sum_i \alpha_{ij} Xi$$

$$\frac{C_j}{n} = \beta_1 P + \beta_2 T + \sum_i \beta_{ij} Xi$$

where n is the number of stations; L_j and C_j denote the number of employees and the amount of nonlabor costs respectively in cost category j; P denotes the num-ber of passengers; T the tons of cargo; and the X_i are independent variables des-cribing the route system. The following measures of output or activity from the local service carriers were tried as independent variables X_i:

1. the number of aircraft departures
2. the average distance between terminals.

(The cross-sectional data for the 13 U.S. local-service carriers was for the year 1966; several mergers in 1967 much reduced the sample size after that date.)

The estimated coefficients α_1, α_2, β_1 and β_2 can be used to derive cost elas-ticities as a function of changes in the level or mix of output. The reliability of the individual slope coefficients showing the marginal cost of cargo and passenger operations (the coefficients of cargo and passenger output respectively in each equation) depends on the existence of sufficient covariation in the sample to avoid the indeterminancy arising from multicollinearity.

A special problem is posed by the local-service carriers' method of reporting costs and employees. Total cost, number of employees, and labor cost are reported for each of the several major functional categories of costs (j - 1,4). Nonlabor costs in each category were derived by subtracting the costs of labor assigned to that account. In addition, however, certain employees are not included in any of the four categories. (These employees may well reflect the true common cost problem where assignment to a category is often quite arbitrary.) This class of "unaccountable" employees has been labeled "other employees," and a separate equation estimated for them. Subtracting "assigned" labor cost from total cost in each functional account and aggregating over all categories overstates nonlabor costs by the amount of this "unaccountable" labor. Accordingly, this must be subtracted from nonlabor costs as defined above in determining total nonlabor cost. Total indirect costs for the firm associated with operations at a given *terminal* serving routes denoted by variables X_i and at passenger and cargo output levels P and T respectively is:

$$\text{Total labor costs per station} = \sum_j W_j \left(\frac{L_j}{n}\right) = \sum_j W_j \left(\alpha_{1j}P + \alpha_{2j}T + \sum_j \gamma_{ij}Xe\right)$$

$$\text{Total nonlabor costs per station} = \left[\sum_j p\left(\frac{C_j}{n}\right)\right] - U$$

$$= \left[\sum_j p(\beta_{1j}P + \beta_{2j}T + \sum_i o_i X_{ij})\right] - U$$

where U is unaccountable labor; W_j is labor's wage in category j; and P is the relative price of nonlabor input prices between the less developed countries and the United States.

Additional assumptions are required to allocate these average costs-per-station associated with the two terminals in question to the links originating or terminating service at those terminals. The appropriate assignment of terminal costs to particular links will be somewhat arbitrary since many of these costs are truly common costs. This again reflects a "systems" or network problem for which there are no totally satisfactory answers. The regression equations use data at the firm level of aggregation; both the costs-per-station explained by the model as a function of traffic and route system variables and these latter variables refer to firm averages. Clearly additional and strong assumptions will be required in using these average costs-per-station as a basis for costs in particular links.

The obvious first step is to estimate the marginal costs of cargo and passenger traffic on the link of operating the two stations using the coefficients for those variables in the above equations. There remains a significant component of costs-per-station represented by the intercept term and the several nontraffic variables in the equation which do not vary with traffic levels, essentially a "fixed" as opposed to "variable" cost. These costs must be assigned to all links which a given airport services. Accordingly, the model includes two parameters which denote the share of fixed costs for each terminal that are to be attributed to the link in question. Denoting these parameters K_1 and K_2 respectively, the indirect costs associated with a given *link* are of the following form:

Total labor and nonlabor
costs per link

$$= \sum_j [(W_j \alpha_{1j} + {}_p\beta_{1j})P + (W\alpha_{2j} + {}_p\beta_{2j})T]$$

$$+ (K_1 + K_2) [\sum_j W_j \sum_i (\gamma_{ij} X_i) + \sum_j p \sum_i (\alpha_{ij} X_i) - U]$$

In this equation the output variables P^* and T^* refer to passenger and cargo flows on the particular link in question. Presumably, the number of links the airports serve will be the basis for determining K_1 and K_2. (No restrictions on the K's is necessary in the model. The sum of the K's could exceed one, assigning to the link more than the total indirect operating costs of *all* operations to and from the two airports.) It might be appropriate for the weights K to reflect density of operations on links as well as the number of links, though the density of operations has already been included directly in the equation by the variables P and T.

Fixed Facility Costs

These costs include navigation and communication equipment, airstrips, and terminals. All of these costs are related to aircraft type. Electrical and ground equipment include all equipment and facilities not normally owned or maintained as part of airline operations, but rather as part of airport and airway operations. Ground-based communications and navigation equipment, airport fixtures such as lighting systems and weather instruments, the control tower, and ground maintenance vehicles are included in this category. The amount of ground instrumentation required will depend on the type of operation – day, day/night; fair weathei (VFR) – visual flight rules; or fair/poor weather (IFR) – instrument flight rules. Aircraft utilization and the reliability of service can be increased at the cost of more sophisticated ground equipment. The trade-offs between weather (including hours of daylight), terrain, and ground instrumentation (as it affects aircraft utilization or the number of days in which an airport can be used) are complex, and depend to a large extent on local circumstances. The model costs four broad classes of flying conditions separately, day or day/night, and VFR versus IFR.

Estimates of current unit cost of new equipment have been provided by the
FAA Logistics Service and recommended numbers of units of each type and
personnel requirements have been developed by the FAA Regional Aviation Assistance Group. The forecasts of required equipment for various environments and
terrain types are best estimates of what would be required in a developing country based upon the extensive experience of this group in designing airways in
Latin America. This cannot, of course, replace engineering analysis and a full
study of requirements at actual locations.

Personnel requirements depend also on the number and types of equipment
and facilities utilized. The estimates provided are considered reasonable estimates
of staffing levels for the several possible degrees of system complexity. Cost of
maintenance materials is available on an annual basis; and, as with initial equipment purchase cost, U.S. prices for such equipment is assumed to be close to the
net cost to foreign countries for such items. The international nature of this
market has been further substantiated by FAA personnel in informal conversa-
tions, in which we learned that foreign airlines requesting bids from manufacturers
in several countries often receive surprisingly close prices for equipment of
similar capability. The United States and Great Britain are the major suppliers to
the developing nations of most of the highly technical equipment in this category.
Most of these nonlabor costs, then, must be counted as foreign exchange.

Runway requirements depend on temperature and altitude; higher temper-
atures and higher altitudes require longer runways. FAA runway length requirements charts were represented in the model by linear equations, which indicate
the approximate length of runway as a function of aircraft type, elevation,
temperature, and gradient. These linear approximations are reasonably accurate,
though they are not as good as a careful derivation of runway requirements at a
particular site. Representing runway requirements by these equations in the
model allows quick estimation of airstrip requirements. It is assumed that a single
runway utilized for both takeoff and landing will be sufficient for the traffic
densities considered. Pavement configurations include the runway and apron, and
a parallel taxiway for all airports but the DC-3 class.

These estimates of runway length and width, together with estimates of pavement costs are the basis for determining runway costs in the model. Pavement
types and costs vary widely. Both asphalt and concrete are used depending on
prevailing temperature levels and the relative costs of each type of surface. In some
cases, where terrain is extreme, transporting concrete for runway construction
can be expensive. Unit pavement costs at the two airports in question are an input
to the model.

The cost of land acquisition and general clearing is very specific to the situation, hence cost estimating equations cannot be derived. Terrain will much affect
airstrip construction costs. Similarly, the cost of tower and terminal buildings are
very specific to the situation. Quality of service desired, climate, local expecta-
tions, volume of traffic, and links with other modes of transportation will all

affect the kinds of structures to be built. The total cost of appropriate structures is an input to the model. For the sample runs a single combined tower/terminal building has been designed and costed for each of the locations.

Since all of these fixed facilities serve more than one link, a pro rata assignment of costs to links must be made. The model includes three parameters for this purpose. Two parameters represent the share of fixed airport facilities assigned to the link. The third parameter denotes the share of airways and navigational aid costs assigned to the link. This last category is unquestionably a common cost in the best sense of the word. Whatever share is assigned to the link is likely to be somewhat arbitrary. However, these assignments are necessary if the total costs of a link are to be determined by the model. If a large number of links are costed by repeated use of the model as a means of evaluating a system of links, then there is less need to make these somewhat arbitrary assignments of costs to particular links.

Program Input and Operation

This program is written in G level IBM Fortran IV for the 360/65 computer. It requires about 73,000 bytes of core. No scratch tapes or disk storage are needed. Data input is by card (logical unit 5) and output is to the printer (logical unit 6). The deck as supplied contains no control cards. The user must supply such cards as his particular computer's configuration may require.

The data cards follow the program deck. One program run can generate many output reports as determined by the data deck.

For the first report of a run, the program requires data cards for all 93 input variables. It prints an error message for each missing card but continues the run. If two values are entered for the same variable, an error message is printed. The last value read is used.

The last card read for each report contains the number 5555 in columns 1 to 4. The next cards are used as data for the following report. For the second and subsequent reports, cards need only be entered for changed values of variables. If, for example, the interest rate remains constant for all the reports during a run, it need only be entered for the first report of the run.

The data for the last report in the run must be followed by a card containing the number 9999 in columns 1 to 4 instead of 5555. This will be the last card read in the data deck.

The data cards for any *one* report may be entered in any order. Card columns 1 to 4 contain the variable number, right justified, card columns 5 to 21 contain the variable value in either F (with decimal point) or E (with exponent) format. (See Table E-1).

Variables 9 and 58 use special formats. Four values must be entered for variable 9: the service utilization for each value of flight condition. Two cards are used. The first card contains 0009 in columns 1 to 4. The second card contains the four values in either F or E format in columns:

1–8   VFR day only
9–18   VFR day/night
19–28 IFR day
29–38 IFR day/night

Variable 58 contains the 80-character report title. Two cards are again required; the first contains a 0058 in columns 1 to 4. The second card contains the 80-character title.

The two cards for variable 9 and for variable 58 must be placed together in the data deck; the variable number first, followed immediately by the card containing the variable values or the report title.

Preliminary Calculations:
Block Time and Fleet Requirements

The first step in the model is to calculate block time over the link for the aircraft in question. Together with assumptions about aircraft utilization and passenger and cargo load factors, this determines the number of aircraft needed to serve the given traffic. These calculations are shown below in equations 1 to 8.

Although block time averages are available for United States air carriers by aircraft type and distance, an unknown portion of the total block time unavoidably includes waiting time due to ground congestion, which is likely to be more severe in the United States than for the low-volume routes considered in this study. Hence, flight-time estimating equations are preferred here with an additional fixed component per flight added to represent taxi time. Ten minutes (5 for takeoff, 5 for landing) appears to be a conservative estimate for this figure as there is unlikely to be significant ground congestion for the scale of operations anticipated.

The demand to be served is specified on an annual basis, both passenger and cargo flows. Total passengers per year is for one direction only, assumed to be equal for both directions. Cargo tonnage and volume is defined as the maximum of shipments in either direction, which, in turn, affects capacity required. It is assumed that cargo will be carried first by passenger flights in the hold area. All-cargo flights will then be utilized to carry the residual not carried on passenger flights. Cargo capacity of all-passenger (or combination aircraft) flights is expressed as the fraction of all-cargo version capacity that can be carried by the passenger version of the aircraft, both in weight and volume. Cargo capacities for aircraft are stated as both weight and volume limits; either may be the constraining dimension, depending on the average density of the freight carried.

The fleet size required to transport the required number of passengers and tons between the two airports is highly dependent upon daily service utilization

Table E-1
Input Parameters

Variable
Number   *Description*

Link Characteristics

1	Passengers per year
2	Tons per year
3	Cubic feet per year
4	Passenger load factor
5	Weight load factor
6	Volume load factor
7	Nonrevenue factor
9	Hours service utilization per day (special input format used – 4 values needed: VFR day, VFR day/night, IFR day, IFR day/night)
10	Distance between airports (miles)
11	Dollars of GP&E per dollar of flight equipment investment
12	Terrain type (1 = flat, 1 = hilly, 3 = mountainous)
13	Elevation at airport 1 (feet)
14	Elevation at airport 2 (feet)
15	Peak temperature at airport 1 ($^{\circ}$F)
16	Peak temperature at airport 2 ($^{\circ}$F)

Airplane Characteristics

19	Plane type (1 = small piston, 2 = large piston, 3 = turbo prop, 4 = jet)
20	Size of crew
21	Average crew block hour pay
22	Passenger capacity
23	Weight capacity (tons)
24	Volume capacity (cubic feet)
25	Fraction of all cargo weight capacity in passenger plane
26	Fraction of all cargo volume capacity in passenger plane
27	Average passenger load time (hours)
28	Average freight load time (hours)
29	Gallons of fuel used/block hour
30	Number of engines
31	Weight of one engine (pounds)
33	Empty weight of airframe (pounds)
34	Hours between overhauls
35	New cost of airplane less engines
36	Total new cost of engines
37	Used cost of complete plane
38	Aircraft life remaining (years)
39	Salvage value of plane
40	Constant, A for flying-hours equation, $F = A + B * D$
41	Coefficient of distance, B for flying-hours equation
42	Current to original relative price of engine parts
43	Current to original relative price of airframe parts
44	Relative maintenance labor efficiency, U.S. to local
58	Report title – 80 columns (special input format card)

Factor Prices

45	Gallon cost of aviation gasoline
48	Gallon cost of piston oil
50	Maintenance labor rate
51	Cost of capital

Table E-1 (cont.)

Variable
Number   Description

52	Annual hull insurance cost per dollar of plane value
53	Passenger plane liability rate per mile of plane travel
54	Freight plane liability rate per mile of plane travel
59	Nonlabor cost relative price factor foreign to U.S.

Indirect Employees Annual Wages

94	Passenger servicing employees
95	Aircraft and traffic servicing employees
96	Promotion and sales employees
97	General and administrative employees
98	Nonassigned labor

Fraction of Costs in Foreign Exchange

55	Fuel and oil
56	Airframe material
57	Engine material
83	Airport capital
84	Airfleet capital
85	Ground equipment and navigation aids
86	Ground vehicles
87	Aircrew wages
88	Maintenance wages
89	Indirect labor cost

Airport and Airway Data

64	Annual wages radio operator
65	Annual wages flight service specialist
66	Annual wages air traffic controller
67	Annual wage electronic tech
68	Annual wage electro-mech
69	Annual wage weather forecaster
70	Annual wage airport management
71	Annual wage crash and rescue personnel
72	Annual wage unskilled
73	Runway gradient in degrees at airport 1
74	Runway gradient in degrees at airport 2
75	Airport 1, acquisition and clearance costs
76	Airport 2, acquisition and clearance costs
77	Runway cost of airport 1, pavement $/square yard
78	Runway cost of airport 2, pavement $/square yard
79	Airport building cost airport 1
80	Airport building cost airport 2
90	Ground electrical equipment life
91	Ground vehicles life
92	Airport building life
93	Airport runway life

Proportion of Capital and Operating Expense Charged to Link

99	Airport 1
100	Airport 2
101	Airway

and average load factor. Service utilization is defined as the total number of hours per day that the airplane is in use. The annual number of flight days depends upon local climatic conditions and the level of sophistication of navigational equipment chosen. Load factors are expressed as fractions and represent the fraction of capacity that is utilized, on average, and is dependent to a large extent on efficiency of scheduling. Fractional numbers for fleet may be either raised to the next larger integer for single-link operations, or left in the fractional form for later aggregation with other air-link requirements.

Nonrevenue factor, henceforth abbreviated NFR, is included to reflect the small percentage of flights which do not directly contribute to revenue, such as training, and testing flights, and movements to overhaul facilities. This appears to average about 3 percent in IATA statistics.

Direct Operating Costs

Nature of the Model. The direct costs of aircraft operation are based on a modification of the ATA model. All costs are first determined on a block hour basis, then scaled according to the level of demand to yield total costs. Turbine and turboprop aircraft operating costs are based on the 1967 revision of the ATA model, whereas piston costs are based on the 1960 version. Definition of variables and the equations for each cost component appear below (equations 9 to 50). A few remarks will indicate the substance of our modifications of the ATA cost model.

Crew Costs. The equation for crew costs in the air model determines costs from crew size and crew costs per block hour. Both variables depend on aircraft type. Average crew costs per block hour will depend on both the wage and the average utilizations of flight crews. Crew costs are given in equations 9 to 11 below.

Oil and Fuel Costs. Oil and fuel costs are derived straightforwardly from ATA estimating equations. The 1960 equations are used for piston and the 1967 revision for turbine craft.[4] Difference among countries for fuel costs will arise because of variation in fuel prices. Fuel costs are given in equations 12 to 14.

Maintenance. Maintenance costs in the ATA model are broken into airframe and engine maintenance. Both labor and material costs are determined separately.

---

4. Air Transport Association of America, *Standard Method of Estimating Comparative Direct Operating Costs of Transport Airplanes,* June 1960 (revised, December 1967).

A conversion from costs per air-mile to costs per block hour is accomplished by multiplying the former cost expressions by D/T_b where D is either T_b x (block velocity) or T x (air speed).

In addition, an overhead charge is added, a proportional markup of labor and material costs. Two basic modifications were made in the ATA model, the inclusion of variables denoting labor efficiency (labor productivity relative to United States productivity) and current prices of airframe and engine parts relative to their original prices.

Maintenance labor costs are determined by equations 15 to 25. For piston aircraft, the direct labor required for aircraft maintenance is linearly related to aircraft cost and aircraft weight. In the case of turbine aircraft maintenance, maintenance hours/block hour is also related to block hours per flight cycle. Labor requirements for engine maintenance is largely determined by the time between major overhauls. Piston engine labor maintenance is determined by engine weight and number of hours between overhauls. Maximum takeoff thrust, π, and number of flight cycles determine the labor input required for turbine engine maintenance. All labor requirements as derived by the ATA equations are then weighted by a labor productivity variable, the ratio of labor productivity in the United States to the level in the country in question.

Airframe and engine material cost is a gross approximation, including both routine maintenance and overhaul material requirements. The current price of parts actually used relative to the original price of airframe and engine parts, Pa or Pe respectively, is included to reflect the fact that for older aircraft used or rebuilt components may be commonly utilized for replacement purposes. It should be recognized that maintenance material cost, as well as maintenance labor costs, are forecasts of airplane "lifetime average" costs and therefore cannot reflect perfectly all of the time-phasing aspects of major overhauls.

For piston aircraft, a simple linear relationship is postulated between cost per block hour and new cost of airplane, presumably on the theory that the greater the cost of the airplane, the greater the cost (and possibly number) of parts to be replaced per unit time. For turbine engines, the latest ATA revision separates cost into one component that is proportional to time used, and one that is proportional to the number of flight cycles that occur over a period of time. Equations 26 to 35 denote the costs of material prices.

Finally, a "maintenance burden" or fixed maintenance charge is determined, a proportion of labor and material costs. The ATA equations were used in this case. This is shown in equations 36 and 37.

Insurance. Total insurance cost per airplane consists of a hull insurance component, which is an annual percentage of airplane value plus a public liability and property damage component which is based on aircraft mileage. Insurance rates depend upon aircraft type, country, and type of operation (see equations 38 to 42).

Depreciation. Depreciation costs are based upon finite aircraft life using the CRF formula. This formula determines an annual charge equivalent to repayment of interest and principal on a straight time basis over the assumed life of the investment (see equations 43 to 45).

Ground Property and Equipment.   Ground equipment costs are assumed to be a constant proportion of aircraft investment. The estimate of costs of maintaining this investment is based on a study by Operations Research, Inc.[5] Maintenance costs are related to the value of ground equipment and the volume of direct labor employed in flight equipment maintenance. The assumption justifying the latter relationship is that the bulk of ground property and equipment maintenance is occasioned in support of the principal function of maintaining flight equipment (see equations 46 to 48).

Equations for Direct Operating Costs.

1. $RFKTRO$ = $2 * [PASS/(PASSLD * PASSCP)]$
   $RFLYRP$ = Revenue passenger flights per year
   $PASS$ = Number of passengers per year in either direction
   $PASSLD$ = Passenger load factor
   $PASSCP$ = Plane passenger capacity

2. $$RFLYRC = \text{Max}\left\{\left[\text{Max}\left\{\frac{2 * TONS}{TONLD * TONPLN} - A1 * RFLYRP\right\}, \left\{\frac{2 * VOL}{VOLD * VOLPLN} - A2 * RFLYRP\right\}\right], [\Phi]\right\}$$

   $TONS$ = Total shipped tons per year in either direction — use maximum of tonnage in either direction
   $TONLD$ = Cargo weight load factor
   $TONPLN$ = Plane weight capacity
   VOL = Total shipped volume per year in either direction — use largest volume shipped in either direction
   $VOLLD$ = Volume load factor
   $VOLPLN$ = Plane volume capacity
   $A1$ = Fraction of all cargo weight capacity represented by passenger craft cargo weight capacity
   $A2$ = Fraction of all cargo volume capacity represented by passenger craft cargo volume capacity
   $RFLYRC$ = Cargo revenue flights per year

3. TF = $A + B * D$
   TF = Flight time between terminals

---

5. *Cost Estimating Relations for Subsonic Aircraft,* Operations Research, Inc., 1964, prepared under Contract SD–275 for the Department of Transportation.

	A,B	=	Coefficients of flight time equation
	D	=	Distance between terminals
4.	TB	=	$TF + 0.17$
	TB	=	Block time = flight time plus allowance for takeoff, landing and taxi time.
5.	ABH	=	$TB * (RFLYRP + RFLYRC) * ANRF$
	ABH	=	Annual block hours for fleet
	$ANRF$	=	Nonrevenue factor (greater than 1)

6. $PLANFR$ =

$$PLANFR = \frac{RFLYRC * (ANRF*TB + FLDT)}{SERVHR\,(IFR) * DAYS}$$

	$PLANFR$	=	Freight planes requires
	$FLDT$	=	Average of freight load and unload time for a plane
	$DAYS$	=	Days of service per year — set to 365 by program
	$SERVHR$	=	Hours of service utilization per day. A four-value array is read in. The correct value is chosen by the subscript IFR which ranges from 1 to 4 for VFR day only, VFR day/night, IFR day only, IFR day/night.

$$PLANPS = \frac{RFLYRP * (ANRF * TB + PLDT)}{SERVHR\,(IFR) * DAYS}$$

	$PLANPS$	=	Passenger planes required
	$PLDT$	=	Average of passenger load and unload time
8.	$FLEET$	=	$PLANFR + PLANPS$
	$FLEET$	=	Total number of planes needed
9.	$C1$	=	$CRWSZ * CWAGE$
	$C1$	=	Flight crew costs per block hour
	$CRWSZ$	=	Crew size
	$CWAGE$	=	Average pay/block hour
10.	$C1F$	=	$C1 * ABH$
	$C1F$	=	Fleet flight crew costs per year
11.	$C1L$	=	$C1F/WAGE$
	$C1L$	=	Fleet flight crew man-hours per year

12a. Piston Aircraft

$$C2 = FUEL * CGAS + \frac{FUEL * WGAS * CPOIL}{70 * WPOIL}$$

12b. Turboprop and Jet

$$C2 = FUEL * CFUEL + ENGINE * 0.135 * CTOIL$$

$C2$	=	Fuel and oil costs per block hour
$FUEL$	=	Gallons of fuel used per block hour per plane
$ENGINE$	=	Number of engines per plane
$WGAS$	=	Gasoline weight pounds per gallon = 5.9 by data statement
$WPOIL$	=	Piston oil weight pounds per gallon = 7.5 by data statement
$CPOIL$	=	Gallon cost of piston oil
$CFUEL$	=	Temporary variable; set equal to $CKERO$ for turboprop or $CJP4$ for jet
$CKERO$	=	Gallon cost of kerosene
$CJP4$	=	Gallon cost of JP4 fuel
$CTOIL$	=	Gallon cost of turbine engine oil

13. $C2F$ $= C2 * ABH$

   $C2F$ = Fleet fuel and oil costs per year

14. $C2G$ $= FUEL * ABH$

   $C2G$ = Fleet fuel consumption in gallons per year

15a. Piston Aircraft

$$C3 = \left(1.7 + \frac{0.067 * WA}{1000}\right) * RWAGE * RLE$$

15b. Turboprop and Jet

$$C3 = \frac{TFLHR * TF}{TB} + \frac{TFCYR}{TB} * RWAGE * RLE$$

$C3$	=	Airframe labor costs per block hour
WA	=	Basic empty weight of airframe in pounds
$RWAGE$	=	Maintenance labor rate per hour
RLE	=	Relative maintenance labor efficiency U.S. to foreign (generally greater than one)

16. $TFLHR$ $= \dfrac{0.05 * WA}{1000} + 6 - \dfrac{630}{120 + WA/1000}$

   $TFLHR$ = Labor man-hours per flight-hour

17. $TFCYR$ $= 0.59 * TFLHR$

   $TFCYR$ = Labor man-hours per flight cycle

18. $C3F$ $= ABH * C3$

   $C3F$ = Airframe labor costs per year

19. $C3L$ $= \dfrac{C3F}{RWAGE}$

   $C3L$ = Airframe labor man-hours per year

20a. Piston Aircraft

$$C4 = ENGINE * TEBH * RWAGE * RLE$$

20b. Turboprop and Jet

$$C4 = ENGINE * \left(TEBY + \frac{TEFY}{TB} \right) * RWAGE * RLE$$

$C4$ = Direct engine maintenance per block hour
$TEBH$ = Labor man-hours per block hour

21a. Piston Aircraft

$$TEBH = \left(0.30 + \frac{0.70}{AK2} \right) * \left(\frac{ENGWT}{1000} \right) * \left(0.2495 + 0.765 * \frac{ENGWT}{1000} \right)$$

21b. Turboprop

$$TEBH = \frac{TF}{TB} * \left[0.6 + 0.027 \left(\frac{THRUST}{1000} \right) \right]$$

21c. Jet

$$TEBH = \frac{TF}{TB} * \left[0.65 + 0.03 \left(\frac{THRUST}{1000} \right) \right]$$

$ENGWT$ = Engine weight
$THRUST$ = Takeoff thrust in pounds

22. $$AK2 = 0.76 * \frac{HBTO}{100} + 0.164$$

$AK2$ = Coefficient in equation 22a
$HBTO$ = Hours between overhauls

23. $$TEFY = 0.3 + 0.03 \left(\frac{THRUST}{1000} \right)$$

$TEFY$ = Labor man-hours per flight cycle

24. $C4F = C4 * ABH$
$C4F$ = Fleet engine labor cost per year

25. $$C4L = \frac{C4F}{RWAGE}$$

$C4L$ = Fleet engine labor man-hours per year

26a. Piston

$$C5 = PA * \left(3.0 + 0.00475 * \frac{CNEWAR}{1000} \right)$$

26b. Turboprop and Jet

$$C5 \quad = PA * \left(CMFH * \frac{TF}{TB} + \frac{CMFC}{TB} \right)$$

PA = Relative price of used to new airframe parts
$CNEWAR$ = New cost of airplane less engines

27. $CMFC \quad = 6.24 * \dfrac{CNEWAR}{1,000,000}$

$CMFC$ = Material cost per flight cycle

28. $CMFH \quad = 3.08 * \dfrac{CNEWAR}{1,000,000}$

$CMFH$ = Material cost per flight hour

29. $C5F \quad = C4 * ABH$
      $C5F \quad$ = Fleet direct airframe material cost per year

30a. Piston
      $C6 \quad = CMBH * ENGINE$

30b. Turboprop and Jet

$$C6 \quad = \left(CMFH * \frac{TF}{TB} + \frac{CMFC}{TB} \right) * ENGINE * PE$$

$C6$ = Direct engine material cost per block hour
$CMBH$ = Material cost per block hour
PE = Relative price of used to new engine parts

31. $CMBH \quad = \left(\dfrac{CNEWAN}{1000} \right) * \left(\dfrac{0.0004274 * CNEWAN}{1000} \right.$

$$\left. + 0.08263 \right) * \left(0.1 + \frac{0.9}{AK3} \right)$$

$CNEWAN$ = New cost of single engine

32. $AK3 \quad = \dfrac{0.076 * HBTO}{100} + 0.164$

$AK3$ = Temporary variable in piston

33. $CMFC \quad = 2.0 * \dfrac{CNEWAN}{100,000} \quad$ For equation 30b

34. $CMFH$ $= 2.5 * \dfrac{CNEWAN}{100,000}$ For equation 30b

35. $C6F$ $= C6 * ABH$
    $C6F$ $=$ Direct engine material cost per year

36a. Piston
    $C7$ $= 0.89 * (C3 + C\$) + 0.223 * (C5 + C6)$

36b. Turboprop and Jet
    $C7$ $= 1.8 * (C3 + C4)$
    $C7$ $=$ Applied maintenance burden per block hour for flight equipment

37. $C7F$ $= C7 * ABH$
    $C7F$ $=$ Fleet applied maintenance burden for flight equipment

38. $AMILEP$ $= RFLYRP * D$
    $AMILEP$ $=$ Number of miles flown in one direction per year by passenger planes

39. $AMILEF$ $= RFLYRC * D$
    $AMILEF$ $=$ Number of miles flown in one direction per year by cargo planes

40. $C8TP$ $= HULL * COST * PLANPS + AMILEP * RLIABP$
    $C8TP$ $=$ Passenger fleet insurance cost
    $HULL$ $=$ Annual hull insurance rate (dollars per dollar of plane value)
    $COST$ $=$ Cost of used airplane
    $RLIABP$ $=$ Liability rate per mile for passenger planes

41. $C8TF$ $= HULL * COST * PLANFR + AMILEF * RLIABF$
    $C8TF$ $=$ Freight fleet insurance cost
    $RLIABF$ $=$ Liability rate per mile for freight planes

42. $C8T$ $= C8TP + C8TF$
    $C8T$ $=$ Fleet total insurance cost

43. P $= \dfrac{1}{1 + R}$

    P $=$ Discount rate
    R $=$ Interest rate per year

44. $C9$ $= (COST - SCRAP * P^{YL}) * \left[\dfrac{1 - P}{P(1 - P^{YL})} \right]$

	C9	= Annual depreciation and capital costs per plane
	SCRAP	= Scrap value of airplane
	YL	= Economic life of airplane in years
45.	*C9F*	= *FLEET* * C9
	C9F	= Fleet annual depreciation and capital costs
46.	C10	= 0.0251 * (*C3F* + *C4F*) + 0.0345 * *AK4* * *COST* * *FLEET*
	C10	= Annual system maintenance cost of ground property and equipment per dollar of flight equipment invested
47.	C11	= *ANNUAL* [*R*,*Y*1,(*AK4* * *COST* * *FLEET*)]
	C11	= Annual capital cost of ground property and equipment
	*Y*1	= Ground electrical equipment life

48. $$ANNUAL = \frac{C * R * (1 + R)}{(1 + R)Y - 1}$$

ANNUAL   (*R*,*Y*,*C*) is the capital recovery function on *R*, interest *Y*, life, and *C*, cost giving the annual capital cost

49. *CDIR* = *C2F* + *C5F* + *C6F* + *C7F* + *C8T* + *C9F* + C10 + C11
     CDIR = Total direct cost

50. *CLAD* = *C1L* + *C3L* + *C4L*
     CLAD = Total direct labor man-hours

Indirect Operating Costs

Indirect airline costs were separated into several objective account categories, with each objective account divided into labor and nonlabor components. The United States CAB objective account categories for Class II and III airlines include Passenger Servicing, Aircraft and Traffic Servicing, Promotion and Sales, and General and Administrative Expenses. Data for 1966 were used.

Indirect Cost Equations for Local Service Operations.   The estimated equations relating employees per station and nonlabor costs per station are listed below. R_c^2 denotes the percent of the total variance of the dependent variable explained by the equation, adjusted for degrees of freedom; and statistics are shown in parentheses.

1.   Passenger Servicing
     (no. of employees) = 0.654 + 0.0000672(no. of passengers)
                              (10.60)

$$R_c^2 = 0.8946$$

(nonlabor costs) = –463 + 396(av. stage length)
(2.98)
+ 9822(no. of passenger-service employees)
(2.64)

$$R_c^2 = 0.7314$$

2. Aircraft and Traffic Servicing
(no. of employees) = 3.55 + 0.183(no. of tons)
(3.54)
+ 0.00181(no. of departures per year)
(2.30)

$$R_c^2 = 0.7248$$

(nonlabor costs) = 17400 + 2.4(no. of passengers)
(7.45)
+ 91.5(no. of tons)
(2.99)
+ 8.55 (no. of departures per year)
(2.01)
– 4530(no. of aircraft-servicing employees)
(3.80)

$$R_c^2 = 0.9371$$

3. Promotion and Sales
(no. of employees) = –3.05 + 0.00012(no. of passengers)
(3.90)
– 0.0009(no. of tons) + 0.0306(av. stage length)
(0.39)   (2.12)

$$R_c^2 = 0.8214$$

(nonlabor costs) = –31700 + 0.946(no. of passengers)
(3.33)
+ 33.2(no. of tons) + 323(av. stage length)
(1.47)   (2.42)

$$R_c^2 = 0.8570$$

4. General and Administrative

(no. of employees) = 0.013 $\begin{bmatrix}\text{employees in passenger servicing, aircraft and}\\ \text{traffic servicing, and promotion and sales}\end{bmatrix}$
(Note: This equation is not estimated econometrically.)

(nonlabor costs) = 3400 + 0.239 $\begin{bmatrix}\text{employees in passenger servicing,}\\ \text{aircraft and traffic servicing, and}\\ \text{promotion and sales}\end{bmatrix}$
(6.31)

$$R_c^2 = 0.7440$$

5.   Nonassigned Labor
      (no. of employees) = 0.650 + 0.265 (all assigned labor)
                                    (7.20)

$$R_c^2 = 0.7931$$

      (cost of nonassigned employees) = − 3790 + 2470 (all assigned labor)
                                    (7.35)

$$R_c^2 = 0.8002$$

Air Model Indirect Operating Cost Equations

General Parameters

1. *PABT*   = $2 * PASS$
    PABT   = number of passengers carried each year
    PASS   = number of passengers carried one way

2. *TONT*   = $2 * TONS$
    TONT   = number of tons of cargo carried each year
    TONS   = tons of cargo carried one way per year

3. *DEPT*   = $RFLYRP + RFLYRC$
    DEPT   = number of departures per year
    RFLYRP   = passenger revenue flights per year
    RFLYRC   = cargo revenue flights per year

4. *SH*   = $SH1 + SH2$
    SH   = share of indirect costs to be allocated to this link
    SH1   = share of costs to be allocated to airport 1
    SH2   = share of costs to be allocated to airport 2

Passenger Servicing

5. *PASEMP*   = $0.654 * SH + 0.0000672 * PABT$
    PASEMP   = number of employees

6. *PASCST*   = $PASEMP * W1$
    PASCST   = annual labor cost
    W1   = annual wage

7. *PASNLB*   = $-46300 * SH + 396 * D * SH + 9822 * PASEMP$
    PASNLB   = nonlabor cost

Aircraft and Traffic Servicing

8. $ATEMP$ = $3.55 * SH + 0.0183 * TONT + 0.00181 * DEPT$
    $ATEMP$ = number of employees

9. $ATECST$ = $ATEMP * W2$
    $ATECST$ = annual labor cost
    $W2$ = annual wage

10. $ATNLB$ = $17400 * SH + 2.4 * PABT$
    $+ 91.5 * TONT + 8.55 * DEPT - 4530 * ATEMP$
    $ATNLB$ = nonlabor cost

Promotion and Sales

11. $PSEMP$ = $-3.05 * SH + 0.00012 * PABT$
    $-0.0009 * TONT + 0.0306 * SH * D$
    $PSEMP$ = number of employees

12. $PSECST$ = $PSEMP * W3$
    $PSECST$ = annual labor cost
    $W3$ = annual wage

13. $PSNLB$ = $-31700 * SH + 0.946 * PABT$
    $+ 33.2 * TONT + 323 * SH * D$
    $PSNLB$ = nonlabor cost

General and Administrative

14. $GAEMP$ = $0.013 * (PASEMP + ATEMP + PSEMP)$
    $GAEMP$ = number of employees

15. $GAECST$ = $GAEMP * W4$
    $GAECST$ = annual labor cost
    $W4$ = annual wage

16. $GANLB$ = $3400 * SH + 0.239 * (PASNLB + ATNLB + PSNLB)$
    $GANLB$ = nonlabor cost

Nonassigned Employees

17. $GNOEMP$ = $0.650 * SH + 0.265 * (PASEMP + ATEMP + PSEMP + GAEMP)$
    $GNOEMP$ = number of employees

18. $GNOCST$ = $GNOEMP * W5$
     $GNOCST$ = annual labor cost
     $W5$ = annual wage

Nonassigned Labor

19. $GNCST$ = $-3790 * SH + 2470 * (PASEMP + ATEMP + PSEMP + GAEMP)$
     $GNCST$ = annual labor cost

Summary Totals

20. $TOTANL$ = $(PASNLB + ATNLB + PSNLB + GANLB - GNCST) * PS$
     $TOTANL$ = total annual indirect airline nonlabor cost
     PS = relative price factor of nonlabor cost, U.S. to foreign

21. $TOTEMP$ = $PASEMP + ATEMP + PSEMP + GAEMP + GNOEMP$
     $TOTEMP$ = total number of airline indirect employees

22. $TOIEMC$ = $PASCST + ATECST + PSECST + GAECST + GNCST$
     $TOIEMC$ = total annual indirect labor cost

23. $TOTANX$ = $TOTANL + TOIEMC$
     $TOTANX$ = total indirect cost including labor

Fixed Facility Costs

Fixed facility costs include electrical equipment, air strips, and terminal facilities.

Model Structure. The required inputs for specifying airport, electrical, and ground equipment and personnel are:
a. airplane type
b. type of operations: day, day/night
c. weather: fair, fair/poor
d. distance between terminals
e. runway length
f. taxiway length
g. flat (1), hilly (2), or mountainous (3)
The two terminals need not have identical facilities and personnel levels, as for example if one is located in a frequently fog-bound area (required pavement

DC-3

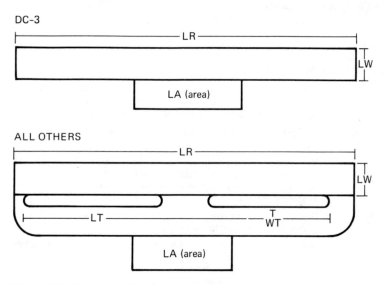

Figure E-1. Pavement Configurations

lengths may also differ at the two locations owing to temperature, elevation, and gradient differences.

Two different flight conditions are included in the model: (1) Instrument Flight Rules (IFR) — generally flight conducted with less than 1000 feet ceiling or distance from clouds and a visibility of less than 3 miles (5 miles in some cases); and (2) Visual Flight Rules (VFR) — flight conducted by visual reference to recognizable objects.

For a given airplane type, terrain, and operation, the model specifies the number of units of each equipment and facility type and then multiplies by the unit prices to arrive at a cost figure. Table E-2 lists electrical equipment required and an estimate of its unit cost. Annual charges to cover these investment costs using the CRF.

Airport personnel costs are obtained by multiplying the number of persons required in each labor class by the prevailing average annual pay for the class in the country and aggregating. Table E-3 lists airport personnel and describes their function briefly. Both staffing levels and nonlabor operating costs are prepared from formulas developed by FAA systems Maintenance Service. These are shown in Table E-4.

Two sorts of runway specifications were employed, as shown in Figure E-1. The cost of runways is based on the amount of air field pavement required. Runway length and width are determined by aircraft choice, altitude, temperature, and runway gradient.

Table E-2
Airport Equipment Requirements

Equipment		Construction and Installation Costs
A.	**Navaids – Air Navigation Aids**	
	NDB-1 — High-power nondirectional radio beacon (500–1000 watts), with voice transmission capability. Airborne equipment indicates bearing of ground transmitter.	$ 90,000
	NDB-2 — Low-power NDB (25–50 watt), with voice transmission capability.	17,550
	VOR — Very-high-frequency omnidirectional radio range, with voice transmission capability. Airborne equipment indicates azimuth position of aircraft relative to ground station.	73,000[a]
	DME — Distance measuring equipment. Airborne equipment gives distance to ground station.	70,000[b]
	ILS — Instrument landing system. Airborne equipment indicates lateral and vertical angle of approach to runway. ILS associated lighting aids are included elsewhere in the breakdown.	150,080[c]
	ILS MKR BCN — Marker beacon (75 mc). Airborne equipment indicates when aircraft is over station.	9,500
B.	**Airport Lighting**	
	ROTATING BCN — Rotating airport light, to facilitate location of airport at night or in low visibility conditions.	2,490[d]
	RUNWAY LIGHTS — Lighting system, to outline runway in darkness or bad weather.	0.90[e]
	TAXIWAY LIGHTS — Lighting system, to outline taxiways in darkness or bad weather.	0.90[e]
	ALS — Approach lighting system, to provide visual guidance to runway (usually associated with ILS).	195,000
	SALS — Simple approach lighting system. (Less extensive version of ALS, not necessarily associated with ILS.)	56,000
	VASIS — Visual approach slope indicator system, to give angle-of-descent guidance.	20,000[f]
	REIL — Runway-end identifier lights. High-intensity lights to facilitate location of landing end of runway.	9,500
C.	**Meteorology**	
	WX OBSVN — Service-requiring group of weather instruments adequate to take minimal weather observations.	1,875
	WX FCST — Service-requiring more extensive group of weather instruments adequate to take surface and upper-air forecasting information.	34,675[g]
	RVR — Runway visual range. Service-requiring instruments for determining visibility on runway. (Includes transmissometer and associated equipment.)	31,000
D.	**Communications**	
	VHF A/G — Very-high-frequency transmitter/receiver radio. (One unit shown per frequency. Figure in table includes one tuneable receiver at each station.)	2,875[h]

Equipment		Construction and Installation Costs
	SSB (4 CHAN) 4-Channel, single-side band high-frequency radio capable of transmitting and receiving voice and/or teletype on four frequencies.	\$ 13,500[i]
	ISB (6 CHAN) 6-Channel, independent-side band high-frequency radio transmitter and receiver similar to SSB but with greater capacity.	26,000[i]
	TLTP (MOD 28) Teletypewriter Model 28 (includes tape cutter and reperforator).	2,925[j]
	HF VOICE Radio send/receive equipment for single-frequency circuit.	26,000[k]
E.	*Air Traffic Control*	
	TWR EQUIP Air-Traffic control tower equipment (light gun, altimeter, crash telephone, flares, adjustable intensity lights, and airport light controls).	153,550[l]
	RADAR ASR-7 Airport surveillance radar equipment (FAA Model ASR-4 or -5 most likely to be available for export). Including tower cost.	1,083,760[m]
	ATCRBS Air-traffic control radar beacon system. Referred to as secondary radar. (Requires special airborne receiver/transmitter.)	
F.	CRSH/RES-1 Simple crash and rescue vehicle, ½ to 3-ton capacity, equipped with foam and/or dry powder, forcible entry tools tools, ladders.	6,500
	CRSH/RES-2 More sophisticated crash and rescue vehicle, similar to Ansul Mangun Model 480 or truck with 100 gallons foam chemical and 1000 gallons of water for 500 GPM discharge	21,000
	SERVICE Service vehicle. ½- to 1-ton pickup truck, radio equipped.	5,500
	ILS MTNC Maintenance vehicle equipped with receiver to check alignment to ILS localizer course.	6,500

Sources: Equipment requirements: FAA Regional Aviation Assistance Group; Cost data: FAA Logistical Service, except where noted.

[a] Single set of electronic equipment; no standby equipment.

[b] At the ILS.

[c] Cost of major air-traffic-control navigation facilities, Planning Research Corp., June 1964, Report No. RD-64-60.

[d] Cost per linear foot installed by airport operator. Cost varies with length of runways, taxiways, etc.

[e] "4-box" VASI — two lights each in upwind and downwind bars.

[f] Rotating beam ceilometer, hygrometer/thermometer, and wind speed/direction indicator, etc.

[g] One each 150 watt fixed tuned transmitter and receiver per frequency.

[h] 200-watt equipment.

[i] One each automatic send/receive unit.

[j] One each 5 kw unit.

[k] Medium traffic level nonradar tower; includes communications, weather, and other equipment; does not include radar or tower structure as such.

[l] Cost is for a solid state ASR-7 with beacon, etc.

Table E-3
Airport Personnel and Their Function

RADIO OPERATOR	Radio Operator of limited technical knowledge, able to send and receive administrative messages via air/ground radio. Journeyman-level personnel should have one month formal training and three months on-the-job training.
FLT SVC SPC	Flight Service Specialist, capable of operating radio and teletype equipment, knowledgeable in pilot briefing and trained to take surface weather observations. Journeyman-level personnel should have 4 months formal training and 8 months on-the-job training.
ATC TWR FSS	Air-traffic controller trained to control airport traffic as well as perform functions of FLT SVC SPC above. Journeyman-level personnel should have 9 months formal training plus 1 year on-the-job training.
ELECTRONIC TECH	Electronic technician trained to maintain all NAVAIDS and communications equipment utilized at or adjacent to the facility. Journeyman-level technicians should have at least 6 years of generalized electronic experience/training, plus 6 months of specialized training at the FAA Academy. If radar equipment is involved, 6 months additional training at the FAA Academy is necessary.
ELECTRO MECH	Electro-mechanical technician trained to maintain airport lighting systems, engine generators, etc. Incumbent should be a journeyman reciprocating-engine mechanic as well as a journeyman electrician.
WX FCSTR	Weather forecaster trained to produce forecasts based on observations taken by ATC and FSS specialists as well as other sources. Journeyman-level personnel should have a 4-year college course plus 1 year of on-the-job training.
APT MGMT	Airport management personnel — includes manager, attendants, etc.
CRSH/RESC	Crash and rescue personnel trained to fight fires of all origins and in forcible entry of disabled aircraft for rescue purposes.
UNSKILLED	Laborers to cut grass, remove debris from runways, etc.

Source: FAA Regional Aviation Assistance Group.

Fixed Facility Cost Equations.

1. $WT2$ = $WT1 = 75$
   $WT1$ = Taxiway width (ft.) — airport 1
   $WT2$ = Taxiway width (ft.) — airport 2

2. $ALA2$ = $ALA1 = 350 * 600$
   $ALA1$ = Area of load apron — airport 1
   $ALA2$ = Area of load apron — airport 2

3a. $T1$ = $TEMPK1 - 59$

3b. $T2$ = $TEMPK2 - 59$
   $T1$ = Corrected maximum temperature — airport 1
   $T2$ = Corrected maximum temperature — airport 2

$TEMPK1$ = Maximum Fahrenheit temperature — airport 1
$TEMPK2$ = Maximum Fahrenheit temperature — airport 2

4a. Small Piston (DC-3)
$WR2$ = $WR1 = 100$

4b. Larger Planes
$WR2$ = $WR1 = 150$
$WR1$ = Runway width (ft.) — airport 1
$WR2$ = Runway width (ft.) — airport 2

5a. $ALR1$ = $(1 + a * G1) * (b + c * ELEV1 + D * T1)$

5b. $ALR2$ = $(1 + a * G2) * (b + c * ELEV2 + d * T2)$
$ARL1$ = Runway length (ft.) — airport 1
$ARL2$ = Runway length (ft.) — airport 2
$G1$ = Runway gradient (degrees) — airport 1
$G2$ = Runway gradient (degrees) — airport 2
$ELEV1$ = Elevation (ft.) — airport 1
$ELEV2$ = Elevation (ft.) — airport 2
$a,b,c,d,$ = Coefficients which depend on plane type

Small Piston	a	= 0.2	c	= 0.105
(DC-3)	b	= 4040	d	= 0
Large Piston	a	= 0.2	c	= 0.210
(DC-6)	b	= 5600	d	= 0
Turboprop	a	= 0.2	c	= 0.175
(L-166)	b	= 4900	d	= 50
Jet (DC-9)	a	= 0.1	c	= 0.65
	b	= 5450	d	= 18

6a. $ALT1$ = $f * ALR1$

6b. $ALT2$ = $f * ALR2$
$ALT1$ = Taxiway length (ft.) — airport 1
$ALT2$ = Taxiway length (ft.) — airport 2
f = 0 for small piston (DC-3)
f = 1.3 for all other types

7a. $CST1$ = $\{[ALR1 * WR1 + ALT1 * WT1 + ALA1] * \dfrac{CPAVE1}{9} + CSBLG1\} * SH1$

7b. $CST2$ = $\{[ALR2 * WR2 + ALT2 * WT2 + ALA2] * \dfrac{CPAVE2}{9} + CSBLG2\} * SH2$

Table E-4
Navigation Aids, Equipment and Personnel Requirements for an Airway Segment 100–300 Miles Long with Two Terminals and Aircraft Type to and Including Short-Haul Jet[a]

Equipment	Unit Cost	Flat Day VFR	Flat Day IFR	Flat Day/Night VFR	Flat Day/Night IFR	Hilly Day VFR	Hilly Day IFR	Hilly Day/Night VFR	Hilly Day/Night IFR	Mount. Day VFR	Mount. Day IFR	Mount. Day/Night VFR	Mount. Day/Night IFR	ATC Tower	Flight Plan & NOTAM	WX OBSVN or FCST	Point to Point & A/G Radio	AFTN TLTP	Speech Circuit to FIC	Long Range Air/GND
NAVAIDS																				
NDB #1	2									1	2	2	1							
NDB #2		2		2		2		2		2		1								
VOR	2	2		2		3		3		3		3								
DME	1	2		2	1	3		3	2	3		3	2							
ILS									1				1							
Mkr Bcn				1		1		1		2		2								
Airport Lighting																				
Rotating Bcn	2	2		2		2		2		2		2								
Runway Lights	2	2		2		2		2		2		2								
Taxiway Lgts	2	2		2		2		2		2		2								
ALS																				
SALS					1			1												
VASIS								2	2			2	2							
REIL									1				1							
Meteorology																				
WX OBSVN		2		2		2		2		2		2				X				
WX Forecast																X				
RVR													1	X						
Communications																				
VHF A/G	4	6	4	6		4	6	4	6	4	6	4	6	X						
SSB (4 Chan)	2	2		2		2		2		2		2				X	X			
ISB (6 Chan)	2	2		2		2		2		2		2			X		X			
TLTP (Mod 28)	2	2		2		2		2		2		2			X				2	
*HF Voice	2	2		2		2		2		2		2		X			X	2		2

Types of Service — "May be Combined Facility": ATC Tower, Flight Plan & NOTAM, WX OBSVN or FCST, Point to Point & A/G Radio. "Comm. Tie-In For International (Optional)": AFTN TLTP, Speech Circuit to FIC, Long Range Air/GND.

ATC									
Twr Equip	2	2	2	2	2	2	2		X
Radar ASR-5					1	1	1		X
ATCRBS					1	1	1		X
Airport Vehicles									
Crash/Res #1	2	2	2	2	2	2	2		
Crash/Res #2	2	2	2	2	2	2	2		
Service	2	2	2	2	2	2	2		
ILS MTNC	2	2	2	2	2	1	1		
Personnel									
Radio Operator									4
Flt Svc Spc									2
ATC Twr/FSS	12	30	12	30	12	30	12	30	2
Electronic Tech	3	4	4	4	4	5	9	11	X
Electro-Mech	2	2	2	2	2	2	2	2	X
WX Fcstr								3	X
Apt Mgmt	6	8	6	8	6	8	8	8	X
Crash/Rescue	4	6	4	4	4	4	6	6	X
Unskilled	6	6	6	6	6	6	6	6	X

Source: FAA Regional Aviation Assistance Group.

[a] For distances less than 300 miles, use NAVAIDS listed for "Large Piston and Turboprop Aircraft. For distances greater than 300 miles, add one VOR, DME and NDB per 100 miles of airways.

[b] No change for distances of other than 300 miles.

[c] No change for distances of other than 300 miles.

	*CST*1	=	Runway, taxiway, and pavement costs allocated to airport 1
	*CST*2	=	Runway, taxiway, and pavement costs allocated to airport 2
	*CSBLG*1	=	Cost of terminal building — airport 1
	*CSBLG*2	=	Cost of terminal building — airport 2
	*CPAVE*1	=	Cost of airfield 1 pavement per square yard
	*CPAVE*2	=	Cost of airfield 2 pavement per square yard
	*SH*1	=	Share of airport 1 allocated to link
	*SH*2	=	Share of airport 2 allocated to link

8a. $ACQ1 = SH1 * ACQQ1$

8b. $ACQ2 = SH2 * ACQQ2$

	*ACQ*1	=	Link's acquisition and clearing cost — airport 1
	*ACQ*2	=	Link's acquisition and clearing cost — airport 2
	*ACQQ*1	=	Unallocated acquisition and clearing cost — airport 1
	*ACQQ*2	=	Unallocated acquisition and clearing cost — airport 2

9a. $CBLD1 = SH1 * CSBLG1$

9b. $CBLD2 = SH2 * CSBLG2$

| | *CBLD*1 | = | Cost of terminal building allocated to link — airport 1 |
| | *CBLD*2 | = | Cost of terminal building allocated to link — airport 2 |

10a. $CSTT1 = CST1 + ACQ1 + CBLD1$

10b. $CSTT2 = CST2 + ACQ2 + CBLD2$

| | *CSTT*1 | = | Total of airport 1 acquisition, clearing, and paving cost allocated to link |
| | *CSTT*2 | = | Total of airport 2 acquisition, clearing and paving cost allocated to link |

11. $CSTTT = CSTT1 + CSTT2$

| | *CSTTT* | = | Total for both airports of acquisition, clearing, and paving cost allocated to link |

12a. $ACBLD1 = ANNUAL\ (R,\ Y3,\ CBLD1)$

12b. $ACBLD2 = ANNUAL\ (R,\ Y3,\ CBLD2)$

	ANNUAL (*R,Y,C*)	=	Subroutine to calculate capital recovery costs given:
			R = interest rate per year
			Y = life in years, and
			C = cost
	*Y*3	=	Life of terminal building in years

13a. $ACN1 = R * ACQ1$

13b. $ACN2$ = $R * ACQ2$

$ACN1$ = Airport 1 annual acquisition costs (interest only, no principal)

$ACN2$ = Airport 2 annual acquisition costs (interest only, no principal)

14a. $CCN1$ = $ANNUAL\ (R,\ Y4,\ CST1)$

14b. $CCN2$ = $ANNUAL\ (R,\ Y4,\ CST2)$

$CCN1$ = Runway and taxiway annual cost — airport 1

$CCN2$ = Runway and taxiway annual cost — airport 2

$Y4$ = Runway life (years)

15a. $CSTN1$ = $ACN1 + CCN1 + ACBLD1$

15b. $CSTN2$ = $ACN2 + CCN2 + ACBLD2$

$CSTN1$ = Annual cost of airport 1

$CSTN2$ = Annual cost of airport 2

16. $CSTTN$ = $CSTN1 + CSTN2$

$CSTTN$ = Annual cost of both airports

Table E-5
Air Model Printout: DC-9, Other Scenario

DC-9 IN COUNTRY A   00261700   PAGE   1

INPUT PARAMETERS

PASSENGER/YEAR	1000.
CARGO TONS/YEAR	73.
CARGO CU.FT./YEAR	11231.
COST OF CAPITAL	0.08

CHANGES ARE FLAGGED BY   ##

**********LINK CHARACTERISTICS**********

1	PASSENGERS PER YEAR	1000	##
2	TONS PER YEAR	73	##
3	CUBIC FEET PER YEAR	11231	##
4	PASSENGER LOAD FACTOR	0.40	##
5	WEIGHT LOAD FACTOR	0.45	##
6	VOLUME LOAD FACTOR	0.45	##
7	NON-REVENUE FACTOR	1.03	##
10	DISTANCE BETWEEN AIRPORTS (MILES)	300	
11	DOLLARS OF GP&E PER DOLLAR OF FLIGHT EQUIPMENT INVESTMENT	$ 0.08	##
12	TERRAIN TYPE	FLAT	
13	ELEVATION AT AIRPORT 1 (FEET)	10	##
14	ELEVATION AT AIRPORT 2 (FEET)	500	##
15	PEAK TEMPERATURE AT AIRPORT 1 (DEG F)	80	##
16	PEAK TEMPERATURE AT AIRPORT 2 (DEG F)	90	##

**********AIRPLANE CHARACTERISTICS**********

19	PLANE TYPE TURBO-JET (DC-9)		
20	SIZE OF CREW	2	
21	AVERAGE CREW BLOCK HOUR PAY	$ 24.00	
22	PASSENGER CAPACITY	105	
23	WEIGHT CAPACITY (TONS)	12	
24	VOLUME CAPACITY (CUBIC FEET)	4050	
25	FRACTION OF ALL CARGO WEIGHT CAPACITY IN PASSENGER PLANE	0.15	
26	FRACTION OF ALL CARGO VOLUME CAPACITY IN PASSENGER PLANE	0.15	
27	AVERAGE PASSENGER LOAD TIME (HOURS)	0.25	
28	AVERAGE FREIGHT LOAD TIME (HOURS)	0.75	
29	GALLONS OF FUEL USED/BLOCK HOUR	871.0	
30	NUMBER OF ENGINES	2	
31	WEIGHT OF ONE ENGINE (POUNDS)	3156	
32	TURBO-PROP AND JET THRUST (POUNDS)	14000	
33	EMPTY WEIGHT OF AIRFRAME (POUNDS)	45300	
34	HOURS BETWEEN OVERHAULS	5000	
36	TOTAL NEW COST OF ENGINES	$ 431100.00	

DC-9 IN COUNTRY A

	PASSENGER/YEAR	1000.
	CARGO TONS/YEAR	73.
	CARGO CU.FT./YEAR	11231.
	COST OF CAPITAL	0.08

35	NEW COST OF AIRPLANE LESS ENGINES	$6069900.00
37	USED COST OF COMPLETE PLANE	$3000000.00
38	AIRCRAFT LIFE REMAINING (YEARS)	13
39	SALVAGE VALUE OF PLANE	$ .00
40	CONSTANT, A FOR FLYING HOURS EQUATION F=A+B*D	0.260
41	COEFFICIENT OF DISTANCE, B FOR FLYING HOURS EQUATION	0.0029
42	CURRENT TO ORIGINAL RELATIVE PRICE OF ENGINE PARTS	1.00
43	CURRENT TO ORIGINAL RELATIVE PRICE OF AIRFRAME PARTS	1.00
44	RELATIVE MAINTENANCE LABOR EFFICIENCY, US TO LOCAL	1.0 ##

*********FACTOR PRICES*********

47	GALLON COST OF JP-4 JET FUEL	$ 0.21 ##
49	GALLON COST OF TURBINE OIL	$ 1.00 ##
50	MAINTENANCE LABOR RATE	$ 1.44 ##
51	COST OF CAPITAL	0.08 ##
52	ANNUAL HULL INSURANCE COST PER DOLLAR OF PLANE VALUE	$ 0.180 ##
53	PASSENGER PLANE LIABILITY RATE PER MILE OF PLANE TRAVEL	0.250E-01
54	FREIGHT PLANE LIABILITY RATE PER MILE OF PLANE TRAVEL	0.100E-02
59	NONLABOR COST RELATIVE PRICE FACTOR FOREIGN TO US	0.67 ##

*********INDIRECT EMPLOYEES ANNUAL WAGES*********

94	PASSENGER SERVICING EMPLOYEES	3500.00 ##
95	AIRCRAFT AND TRAFFIC SERVICING EMPLOYEES	3500.00 ##
96	PROMOTION AND SALES EMPLOYEES	3500.00 ##
97	GENERAL AND ADMINISTRATIVE EMPLOYEES	3500.00 ##
98	NON-ASSIGNED LABOR	3500.00

********* FRACTION OF COSTS IN FOREIGN EXCHANGE*********

55	FUEL AND OIL	0.80 ##
56	AIRFRAME MATERIAL	0.90 ##
57	ENGINE MATERIAL	1.00
83	AIRPORT CAPITAL	0.30
84	AIRFLEET CAPITAL	1.00
85	GROUND EQUIPMENT & NAVIGATION AIDS	1.00
86	GROUND VEHICLES	1.00
87	AIRCREW WAGES	0.0
88	MAINTENANCE WAGES	0.0
89	INDIRECT LABOR COST	0.0

Table E-5 (continued)

DC-9 IN COUNTRY A

00261700   PAGE 3

PASSENGFR/YEAR	1000.
CARGO TONS/YEAR	73.
CARGO CU.FT./YEAR	11231.
COST OF CAPITAL	0.08

**********AIRPORT AND AIRWAY DATA**********

64	ANNUAL WAGES RADIO OPERATOR	$	2800.00	##
65	ANNUAL WAGES FLT SVC SPC	$	5200.00	##
66	ANNUAL WAGES ATC TWR FSS	$	5200.00	##
67	ANNUAL WAGE ELECTRONIC TECH.	$	6800.00	##
68	ANNUAL WAGE ELECTRO-MECH.	$	4000.00	##
69	ANNUAL WAGE WX FCSTR	$	6800.00	##
70	ANNUAL WAGE APT MGMT	$	5200.00	##
71	ANNUAL WAGE CRSH/RESC	$	2800.00	##
72	ANNUAL WAGE UNSKILLED	$	2800.00	##
73	RUNWAY GRADIENT IN DEGREES AT AIRPORT 1		0.0	
74	RUNWAY GRADIENT IN DEGREES AT AIRPORT 2		0.0	
75	AIRPORT 1 ACQUISITION AND CLEARANCE COSTS		1000000.00	
76	AIRPORT 2 ACQUISITION AND CLEARANCE COSTS		100000.00	
77	RUNWAY COST OF AIRPORT #1 PAVEMENT $/SQ. YD.		3.00	
78	RUNWAY COST OF AIRPORT #2 PAVEMENT $/SQ. YD.		3.00	
79	AIRPORT BLDG. COST APT. #1		100000.00	
80	AIRPORT BLDG. COST APT. #2		100000.00	
90	GROUND ELECTRICAL EQUIPMENT LIFE		15	
91	GROUND VEHICLES LIFE		8	
92	AIRPORT BUILDING LIFE		20	
93	AIRPORT RUNWAY LIFE		20	

**********PROPORTION OF CAPITAL AND OPERATING EXPENSE CHARGED TO LINK**********

99	AIRPORT 1	0.05
100	AIRPORT 2	0.20
101	AIRWAY	0.10

DC-9 IN COUNTRY A

00261700   PAGE 4

PASSENGER/YEAR   1000.
CARGO TONS/YEAR   73.
CARGO CU.FT./YEAR   11231.
COST OF CAPITAL   0.08

********** AIR FLEET PERFORMANCE **********

	VFR – DAY ONLY	VFR – DAY/NIGHT	IFR – DAY ONLY	IFR – DAY/NIGHT
*FLIGHT STATISTICS**				
DISTANCE(MILES)	300.00	300.00	300.00	300.00
UTILIZATION (HOURS/DAY)	7.50	9.00	9.00	10.75
FLIGHT TIME(HOURS)	1.13	1.13	1.13	1.13
BLOCK TIME (HOURS)	1.30	1.30	1.30	1.30
TOT ANNUAL BLK HRS	88.74	88.74	88.74	88.74
PASGR REV FLIGHT/YR	47.62	47.62	47.62	47.62
FRGHT REV FLIGHT/YR	18.65	18.55	18.65	18.65
PASSGR PLANES REQD.	0.03	0.02	0.02	0.02
FRGHT PLANES REQD.	0.01	0.01	0.01	0.01
*****AIRCREW*********				
CREW-HOURS PER YEAR	177.47	177.47	177.47	177.47
COST/YEAR	4259.35	4259.35	4259.35	4259.35
*****OIL FUEL*****				
GALLONS OF FUEL/YEAR	77289.38	77289.38	77289.38	77289.38
COST/YEAR	16254.73	16254.73	16254.73	16254.73
AIRPLANE MAIN.				
AIRFRAME MAN-HOURS	417.93	417.93	417.93	417.93
AIRFRAME LABOR COST	601.81	601.81	601.81	601.81
ENGINE MAN-HOURS	141.23	141.23	141.23	141.23
ENGINE LABOR COST	203.37	203.37	203.37	203.37
AIRFRAME MATL. COST	4027.40	4027.40	4027.40	4027.40
ENGINE MATL. COST	2839.64	2839.64	2839.64	2839.64

Table E-5 (continued)

DC-9 IN COUNTRY A

00261700　　PAGE 5

PASSENGER/YEAR	1000.
CARGO TONS/YEAR	73.
CARGO CU.FT./YEAR	11231.
COST OF CAPITAL	0.08

	VFR – DAY ONLY	VFR – DAY/NIGHT	IFR – DAY ONLY	IFR – DAY/NIGHT
*******BURDEN*******	1449.32	1449.32	1449.32	1449.32
ANNUAL CAPITAL &				
****OTHER COSTS*****				
COST OF CAPITAL	0.08	0.08	0.08	0.08
ECONOMIC LIFE YRS	13.00	13.00	13.00	13.00
CAPITAL COST/PLANE	367934.88	367934.88	367934.88	367934.88
FLEET CAPITAL COST	15406.89	12839.07	12839.07	10748.99
GROUND PROPERTY &				
EQUIPMENT COST				
MAINTENANCE	366.93	309.14	309.14	262.10
CAPITAL	1174.11	978.42	978.42	819.14
PASS. LIABILITY INS.	15283.14	12795.47	12795.47	1070.63
FRGHT LIABILITY INS.	7691.52	6410.54	6410.54	5367.87
TOTAL INSURANCE COST	22974.66	19206.01	19206.01	16138.50
**TOTAL DIRECT COST*	64493.68	57903.73	57903.73	52539.83
TOTAL DIRECT LABOR				
MANHOURS/YEAR	736.63	735.63	736.63	736.63

DC-9 IN COUNTRY A

00261700   PAGE 6

	PASSENGER/YEAR	1000.
	CARGO TONS/YEAR	73.
	CARGO CU.FT./YEAR	11231.
	COST OF CAPITAL	0.08

********** INDIRECT COST **********

	EMPLOYEES	LABOR COST
PASSENGER SERVICING	0.30	1042.65
AIRCRAFT AND TRAFFIC SERVICING	3.68	12871.36
PROMOTION AND SALES	1.64	5743.84
GENERAL AND ADMINISTRATIVE	0.07	255.63
OTHER EMPLOYEES	1.67	5847.41
	----------	----------
**** TOTAL LABOR	7.36	$ 33029.45
	----------	----------
**** TOTAL ANNUAL INDIRECT NONLABOR COST		$ 33706.36

**** TOTAL ANNUAL INDIRECT COST		$ 66735.75

Table E-5 (continued)

DC-9 IN COUNTRY A   00261700   PAGE 7

	PASSENGER/YEAR	1000.
	CARGO TONS/YEAR	75.
	CARGO CU.FT./YEAR	11231.
	COST OF CAPITAL	0.08

SHARE OF AIRPORT COSTS ALLOCATED TO LINK

	AIRPORT 1		AIRPORT 2	
	ANNUAL	TOTAL	ANNUAL	TOTAL
AIRPORT ACQUISITION AND CLEARING COSTS	$ 4000.00	$ 50000.00	$ 1600.00	$ 20000.00
AIRPORT BUILDING	$ 509.26	$ 5000.00	$ 2037.04	$ 20000.00
RUNWAY,TAXIWAY,APRON BASE AND PAVEMENT	$ 3317.05	$ 32567.28	$ 14105.96	$ 138494.31
TOTAL AIRPORT COSTS	$ 7826.30	$ 87567.19	$ 17743.00	$ 178494.19

****SUMMARY****
BOTH AIRPORTS $ 25569.30 $ 266061.38

DC-9 IN COUNTRY A

00261700   PAGE   8

PASSENGER/YEAR   1000.
CARGO TONS/YEAR   73.
CARGO CU.FT./YEAR   11231.
COST OF CAPITAL   0.08

SHARE OF NAVIGATION, EQUIPMENT, AND PERSONNEL REQUIREMENTS ALLOCATED TO LINK

	VFR DAY ONLY UNITS	VFR DAY ONLY COST	IFR UNITS	IFR COST	VFR DAY/NIGHT UNITS	VFR DAY/NIGHT COST	IFR UNITS	IFR COST	IFR UNITS	IFR COST
NAVAIDS										
NDB #1	0	0.0	2	17999.99	2	17999.99	2	17999.99	2	17999.99
NDB #2	2	3510.00	0	0.0	0	0.0	0	0.0	0	0.0
VOR	0	0.0	2	14599.99	0	0.0	2	14599.99	2	14599.99
DME	0	0.0	1	7000.00	0	0.0	1	7000.00	1	7000.00
ILS	0	0.0	0	0.0	0	0.0	0	0.0	0	0.0
MARKER BEACON	0	0.0	0	0.0	0	0.0	0	0.0	0	0.0
SUBTOTAL		3510.00		39599.98		17999.99		39599.98		39599.98
AIRPORT LIGHTS										
ROTATING BEACON	0	0.0	2	498.00	2	498.00	2	498.00	2	498.00
RUNWAY LIGHTS	0	0.0	2	2190.15	2	2190.15	2	2190.15	2	2190.15
TAXIWAY LIGHTS	0	0.0	0	0.0	2	2847.19	2	2847.19	2	2847.19
ALS	0	0.0	0	0.0	0	0.0	0	0.0	0	0.0
SALS	0	0.0	0	0.0	0	0.0	0	0.0	0	0.0
VASIS	0	0.0	0	0.0	0	0.0	0	0.0	0	0.0
REIL	0	0.0	0	0.0	0	0.0	0	0.0	0	0.0
SUBTOTAL		0.0		2688.15		5535.33		5535.33		5535.33
METEOROLOGY										
WX OBSERVER	0	0.0	2	375.00	0	0.0	2	375.00	2	375.00
WX FORECAST	0	0.0	0	0.0	0	0.0	0	0.0	0	0.0
RVR	0	0.0	0	0.0	0	0.0	0	0.0	0	0.0
SUBTOTAL		0.0		375.00		0.0		375.00		375.00
COMMUNICATIONS										
VHF A/G	4	1150.00	6	1725.00	4	1150.00	6	1725.00	6	1725.00
SSB (4 CHANNEL)	0	0.0	0	0.0	0	0.0	0	0.0	0	0.0
ISB (6 CHANNEL)	2	5200.00	2	5200.00	2	5200.00	2	5200.00	2	5200.00
TTY (ASR28)	0	0.0	2	585.00	0	0.0	2	585.00	2	585.00
HF VOICE	2	5200.00	2	5200.00	2	5200.00	2	5200.00	2	5200.00
SUBTOTAL		11549.99		12709.99		11549.99		12709.99		12709.99

Table E-5 (continued)

DC-9 IN COUNTRY A

	PASSENGER/YEAR	1000.
	CARGO TONS/YEAR	73.
	CARGO CU.FT./YEAR	11231.
	COST OF CAPITAL	0.08

00261700   PAGE 9

	VFR DAY ONLY		IFR		VFR DAY/NIGHT		IFR	
	UNITS	COST	UNITS	COST	UNITS	COST	UNITS	COST
ATC								
TWR EQUIPMENT	2	30709.99	2	30709.99	2	30709.99	2	30709.99
RADAR ASR-5	0	0.0	0	0.0	0	0.0	0	0.0
ATCRBS-TRANSPONDER	0	0.0	0	0.0	0	0.0	0	0.0
SUBTOTAL		30709.99		30709.99		30709.99		30709.99
AIRPORT VEHICLES								
CRASH/RES. #1	2	1300.00	0	0.0	2	1300.00	0	0.0
CRASH/RES. #2	2	400.00	2	400.00	2	400.00	2	400.00
SERVICE	0	0.0	0	0.0	0	0.0	0	0.0
ILS MAINTENANCE	0	0.0	0	0.0	0	0.0	0	0.0
SUBTOTAL		1700.00		400.00		1700.00		400.00
PERSONNEL								
RADIO OPERATOR	0	0.0	0	0.0	0	0.0	0	0.0
FLIGHT SVC SPC.	12	6240.00	30	15599.99	12	6240.00	30	15599.99
ATC TWR/FSS	0	0.0	0	0.0	0	0.0	0	0.0
ELECTRONIC TECH.	3	2040.00	3	2040.00	4	2720.00	4	2720.00
ELECTRO MECH.	0	0.0	2	800.00	0	0.0	2	800.00
WX FORCASTER	0	0.0	0	0.0	0	0.0	0	0.0
AIRPORT MANAGEMENT	6	3120.00	6	3120.00	8	4160.00	8	4160.00
CRASH/RESCUE	4	1120.00	6	1680.00	4	1120.00	6	1680.00
UNSKILLED	6	1680.00	6	1680.00	6	1680.00	6	1680.00
SUBTOTAL		14199.99		24919.99		15919.99		26639.99

DC-9 IN COUNTRY A

00261700   PAGE 10

PASSENGER/YEAR   1000.
CARGO TONS/YEAR   73.
CARGO CU.FT./YEAR   11231.
COST OF CAPITAL   0.08

SHARE OF ANNUALIZED CAPITAL COSTS FOR
NAVIGATION, EQUIPMENT, AND PERSONNEL REQUIREMENTS ALLOCATED TO LINK

	DAY ONLY		DAY/NIGHT	
	VFR	IFR	VFR	IFR
NAVAIDS	410.07	4626.45	2102.93	4626.45
AIRPORT LIGHTS	0.0	314.05	646.69	646.69
METEOROLOGY	0.0	43.81	0.0	43.81
COMMUNICATIONS	1349.38	1484.90	1349.38	1484.90
ATC	3587.84	3587.84	3587.84	3587.84
AIRPORT VEHICLES	295.83	69.61	295.83	69.61
PERSONNEL	14199.99	24919.99	15919.99	26639.99
TOTAL	19843.11	35046.64	23902.65	37099.28

SUMMARY OF TOTAL AND FOREIGN EXCHANGE COSTS

	DAY ONLY				DAY/NIGHT			
	VFR		IFR		VFR		IFR	
	TOTAL	FOR.EXCH.	TOTAL	FOR.EXCH.	TOTAL	FOR.EXCH.	TOTAL	FOR.EXCH.
ANNUAL CAPITAL RECOVERY COSTS	47793.	29895.	49513.	31615.	47369.	29471.	47597.	29698.
OPERATING AND MAINTENANCE COSTS	133913.	42443.	140806.	38674.	131806.	38674.	139412.	35607.
TOTAL ANNUAL COSTS	181706.	72338.	190320.	70289.	179176.	68145.	187009.	65305.
TOTAL INVESTMENT	449203.	262960.	465604.	279361.	446616.	260373.	450046.	263803.

Table E-5 (continued)

DC-9 IN COUNTRY A   00261700   PAGE 11

PASSENGER/YEAR   1000.
CARGO TONS/YEAR   73.
CARGO CU.FT./YEAR   11231.
COST OF CAPITAL   0.08

ANNUAL FOREIGN EXCHANGE COST

	DAY ONLY		DAY/NIGHT		
	VFR	IFR	VFR	IFR	IFR
FUEL & OIL	13003.79	13003.79	13003.79	13003.79	13003.79
AIRFRAME MATERIAL	3624.66	3624.66	3624.66	3624.66	3624.66
ENGINE MATERIAL	2839.64	2839.64	2839.64	2839.64	2839.64
AIRPORT CAPITAL	7670.79	7670.79	7670.79	7670.79	7670.79
FLEET CAPITAL	15406.89	12839.07	12839.07	10748.99	10748.99
GROUND EQUIPMENT & NAVIGATION AIDS	6521.39	11035.47	8665.26	11208.83	11208.83
GROUND VEHICLES	295.83	69.61	295.83	69.61	69.61
AIRCREW WAGES	0.0	0.0	0.0	0.0	0.0
MAINTENANCE WAGES	0.0	0.0	0.0	0.0	0.0
INDIRECT LABOR COST	0.0	0.0	0.0	0.0	0.0
TOTAL COST	49362.98	51083.02	48939.03	49166.29	49166.29

About the Authors

Paul O. Roberts, Jr. is Associate Professor of Transportation and Logistics at Harvard University Graduate School of Business Administration. Current research interests include intercity freight transportation and its management, from both public and private points of view, as well as methods and models for evaluation of urban transportation systems in general. He is a member of the Massachusetts Governor's Task Force on Intercity Transportation and is active in social and political activities affecting local as well as national transportation policy. He received his Bachelor of Science degree in 1955 from the A&M College of Texas in Civil Engineering and has subsequently earned a Masters degree from M.I.T. and his Ph.D. from Northwestern University, both in Transportation Engineering. He served as Assistant Professor of Civil Engineering at M.I.T. for five years before being appointed as Director of Research of the Harvard Transport Research Program and Lecturer in the Department of Economics and the John F. Kennedy School of Government in 1965. He served in this position until his present appointment in 1968. He is a registered professional engineer in the states of Pennsylvania and Massachusetts as well as a member of T.I.M.S., O.R.S.A., and the Highway Research Board.

Donald N. Dewees is a Senior Research Associate at Charles River Associates. He is also writing a doctoral thesis in Economics at Harvard University on the economics of controlling automobile air pollution. He received a B.S. degree in Electrical Engineering from Swarthmore College and later an L.L.B. from Harvard Law School. He has served as staff attorney to the Harvard Urban Mass Transportation Study, as consultant to the Massachusetts Governor's Task Force on Transportation, and as Systems Engineer with the Harvard Transport Research Project on a study of the transportation system of Colombia. He is a member of the Institute of Electrical and Electronic Engineers, the Pennsylvania Bar Association, and the American Economic Association.